Libertarian Philosophy in the Real World

ALSO AVAILABLE FROM BLOOMSBURY

Critical Theory and Libertarian Socialism, Charles Masquelier
Libertarian Anarchy, Gerard Casey
Nozick's Libertarian Project, Mark D. Friedman

Libertarian Philosophy in the Real World

The Politics of Natural Rights

MARK D. FRIEDMAN

BLOOMSBURY
LONDON • NEW DELHI • NEW YORK • SYDNEY

Bloomsbury Academic
An imprint of Bloomsbury Publishing Plc

50 Bedford Square
London
WC1B 3DP
UK

1385 Broadway
New York
NY 10018
USA

www.bloomsbury.com

BLOOMSBURY and the Diana logo are registered trademarks of Bloomsbury Publishing Plc

First published 2015

© Mark D. Friedman, 2015

Mark D. Friedman has asserted his right under the Copyright, Designs and Patents Act, 1988, to be identified as the Author of this work.

All rights reserved. No part of this publication may be reproduced or transmitted in any form or by any means, electronic or mechanical, including photocopying, recording, or any information storage or retrieval system, without prior permission in writing from the publishers.

No responsibility for loss caused to any individual or organization acting on or refraining from action as a result of the material in this publication can be accepted by Bloomsbury or the author.

British Library Cataloguing-in-Publication Data
A catalogue record for this book is available from the British Library.

ISBN: HB: 978-1-47257-340-7
PB: 978-1-47257-339-1
ePDF: 978-1-47257-341-4
ePub: 978-1-47257-342-1

Library of Congress Cataloging-in-Publication Data
A catalog record for this book is available from the Library of Congress.

Typeset by Newgen Knowledge Works (P) Ltd., Chennai, India

To My Three Great Loves: Aracelly, Judah, and Asher

> Liberty and good government do not exclude each other; and there are excellent reasons why they should go together. Liberty is not a means to a higher political end. It is itself the highest political end. It is not for the sake of a good public administration that it is required, but for security in the pursuit of the highest objects of civil society, and of private life. Increase of freedom in the State may sometimes promote mediocrity, and give vitality to prejudice; it may even retard useful legislation, diminish the capacity for war, and restrict the boundaries of Empire.
>
> LORD ACTON, The History of Freedom in Antiquity [1877]

CONTENTS

Preface viii

Introduction 1
1   Natural rights, the minimal state, and its legitimate functions 13
2   Property rights, eminent domain, regulatory takings, and zoning 33
3   Rights of expression and association 49
4   Paternalism 63
5   The regulatory state 77
6   The federal income tax and the federal reserve system 93
7   Corporate welfare and the welfare state 111
8   Public education 125
9   Health care 135
10 Political issues for which there is no doctrinaire libertarian position 151
11 What is to be done? 169

Notes 179
List of useful internet resources 249
Bibliography 253
Index 275

PREFACE

This study is a natural outgrowth of my previous work, *Nozick's Libertarian Project: An Elaboration and Defense*, Continuum International, 2011. There, I argued for the continuing vitality of Nozick's rights-based defense of the (no more than) minimal state. Having completed this task, it seemed worthwhile to explore the public policy implications of his libertarianism, an important question that has received little attention in the literature.

I wish to express my heartfelt appreciation to a number of people in connection with this project. First and foremost, I thank my wife Aracelly for her unwavering understanding and patience, which made this study possible. For their helpful comments on portions of earlier drafts of my manuscript, I wish to thank Tevi Troy, Steve Horwitz, Tom Palmer, Aaron Gordon, Steve Karavitis, and Fernando Téson.

I owe a special debt to Danny Frederick, whose penetrating criticisms deepened my understanding of Nozick's theory of rights, enabling me to make here what I hope is a more cogent and persuasive presentation of this important subject. Of course, the remaining errors and omissions are entirely my own responsibility.

Introduction

By any standard, we live in interesting political times. In just the past several years, our policymakers have undertaken an unusual if not unprecedented series of deep and momentous economic interventions that have affected virtually every American. These include costly bailouts of our banking and automotive industries; huge, debt-fueled federal spending programs intended to "stimulate" growth; the reorganization of our health care system in a way that greatly expands the role of the state; the Federal Reserve's massive, ongoing campaign of quantitative easing; and the comprehensive reregulation of our financial services industry. Yet in the face of this epic display of governmental activism, libertarianism has never been more popular, perhaps at least in part as a response to such policies.

Evidence of this trend is seen in the more than 1.2 million votes garnered by Gary Johnson, the Libertarian Party's candidate in the 2012 United States presidential election; the emergence and influence of the "Tea Party" movement; the mass media exposure given to such self-identified libertarians as John Stossel, Neil Boortz, and Judge Andrew Napolitano; and the continuing strong sales of Ayn Rand's two major novels, *The Fountainhead* [1943] and *Atlas Shrugged* [1957].

Moreover, while only a small percentage of Americans will spontaneously identify themselves as "libertarians," there is persuasive evidence that a much larger number of persons actually hold views consonant with this philosophy. A January 2010 survey of the US electorate reveals that 14 percent are libertarians, based on the respondents' answers to three key, ideologically loaded questions.[1] Other polls indicate that a substantially higher portion of the electorate hold views that are at least somewhat sympathetic to this worldview.

We should not be surprised by the resonance of such ideas in our politics. The central libertarian tenet, that individuals possess certain natural rights (i.e., those we hold simply on account of our status as human beings, including economic liberty), is deeply encoded in our national DNA through the profound influence of John Locke, and other English and French classical liberals, on our founders. In fact, this ideology dominated our political life until the advent of the Great Depression and the New Deal programs of the 1930s.

Locke, natural rights, and the founding fathers

Locke, in his famous *Two Treatises of Government*, argued that even a world devoid of political authority, what he called a "state of nature," is governed by the natural law dictated by the Creator.[2] This law "obliges every one: Reason, which is that Law, teaches all Mankind, who will but consult it, that being all equal and independent, no one ought to harm another in his Life, Health, or Possessions."[3] Therefore, if an individual or group violates the natural law by aggressing against another person, the innocent party has an inherent right of self-defense, and the further right to punish the offender.

Locke imagined that those living in a state of nature would *conditionally* transfer certain of their rights to the government for the purpose of safeguarding their property (which he understood most broadly, to include people's "lives, liberties, and estates"[4]):

[T]he end of the law is . . . to preserve and enlarge Freedom. For in all the states of created beings capable of laws, where there is no law there is no Freedom. *For liberty is to be free from restraint and violence from others*; which cannot be where there is no law: and it is not, as we are told, a liberty for every man to do what he lists [likes]. (For who could be free when every other man's humour might domineer over him?) *But a liberty to dispose, and order as he lists, his person, actions, possessions, and his whole property*, within the Allowance of those laws under which he is, and therein not be the subject of the *arbitrary* Will of another, but freely follow his own. (emphasis added)

Thus, Locke conceives of natural liberty not as a right to the possession of certain goods, but as freedom from the predations of others. Accordingly, the legitimate role of the state is to establish security and the rule of law. If the executive fails in this essential responsibility, the populace is justified in "appealing to Heaven," that is, invoking its natural rights and revolting against him.

For Locke, natural law not only authorizes but also favors the right of the individual to convert land and other raw materials to private ownership:

> God, who hath given the World to Men in common, hath also given them reason to make use of it to the best advantage of Life and convenience. The Earth, and all that is therein was given to Men for the Support and Comfort of their being. And though all the Fruits it naturally produces, and Beasts it feeds, belong to Mankind in common . . . there must of necessity be a means *to appropriate* them some way or other before they can be of any use. (emphasis in original)

Locke's justification of this right of original appropriation starts with the seemingly self-evident proposition that "every Man has a Property in his own Person."

From this premise, he reasons that self-ownership extends to the work of a person's hands, meaning, we are entitled to retain the fruits of our labor. With respect to land, we earn just title by homesteading, that is, by clearing, enclosing, and working it. According to Locke, the acquisition of land by this method does not violate the moral rights of other people, provided that there remains enough land for them to also appropriate by means of *their* labor.

Locke's ideas are echoed in the celebrated preamble to our Declaration of Independence:

> We hold these truths to be self-evident: that all men are created equal; that they are endowed by their creator with certain unalienable rights; that among these are life, liberty and the pursuit of happiness; that to secure these rights, governments are instituted among men, deriving their just powers from the consent of the governed; that whenever any form of government becomes destructive to these ends, it is the right of the people to alter or to abolish it.

This language expresses a particular ethical perspective, highlighted by the recognition of a moral law that transcends and may supersede man-made law, and the selection of the phrase "pursuit of happiness," rather than simply "happiness," "welfare," or some synonym.

The freedom to *pursue* happiness requires only that other people not interfere with our activities, specifically, that they do not attack us, steal our possessions, or otherwise aggress against us, subject, of course, to our treating them with equal respect. Philosophers refer to moral rights of this sort as negative rights.

On the other hand, if we are entitled *to* happiness, and we cannot obtain it by our own efforts, then other people may legitimately be compelled to supply it, even if this requires a substantial sacrifice on their part. Putative moral rights to such goods (not grounded in contract) are called positive or welfare rights. The distinction between the negative and positive conceptions of rights, and a (general) willingness to recognize only the former as just, lies at the heart of contemporary libertarian philosophy.[5]

Beyond Locke's defense of natural rights

In light of the above, it is clear why contemporary libertarians proudly claim Locke as an intellectual forbearer. However, few modern libertarian philosophers are satisfied with Locke's derivation of natural rights and they have therefore felt compelled to offer a more systematic and coherent justification. This effort is absolutely critical to the libertarian cause because without a clearly articulated, defensible account of the ethical foundation of such rights we will be unable to make headway against opposing political ideologies based on different moral presuppositions, such as the value of equality.

For example, assume we start with the seemingly unassailable premise that "individual freedom is a paramount value," and argue from this that state-mandated redistributions are morally offensive because they violate the right of people to dispose as they like of their own property. We will be met with the reply (among others) that "individual freedom" requires substantial resources for its expression, and that in order for all persons to be truly free, we must rearrange the distribution of wealth in order to realize a more egalitarian pattern of holdings. By this logic, the claimed right to retain justly earned income must yield to the right of other individuals to exercise *their* freedom.

A second example is perhaps warranted. Libertarians are committed to freedom of expression, even for stupid, bigoted, and hateful opinions that contribute nothing worthwhile to the proverbial marketplace of ideas. But why does a speaker's "right" to make false and malicious statements outweigh the public's "right" not to be exposed to communication that it finds extremely offensive? Mere talk of individual rights or freedom does not take us very far in resolving such cases in a principled, rational way.

The absence of a carefully drawn theory of libertarianism will, in addition to leaving mysterious the distinguishing characteristics of real and spurious rights, generate further theoretical puzzles. Specifically, as discussed in the next chapter, the libertarian insistence on stringent property rights has been criticized on the ground that there is no satisfactory way to reconcile what appear to be conflicts between such rights, especially with respect to land use.

Finally, without a defensible ethical foundation for rights it will prove impossible to determine their authority when they run up against competing values, rendering the entire doctrine implausible. Thus, libertarianism is frequently criticized for having the implication that it would be morally impermissible for the state to force the rich to pay even a trivial tax in order to save the needy from starvation. I believe that only the truly doctrinaire would be untroubled if the vindication of natural rights had this consequence, even in theory. This difficulty can be resolved by showing that the moral values that underlie libertarian rights are compatible with a narrow range of state action when there is no viable alternative.[6]

This last issue interconnects with the larger question of the moral legitimacy of even the "minimal state," meaning, one devoted almost exclusively to the protection of its citizens from foreign and domestic predators. Those libertarians known as anarcho-capitalists (or individualist anarchists) claim that if, as asserted earlier, coercion employed against innocent persons is morally wrong, then it is *always* wrong, whether employed for purposes of feeding the hungry or for funding national defense and domestic law enforcement.

For reasons that will soon be clear, I believe that the most convincing justification of natural rights is found in the work of the late Robert Nozick, the distinguished Harvard philosophy professor who died prematurely in 2002. His *Anarchy, State, and Utopia* (cited parenthetically in the text hereafter as "*ASU*," plus relevant page reference), published in 1974, is still regarded, in the words of Philip Petit, a respected contemporary philosopher, "as the most coherent statement available of the case for a rights-based defense of the minimal, libertarian state" (footnote omitted).[7] In the following chapter, I briefly summarize Nozick's theory of natural rights, and describe how it resolves the challenges previously identified.[8]

I do not provide here a full-blown exposition and defense of his libertarianism because this is a work of *applied* philosophy and will therefore focus mainly on what Nozick's natural rights doctrine implies about the moral status of our current laws and institutions.[9] I will argue that our state grossly abuses its powers, afflicting us from cradle to grave with its coercive system of public education; suffocating regulations; pervasive corporate welfare and rent-seeking; mandatory entitlement programs; irrational and redistributive tax code; paternalism; and so on *ad nauseam*.

I believe that even those who are already sympathetic to libertarianism do not generally appreciate the *extent* to which their rights are now infringed. This is at least partially attributable to the fact that virtually all of us gained political maturity after the enactment of the New Deal, which may have been the tipping point in the transformation of our state into the Leviathan we live with today. Accordingly, the lack of exposure to any alternative political reality blinds us to the degree to which our natural liberty has been curtailed by the activist state.

While the moral illegitimacy of certain laws from the natural rights perspective is obvious, for example, when the state arbitrarily redistributes wealth from one group to another by means of crop subsidies or forces unwilling workers to pay union dues as a condition of employment, on other occasions the injustice is far more subtle. For example, few ordinary citizens understand the Federal Reserve System and the threat its virtually unfettered discretion poses to our natural rights.

This historical background gives rise to a related problem: the widespread inability to imagine how society would function without our familiar legal/political institutions. For example, most people assume that in the absence of mandatory professional licensure and the protection of the FDA, consumers would be at the mercy of unqualified physicians and unscrupulous, rapacious pharmaceutical companies. However, as argued in Chapter 5, private organizations would fill this gap, and likely do so more effectively.

I wish to make clear at this point that despite my confidence in the superiority of voluntary solutions to social problems, my critique is quite distinct from that made by such laissez faire economists as the late Milton Friedman (sadly, no relation) and libertarian think tanks such as the Cato Institute. Their objection is that most (if not all) of the programs of the interventionist state have not only failed to achieve their stated goals, but are often actually counterproductive. While I wholeheartedly agree with this conclusion, this book employs a separate line of attack.

A different approach is warranted for two reasons. First, rights-based libertarians do not wish to rest their critique of the welfare/regulatory state on either economic theory or the philosophical doctrine of utilitarianism.[10] This is readily seen if we imagine that the state, by grossly violating the rights of certain innocent people, *did* materially improve the overall level of social welfare. Libertarians would nevertheless object to this, because we hold that the demands of justice outweigh such considerations.

Utilitarianism is one form of a broader moral theory known as consequentialism, which holds, as described by academic philosopher Walter Sinnott-Armstrong, that "whether an act is morally right depends only on *consequences* (as opposed to the circumstances or the intrinsic nature of the act or anything that happens before the act)" (emphasis in original).[11] Utilitarians believe that right actions are those that maximize welfare, happiness, preference satisfaction (or the like), while other consequentialists evaluate the rightness of actions on the basis of other (or additional) values.

Although consequentialists contend that persons should have as their objective bringing about the best consequences, they are typically careful to note that due to informational and time constraints, as well as human bias and irrationality, it will generally be counterproductive for moral agents to actually attempt to *calculate* all relevant outcomes before acting. Thus, most consequentialists propose that agents act on the basis of common sense rules of thumb. In principle, such rules could incorporate stringent moral rights because this approach might arguably produce optimal consequences in the long run.

As a matter of fact, consequentialists are generally far less sympathetic to right-based moral arguments than their main philosophical opponents, the deontologists, who deny (at the minimum) that consequences are the *only* thing that matter from the moral perspective.[12] However, there is nothing in consequentialism per se that is inconsistent with libertarianism. Thus, the fundamental conflict in political philosophy is not properly categorized in terms of consequentialism versus deontology, but between those who would sacrifice the interests of the individual for the so-called greater good and those who would not.

A second reason for rejecting utilitarianism as a foundation for the libertarian conception of rights is that there are plenty of Nobel Prize winning economists who object to laissez faire based on such concepts as market failure, negative externalities, public goods, and so forth. The dispute between defenders of free markets such as Friedman, Thomas Sowell, and Richard Epstein and their ideological opponents (e.g., Paul Krugman and Joseph Stiglitz) ultimately gets bogged down in highly technical disagreements about empirical matters and competing interpretations of economic history. These conflicting assumptions and theoretical models mean that for most people the debate between modern and classical liberals ends up being confusing and inconclusive.

Thus, while I will in the following chapters have occasion to describe the failures of our top-down approach to ameliorating social problems and will identify voluntary, private sector solutions, I do so not to "prove" that free market capitalism will maximize overall welfare compared to the ersatz version practiced here today or even more interventionist alternatives. Rather, my more modest and realistic goal is to show, by the use of common sense and by means of relevant examples, that the absence of coercive government programs would not, at the minimum, produce *unacceptably* negative outcomes relative to the alternatives. Even those of us who emphatically reject utilitarianism as a satisfactory moral theory must acknowledge that a rights-based political program that would, if implemented, produce widespread human misery not only is implausible in a theoretical sense, but also would have no chance of ever being enacted.

Before leaving (for now) the subject of economics, and the use I will make of it in this study, I note that Nozick endorses what he calls the "familiar social considerations favoring private property," that is:

> it increases the social product by putting the means of production in the hands of those who can use them most efficiently (profitably); experimentation is encouraged, because with separate persons controlling resources, there is no one person or small group whom someone with a new idea must convince to try out; private property enables people to decide on the pattern and types of risks they wish to bear, leading to specialized types of risk bearing; private property protects future persons by leading some to hold back resources from current consumption for future markets; it provides alternate sources of employment for unpopular persons who don't have to convince any one person or small group to hire them, and so on (*ASU*, 177).

But, importantly, Nozick continues, "These considerations enter a Lockean theory to support the claim that appropriation of private property satisfies the intent behind the 'enough and as good left over' proviso, *not* as a utilitarian justification of property" (Ibid., Nozick's emphasis). In other words, by identifying the social benefits of private ownership, he is rebutting the claim that homesteading is intrinsically unjust because it harms those not fortunate enough to be the *first* to acquire land.

Although natural rights libertarians do not argue for freedom on utilitarian grounds, this does not prevent us from hypothesizing a strong connection between free markets and the general welfare.[13] The virtues of private property described by Nozick in the passage just quoted explain why (for example) North Koreans live something very much like hell on earth, while South Koreans enjoy an ever-increasing prosperity. Even imperfectly secure property rights will correlate wealth and status not with violence and ruthlessness, but with invention, innovation, self-improvement, hard work, and savings.[14]

In this setting, individuals can prosper only by trading with others on a voluntary basis. Participants in such transactions profit by providing goods or services that their counterparts perceive to be of value to them. So, as Adam Smith famously observed some 240 years ago,

> Give me that which I want, and you shall have this which you want, is the meaning of every such offer; and it is in this manner that we obtain from one another the far greater part of those good offices which we stand in need of. It is not from the benevolence of the butcher, the brewer, or the baker that we expect our dinner, but from their regard to their own interest. We address ourselves, not to their humanity, but to their self-love, and never talk to them of our own necessities, but of their advantages.[15]

Sadly, as we examine our society's basic institutions it will become obvious that we generally (to paraphrase Hamlet) honor the practice of free exchange more in the breach than in the observance, and that this tendency has harmful real-world consequences. It might seem odd, and rather too convenient, if the relationship between respect for rights and societal welfare were a mere coincidence. The point of these empirical observations, therefore, is simply to provide a plausible explanation for this connection.

With Nozick's moral/political framework as a guide, I will critique our activist state, at least the most far-reaching and significant elements of it. Unfortunately, our state's involvement in what should be our private spheres is so varied and pervasive that organizing this effort poses a serious challenge, particularly because many statutes and institutions violate our rights in multiple ways and, accordingly, might be placed in a number of different categories.

Thus, some chapters address particular rights that are violated by the state, such as those pertaining to expression and property, while others address the state's intervention in a discrete aspect of life, such as education and health care. Finally, certain state programs are grouped by what appears to be their motivation, namely paternalism. In each case I explain why the particular law or policy under discussion is inconsistent with our natural rights, and describe the libertarian alternative. However, I acknowledge that certain of the prescriptions presented here will appear so radical to most voters that they have no realistic chance of implementation in the foreseeable future.

In such cases, I offer more pragmatic solutions that represent a substantial improvement over the status quo. These proposals should not be regarded as "libertarian," since they still involve the infringement of individual rights. Their only merit is that they violate rights to a lesser extent than does the status quo and that they have some prospect of realization in the not too distant future.

After concluding my critique of our interventionist state, I describe and analyze certain political positions (e.g., "non-interventionism" or more pejoratively "isolationism" in foreign affairs), that are commonly, but erroneously, identified as the *doctrinaire* libertarian stance. Finally, I offer a few concluding thoughts on how we might persuade others to respect natural rights, and how we might proceed if we do not wish to undertake this potentially fruitless task.

I end this introduction with a word or two about terminology. I will from time to time refer herein to the "rule of law." This term is typically used to describe societies that have enacted such constitutional safeguards as due process, equal protection, the separation of powers, and so forth. But while these are necessary elements of the rule of law, they are not sufficient. History shows that constitutions are often ignored or suspended, and their lofty proclamations of rights have frequently proven useless against budding tyrants. This realization prompted the great political economist and theorist F. A. Hayek to elucidate a more penetrating understanding of this concept.

For Hayek, the rule of law exists only in those societies where there is an enduring political consensus that ensures that the law functions solely as a neutral framework enabling citizens to plan and conduct their affairs.[16] It protects honest citizens against force and fraud, and otherwise leaves them alone. A classic example is our traffic code, which lays out "rules of the road" that permit us to get to our desired destinations, without dictating to us where and when we should travel. At the same time, it punishes drunk and reckless drivers, improving safety for all others.

It is natural, I believe, to regard capitalism as the economic order that results from the application of the rule of law to our financial affairs. My dictionary defines it as "an economic system in which investment in and ownership of the means of production, distribution and exchange of wealth is made and maintained chiefly by private individuals or corporations." However, this definition leaves open the possibility that while the bulk of a society's capital might be privately held, the distribution of goods could still be shaped in fundamental ways by crony capitalism and other unjust governmental policies.

In light of this, in his seminal *Capitalism and Freedom*, Friedman felt obliged to employ the phrase "competitive capitalism" to denote "the organization of the bulk of economic activity through private enterprise operating in a free market."[17] The "free market" qualification makes clear that he endorses only *voluntary* exchange, thereby condemning all transactions and holdings that arise from the government's use of its coercive powers to favor certain constituencies. I generally follow Friedman's usage, and one important purpose of this book is to describe the profound differences between the corrupt capitalism that we practice, and its ideal, free market form.

CHAPTER ONE

Natural rights, the minimal state, and its legitimate functions

This chapter outlines Nozick's argument for natural rights and explains why, as a general rule, it recognizes as morally legitimate only our (negative) right against various forms of aggression by other individuals or the state. I argue further that Nozick's framework enables libertarians to provide credible answers to some of the most commonly heard objections lodged against their doctrine. Finally, I identify the few morally permissible activities of the state.

The challenge of providing an ethical foundation for natural rights

The founding fathers owed an enormous intellectual debt to classical liberalism generally, and to John Locke in particular.[1] Locke claims to derive natural rights from the dictates of natural law, a doctrine that remained influential during his era. Mark Murphy, an academic expert in this field, has summarized the "paradigmatic" natural law doctrine as consisting of two theses: "that from the God's-eye point of view, it [natural law] is law through its place in the scheme of divine providence, and from the human's-eye point of view, it constitutes a set of naturally binding and knowable precepts of practical reason."[2]

Locke equivocated between the idea that natural law can be deduced by human reason and that it had to be accepted simply as the Creator's will. Because philosophers have long held that God's existence (and thus the divine will) cannot be established through logic or observation, the latter strategy is unacceptable as a *philosophical* justification of natural rights. Yet, Locke also failed to show that his particular conception of justice could be derived by reason alone. Accordingly, as Nozick concludes, Locke was unable to "provide anything remotely resembling a satisfactory explanation of the status and basis of the law of nature in his *Second Treatise*" (*ASU*, 9). Subsequent generations of libertarian theorists have therefore felt compelled to offer a more convincing defense of natural rights than is found in Locke.

Nevertheless, it is apparent that his basic conception has an undeniable intuitive force. Most of us believe that we would be morally justified (if not obligated) to resist a murderous, tyrannical regime, even one elected through an unquestionably democratic process. But on what nontheological basis can we rightly oppose a duly elected government or disobey its laws? Of course, one possible response is that, as Locke claimed, all persons have natural rights that entitle them to rebel against despots.

Unfortunately, many contemporary libertarians ignore the challenge of providing an ethical foundation for rights, and simply assume the truth of something like Ayn Rand's oft-quoted claim that:

> A civilized society is one in which physical force is banned from human relationships—in which the government, acting as a policeman, may use force *only* in retaliation and *only* against those who initiate force. (emphasis in original)[3]

In a second essay, she expresses the same essential idea in a slightly different way:

> The precondition of a civilized society is the barring of physical force from social relationships—thus establishing the principle that if men wish to deal with one another, they may do so only

by means of *reason*: by discussion, persuasion and voluntary, uncoerced agreement. (emphasis in original)[4]

This moral stance has come to be referred to as the nonaggression principle ("NAP"), but no shibboleth, whatever its virtues, can substitute for a fully worked-out political theory. Even on its face, Rand's formulation of the NAP is plainly incomplete because it does not expressly permit an individual citizen to use force in self-defense or in defense of innocent third parties. Moreover, I think it is clear that at least in *some* circumstances the preemptive initiation of force is morally justified. I believe that Rand in fact understood these things, but they are not expressed in these short passages.

More substantively, all states collect taxes on a nonconsensual basis, and thus arguably are violating the NAP with respect to those citizens who would prefer to do without the state altogether, that is, the anarchists. Nevertheless, Rand upheld the moral legitimacy of the state as the best practical guardian of the rights of its citizens. Therefore, we should understand her principle as prohibiting the *unjustified* (construed in a certain way) initiation or use of force, with the specifics to be filled in by supporting arguments. As so interpreted, I have no quarrel with what I regard as her political ideal, although I reject the logic she relies upon to defend it.

For Rand, the NAP is the product of an elaborate philosophical system she called Objectivism. Thus, her derivation of rights is no stronger than the ethical foundation on which it rests.[5] Having explained elsewhere my reasons for rejecting her moral philosophy, I will not repeat them here.[6]

Nozick's account of rights

In contrast to Rand, Nozick does not attempt to derive libertarian rights in a top-down fashion from an overarching moral philosophy that delineates virtue and vice. Instead, he offers what is essentially a *political* doctrine, that is, a theory regarding the legitimate boundaries of state power. This takes the form of an argument designed to appeal to our deepest convictions regarding the respect owed to us as a "rational agent"; that is, a being able to conform its conduct to the moral law and "to regulate and guide its life in accordance with some overall conception it chooses to accept"

(*ASU*, 48–9).[7] Due regard for this attribute imposes on other people and the state a near-absolute prohibition (which Nozick calls "side constraints") on the use of force or coercion against innocent human beings, meaning those not themselves violating (or unreasonably threatening to violate) the rights of others (see *ASU*, 33–5).

In embracing the side constraint interpretation of rights, Nozick appeals to Immanuel Kant's highly influential notion of persons as "ends in themselves," quoting his second formulation of the categorical imperative: "Act in such a way that you always treat humanity, whether in your own person or in the person of any other, never simply as a means, but always at the same time as an end" (see *ASU*, 32).[8] This precept is violated, says Nozick, when the state uses individuals as mere tools to accomplish some social objective they themselves have not selected. Coercive interference with people's lives fails to accord them the respect and dignity to which they are entitled, and is therefore morally offensive.[9]

This then is the nature of the fundamental divide between libertarians and modern liberals. Except in extraordinary cases, we reject all demands that an innocent person's interests be sacrificed in the name of the group, the community, or the nation. As Nozick eloquently observes:

> There are only individual people, different individual people, with their own individual lives. Using one of these people for the benefit of others, uses him and benefits the others. Nothing more. What happens is that something is done to him for the sake of others. Talk of an overall social good covers this up. (Intentionally?) (*ASU*, 33)

His insistence on the inviolability of human beings is in harmony with our fundamental moral instincts. Most of us would reject forced organ transplants out of hand, even if the welfare gains experienced by those who receive kidneys would greatly outweigh the loss of utility on the part of the unwilling donors (who could get along fine with just a single one). It is true that some people support other kinds of nonconsensual redistributive measures, but it may be that their judgment in these matters is influenced by self-interest, if they are likely to benefit from such things, or by culturally induced biases.

Nozick's argument for natural rights is certainly controversial, but so are all competing political theories, such as those that would promote what is called social (or distributive) justice, egalitarianism, communism, traditionalist values, or theocracy. However, Nozick's theory compares favorably with its rivals in terms of plausibility, coherence, and consistency with facts about the nature of human beings.

Because Nozick's notion of side constraints is intended as a limit on permissible state action, it allows libertarian rights to peacefully coexist with a broad spectrum of views regarding our positive (non-enforceable) moral duties to others. A Nozickian libertarian can consistently hold that we should be generous in support of our needy fellow humans *and* that it is nevertheless wrong for the state to compel persons to do so. Nozick expressly ducks the question of whether this prohibition on compulsion is absolute or "may be violated in order to avoid catastrophic moral horror" (*ASU*, 30n).

The entitlement theory of justice

By means of his entitlement theory of justice, Nozick applies his conception of rights specifically to matters of property. Very briefly, this theory holds that if a person (i) justly acquires previously unowned property ("justice in acquisition") or (ii) receives it in a voluntary transaction (without the use of force or fraud) from a person who justly holds it ("justice in transfer"), then she is entitled to retain it (see *ASU*, 151–2). If all holdings in society satisfy these principles, then the entire distribution is just.

However, as Nozick is quick to point out, this theory is subject to a crucial qualification. If a set of holdings includes property obtained in violation of the first two principles, these wrongs must be corrected ("rectified") before the distribution can be considered just. He discusses the necessary elements and requirements of a satisfactory theory of rectification (*ASU*, 152–3, 158, 230–1), but ultimately admits that he does not have one at hand.

Nozick's theory of just acquisition follows Locke in holding that a person who labors to acquire or improve natural assets in a particular way is entitled to full property rights in them, provided he does not harm others in the process. With respect to wild berries and game, the simple act of harvesting the resource is sufficient.

For land, the paradigm is homesteading, whereby a settler clears and cultivates previously unclaimed land, while leaving, in Locke's words, "enough and as good" for others.

This is obviously an idealized account, and Nozick is certainly under no illusion that our world's actual history conforms to it in any substantial way. The Lockean model nevertheless remains relevant because it rebuts the claim that it is *impossible*, even as a theoretical matter, for property to be reduced to private ownership in a morally pristine way. Moreover, a homesteader's title to his land may be imperfect, yet still be superior to that of any other claimant.

Even so, it might be asserted that Lockean appropriation is unfair to those not around when the land was first claimed. After all, there is little or no land left today for original acquisition. But, this lack of opportunity does not render all contemporary property titles suspect. The reason is that the economic virtues of private ownership are sufficient compensation.

As Nozick observes, societies that recognize and protect private property are likely to be much more prosperous than those that don't. And, in such communities people will be able to purchase or lease all the raw materials, including land, that they require without the hardship of homesteading. You don't need to own a salt mine to obtain all you want of this mineral at an affordable price.

The ethical foundation for original appropriation is the notion of entitlement, which arises from constructive labor. That is, if a person *invests* her time and energy in developing unowned land (a commitment avoided by the timid or lazy), while not worsening the position of others, she has earned ownership of this resource and the right to whatever profits she may obtain from it. I should note here that Nozick does *not* generally condition property rights on meritorious effort, because this would exclude accretions by gift or bequest (as well as luck).[10] Accordingly, he summarizes his theory of justice as, "From each as they choose, to each as they are chosen" (*ASU*, 160).

However, original appropriation is not a matter of being "chosen," but a *unilateral* process that confers just title to a scarce resource that the claimant did not create. Therefore we cannot presume that this process is benign in the way of voluntary exchange, where both parties perceive a benefit; rather, justice demands that title be *earned* by improving the resource, and that the reduction to private property not harm others. Nozick calls this condition the "Lockean proviso" (see *ASU*, 178–80).

Nozick does not have much to say about the principle of justice in transfer. He does not need to, because voluntary exchanges can be defended by means of his arguments for side constraints, combined with his defense of property rights, even where one party enjoys a superior negotiating position. Provided that this advantage is itself not the result of any violation of rights, this disparity does not render the exchange unjust.

Although Nozick does not discuss this point, it seems clear that the principle of justice in transfer may be satisfied in some circumstances even if the transferor has imperfect title. With respect to stolen personal property, while the true owner (or his descendents) is morally entitled to its return, the innocent purchaser for value has a claim superior to that of anyone else. If the identity of the true owner is lost to history, the innocent buyer justly keeps it.

With respect to real property, even if the original homesteader used force or fraud to obtain (raw) land, it does not follow that the descendents of the victim, particularly if they are many generations removed from the crime, can justly reclaim possession (although the state may owe them compensation for this wrong). If the victim did not homestead, but instead merely *used* the land by, for example, harvesting wild game, this would be insufficient to confer just title under the Nozick/Locke model of original appropriation.[11] Thus, a subsequent good faith purchaser whose chain of title runs through the homesteader should retain ownership.

Nozick certainly recognizes that current ownership of land and the distribution of wealth generally have been shaped by past injustice, including crimes against African-Americans and Native Americans. However, for a number of reasons, rectification of these wrongs is now problematic.

First, and most practically, the state is not very good at rectification. President Johnson's "war on poverty" was intended, at least in substantial part, to redress the horrors of slavery and its aftermath. Furthermore, in the name of ameliorating the effects of our past aggression against Native Americans, we now offer them various forms of public assistance. Not only have these efforts failed to narrow the substantial wealth gap that has existed for many generations between whites and members of these communities, but there is ample evidence that because of the perverse incentives that were built into these programs, they have actually done more harm than good.[12] Such long-term governmental largess promotes dependency and social isolation, and thus the kindest policy that we could implement for the victims of past wrongs is to wean them off such aid.

Second, even if our legislators could somehow devise an effective rectification strategy, this enterprise must respect the rights of citizens who were neither the perpetrators of such historical wrongs nor the beneficiaries of them. On Nozick's principles, to which I subscribe, it would be morally impermissible to burden blameless persons with the cost of remedying injustices committed by others. Because the misdeeds in question occurred at least many decades ago, most of the perpetrators and victims are dead. Thus, other than with respect to the return of identifiable property, rectification would have to be enforced against innocent people.

Finally, even putting the earlier arguments aside, as the injustices in question recede into the distant past, the case for rectification becomes correspondingly weaker. If, for example, person *A* has $100,000 stolen from him, it seems very likely (although not certain) that his child *B* will also suffer a material loss. However, it is much less likely that *A*'s grandchild, *C,* will suffer serious harm, as there is by then a greater chance that *A* or *B* will have recovered from the injury, and thus less probable that *C* ends up significantly worse off relative to the imaginary baseline that would have existed in the absence of the injustice to *A*. When we consider the effect of the original injustice on *A*'s great, great, grandchildren, there will quite simply have been too many intervening choices and contingencies for a finding of "proximate cause" to apply.[13]

Once past injustices are rectified, the entitlement theory implies that holdings in a just society need not conform to any preconceived egalitarian pattern. Nozick asserts that whatever the actual set of holdings, "If these distributional facts *did* arise by a legitimate process, then they themselves are legitimate" (*ASU*, 232, his emphasis).

In support of this position, Nozick argues that our natural liberty is incompatible with the very idea of distributive justice (see *ASU*, 160–3). As he illustrates by means of his famous Wilt Chamberlain (a great professional basketball player of the 1960s and early 1970s) argument, indisputably *voluntary* transactions will potentially result in great disparities in wealth, as resources flow to those who can produce highly desirable goods or services.

Nozick asks his readers to imagine a community in which there exists a pattern of holdings that they consider just (perhaps everyone has roughly the same). Then, along comes someone like Wilt and offers to play basketball for a team if it will raise ticket prices by one dollar, and give him the proceeds. This arrangement will soon make Wilt very wealthy. But, both sides of this transaction seem entirely benign: Wilt wishes to play and his fans desire to pay to see him do so. By what moral authority does the state interfere in order to maintain the distribution in place before Wilt arrived?

Indeed, to maintain what egalitarians regard as a just distribution, the state would, in Nozick's memorable phrase, "have to forbid capitalist acts between consenting adults" (*ASU*, 263). In practice, the state typically attempts to do so not by prohibiting exchanges but by using its monopoly of force to redistribute the holdings resulting from them. This process directly interferes with the projects and plans of those affected, and clearly violates the Kantian prohibition against treating persons solely as tools to accomplish some supposedly greater good.

Claims of social justice

Commentators use the term "social justice" in a great variety of ways, and it is evident that there is no uniform, definite meaning in common practice. Generally, it expresses the idea that for a society to be just it must satisfy certain, typically egalitarian, criteria with respect to the distribution of goods.

However, there are serious conceptual problems with the idea of social justice, which can be brought out by contrasting it with our ordinary notions of justice. Aristotle proposed that justice is realized when people get what they deserve.[14] But, if "desert" is assimilated to reward or punishment for "moral merit" (or its absence), it is certainly *not* in our power to ensure that people always or even mostly get what they deserve.

First, there are profound disagreements about what constitutes virtue, and even if we could agree on appropriate criteria, we cannot see into people's motivations or character, nor can we have knowledge of all a person's deeds. Further, some apparent saints suffer unrectifiable tragedies, while what look like mortal sinners enjoy long and healthy lives. Because justice of the sort Aristotle imagines could only be effected by divine omnipotence, we may call this notion "cosmic justice."

With respect to the aspects of justice we can realistically attempt to secure (call this "ordinary justice"), libertarians hold that people are entitled to retain what they receive from others in consensual transactions. A competitive capitalist economy will tend to concentrate wealth in the hands of those who can produce things that are highly valued by others, as they will profit handsomely from the mechanism of voluntary exchange.[15]

Many innocent people will fare poorly in free markets relative to other participants in these same markets. But it seems uncontroversial that if blameless people are dying or suffering greatly because they lack the basic necessities of life, and if other members of their community have the resources to prevent or ameliorate such harm with minimal sacrifice of their own interests, they should voluntarily render aid. And, if there were no other means to this end, it would be permissible for the members of that society to coerce them to do so (provided that the burden of this assistance is shared equitably).

Notice, however, that we need not invoke *social* justice in order to reach this result. Nozick acknowledges that side constraints might have to be overridden if required to avert a moral catastrophe. Moreover, as discussed in more detail below, his Lockean proviso would justify the relaxation of property rights if they harm non-appropriators. Therefore, the notion of social justice is superfluous, as the precepts of ordinary justice are sufficient to command relief for innocent persons in desperate need.

Furthermore, the idea of social justice is confusing and misleading because it implausibly implies that there is some special aspect or type of justice that applies only to a particular group. If the validity of a political theory depends on it satisfying the particular needs of the poor, why does this requirement not also extend to other communities? What about appropriate treatment for the "Average Joe," the talented and entrepreneurial, ethnic/racial minorities, gays, the deeply religious, the disabled, environmentalists, nonconformists and eccentrics, the physically unattractive, and so on?

The claim that there is a special kind of justice, reserved for the worst off, would constitute an independent theory of justice, the ethical foundations of which would have to be specified and defended, reconciled with other competing values, its implications evaluated, and so on. I have not seen such a theory successfully articulated.

Even if we were persuaded that the idea of social justice is coherent, it would still not follow that the state has the moral authority to enforce this ideal beyond what is required to establish ordinary justice. By its very nature, social justice purports to identify conditions *not* brought about by the wrongful acts of moral agents, which would be subject to punishment and rectification under the tenets of ordinary justice. The enforcement of the former would require us not to redress wrongs or to save the innocent from grave harm, but to interfere on a wholesale basis with the *impersonal* outcomes generated by the free market.

These results, like those produced by nature itself, are neither just or unjust, but simply facts of life. Thus, as Hayek writes, "justice, like liberty and coercion is a concept which, for the sake of clarity, ought to be confined to the deliberate treatment of men by other men."[16] This is essentially Nozick's first line of attack against the so-called luck egalitarians, who contend that distributions under laissez faire are morally arbitrary because they will largely be a function of our natural talents and endowments. In their view, these attributes are a matter of brute luck (i.e., risks we did not knowingly take), and thus undeserved. Accordingly, the state is justified in redistributing the rewards that flow from them.[17]

In rebuttal, Nozick offers a series of counterexamples. Thus, persons do nothing to deserve the two healthy kidneys most of us are born with (see *ASU*, 206). Nevertheless, most people would be horrified by forced organ transplants, even if this practice would save lives.

Moreover, he says, if my future wife prefers me to another suitor because of my (undeserved) good looks and intelligence, am I nevertheless not entitled to her love? Should society, in order to correct this putative injustice, subsidize the rejected swain's plastic surgery and special intellectual training? (see *ASU*, 237). This solution must seem absurd, because it does not follow from the fact that something is undeserved (i.e., not distributed on the basis of moral merit), that it can justly be taken from the holder (see *ASU*, 224–6).

Nozick's second argument relies on the undeniable fact that superior natural endowments do not "just happen" to produce wealth; obviously, there are intermediate steps. Before a person can exploit her gifts she must develop them, and beyond this, she must typically offer things that others wish to obtain by means of voluntary exchange. In addition, some holdings arise by gift or bequest, and as a result of luck.

Accordingly, under Nozick's theory of justice, the structure of holdings will not track moral merit, virtue, or the like, but this does *not* make them "morally arbitrary," that is, random or whimsical. To the contrary, they are in large measure the product of the *autonomous choices* that rational agents make in developing their talents, investing their labor and capital, and selecting the recipients of gratuitous transfers (see *ASU*, 158–9, 213–6). And, as a practical matter, it is impossible to segregate out that portion of holdings that result from "dumb" luck.[18] Thus, even accepting the idea that the distribution of holdings cannot be morally arbitrary, luck egalitarians fail to give us any reason why people are not entitled to the holdings generated in a free market economy.[19]

Interpreting the NAP in light of Nozick's conception of rights

Rand's formulation of the NAP precludes the use of "physical force," but the exact contours of this prohibition are too ill-defined to permit it to serve as a useful moral guide. I have adopted Nozick's idea that this prohibition applies to any use of coercion or force by individuals or the state that interferes with the right of rational agents to live as they please, except as required to preserve the equal right of other persons to do the same. This conception of rights enables libertarians to address two of the most commonly heard objections to this doctrine.

Resolving conflicting claims of right

One of the primary philosophical objections to libertarianism is that its understanding of rights is too blunt and inflexible to arbitrate the myriad of cases where they appear to conflict, especially with respect to land use.[20] This problem is perhaps best presented by way of examples. Imagine that landowner A wishes to conduct some activity (e.g., a bonfire, fireworks display, the development of new, experimental explosives, etc.) that poses a substantial *risk* of harming his neighbor B or damaging his property. B objects to A's plans.

Since A has not to this point actually used force against B or injured him in any way, A claims that his property rights allow him to do whatever he likes on his land until such time as he actually harms B or his property. If that time ever comes, he stands ready to compensate B. In response, B avers that he is not interested in compensation, but in his own safety and the quiet enjoyment of his possessions. Accordingly, B asserts that A's proposed activity exposes him to an unacceptable level of risk, and thus violates his rights.

A similarly inconclusive dialogue can be envisioned with respect to pollution. Suppose that A is conducting some economically productive venture on his property that provides employment to many members of the community. A's enterprise unavoidably emits a trace level of air pollution, which poses no threat to human health. As it happens, a few stray particles fall on his neighbor B's land and are inhaled into his lungs. B, a radical environmentalist who objects to even the most *de minimis* level of pollution, claims that A is trespassing on his property, including his lungs, in violation of his rights. He refuses A's offer of generous compensation, and demands that he shutter his business.

At first blush, this objection to the libertarian conception of rights seems quite imposing. However, it assumes without justification that libertarians cannot simply employ community standards to resolve such cases. These norms can be determined by the same methods employed by economists in performing cost-benefit analysis ("CBA"). CBA quantifies in dollar terms the trade-offs that people *actually make* in (among other things) purchasing goods that reduce the risk of certain harms, like optional safety equipment in automobiles. From these patterns, economists can calculate how much we collectively value a small reduction in the risk of dying in an accident.

Similarly, in attempting to price clean air, economists might compare what people pay for otherwise identical residences located in areas with substantially different levels of smog.[21] In this way, they determine the dollar value that people attach to this and other goods. The same technique may be used to ascertain community standards with respect to a wide variety of land use issues, including the risks associated with certain activities.

All rights, including property rights, have great stringency. So, as a general matter the owner of land or other resources must be permitted to conduct whatever activities he likes on or with them, without obtaining the consent of others. We are justified in resorting to community standards only to determine whether a claimed right is real or spurious, *not* to determine the strength of such right, once established.

Returning to my example of A conducting some activity on his land that imposes a substantial risk of harm to B, once we conclude that A's conduct would violate B's rights under community standards, B would be entitled to simply enjoin A's conduct. In other words, B would not be required to sell or trade his permission, even if A offers him compensation substantially above fair market value. This discretion is implied by the notion of side constraints described earlier.

The use of community standards to resolve conflicting claims of right is consistent with underlying libertarian values. It does not run afoul of Kantian principles of respect for rational agents because all persons within a community are held to the same norms. On an intuitive level, it is clear that I am showing appropriate deference to others when the conduct of a suitably beneficial activity exposes them to a trace level of pollution that poses *no* realistic threat to their health. Similarly, it is obvious that this standard is violated when persons are involuntarily subjected to a grave risk of death, unless this exposure was unavoidably necessary to protect a much greater number of innocent human lives.

The problem of fraud

All libertarians hold that fraud is not only morally reprehensible, but also worthy of prohibition and punishment. Accordingly, a failure of libertarian theory to articulate a coherent basis for this stance would count as a serious demerit. Some critics have argued that libertarianism has this flaw.[22]

The NAP, in its literal form, does not provide a clear rationale for condemning fraud because such conduct fits very uneasily under the rubric of the initiation of force or aggression. Nevertheless, many libertarians simply assimilate fraud to theft, and condemn it on this basis.[23] However, I believe that this move is unjustified, because the con man does not steal your property in the same way that a thief does.

The mechanism of fraud is the inducement of action through the *deliberate* misrepresentation or deceit about important facts. Fraud occurs when the victim hands over his/her money or property to the perpetrator. Although the victim does so only because he has been duped, he nevertheless *elects* to entrust his property to the perpetrator. On the other hand, the thief does not need to create false trust; he simply takes what he wants and he need not concern himself with the victim's state of mind. Thus, it remains unclear how the swindler commits "aggression" against his target.

It may be objected at this point that the scammer's aggression consists in retaining property that he unjustly possesses. But this argument begs the question because it still does not explain *why* fraud is unjust, and therefore provides no justification for intervening to retrieve the ill-gotten gains. After all, perfectly competent people enter into contracts that in retrospect prove to be horribly disadvantageous to them. In such cases, libertarians will decry paternalism and affirm personal responsibility. What makes fraud different?

This problem can be resolved if we bear in mind that Nozick's idea of side constraints is derived from Kantian notions regarding the respect due rational agents. Their special status requires that persons not be used solely as a means to an end. This ethical standard precludes not only the use of force and coercion (subject to a limited range of exceptions, such as self-defense), but also victimization by fraud. The perpetrator of the latter *intentionally* prevents the agent from making a free choice, and this fact distinguishes it from other innocent or negligent misrepresentations that may lead people to make disadvantageous decisions.

This idea is captured elegantly by Isaiah Berlin in his famous essay, "Two Concepts of Liberty": "[T]o lie to men, or to deceive them, that is to use them as means for my, not their own, independently conceived ends, even if it is for their own benefit, is, in effect, to treat them as sub-human, to behave as if their ends are less ultimate and sacred than my own."[24] Thus, fraudulent conduct and theft are alike in treating persons in this impermissible fashion, and may both be punished and rectified under libertarian principles, properly understood.

The legitimate functions of the state

Nozick defends the justice of the minimal state, even though it funds itself by means of nonconsensual taxation. The anarcho-capitalists forcefully challenge the logical consistency of this stance. They pointedly ask, "why don't side constraints prohibit the collection from unwilling citizens of levies to finance military defense and law enforcement?" Without a good answer, the minimal state must be regarded as morally objectionable, although it might still be the least evil of all available alternatives.

The anarchist objection will not trouble those who endorse (at least) the minimal state, but do so on the basis of ethical principles that are different than those that underlie natural rights. Thus, utilitarians might simply reply that the practical advantages of the state in terms of promoting the general welfare justify the coercion required to fund it. However, since Nozick embraces side constraints, this rationale is unavailable to him.

Rather, he tries to show that the minimal state, whose charter is limited to "protecting all its citizens against violence, theft, fraud, and to the enforcement of contracts and so on" (*ASU*, 26), could evolve out of a state of nature in a manner that does *not* involve impermissible coercion. This would refute the anarchist claim that states are *intrinsically* evil. Nozick's effort is almost universally (and correctly I believe) regarded as a failure.[25]

However, even though Nozick's justification of the minimal state is unsuccessful, it obviously does not follow that no alternative defense is possible. I believe that the most promising argument for the justice of the minimal state is that the compulsion employed to fund its few legitimate activities stands on a different moral footing than coercive taxation for other purposes. The core functions of the minimal state—protection from foreign attack and criminal violence, and the adjudication of civil lawsuits—establish the basic preconditions for the exercise of rational agency. For Nozick, this attribute is the source of our special normative status.

Accordingly, a state does not act unjustly if it taxes coercively only to support those functions that safeguard our autonomy. And, because military defense is a classic public good (and thus susceptible to the problem of free riders), and because comparable difficulties exist with respect to the supply of law enforcement, it is plausible that neither can be produced by purely voluntary means, or will be available only if some people pay much more than their fair share.[26] Thus, coercive taxation to fund the minimal state may be defended by appealing to fundamental libertarian values.[27]

This brings us to the next logical question regarding the minimal state; that is, does it have a legitimate role as the provider of a social safety net if private efforts at relief fail? This is an important issue, since one of the most frequently heard objections to libertarianism is that it would require us to stand by helplessly while the disadvantaged suffer and even die rather than employ nonconsensual measures to save them. If this were the implication of libertarian principles it would, I acknowledge, render this doctrine implausible, but this is not the case. There are two distinct rationales that vindicate this claim.

The first rationale relies entirely on moral considerations that are internal to (and thus perfectly consistent with) the Locke/Nozick justification of individual property rights. For Locke, the right to reduce land and other external resources from a state of nature to private ownership is an incident of our natural right of self-preservation. Thus, he holds that we need not obtain the consent of others before doing so because "If such consent as that was necessary, Man had starved, notwithstanding the Plenty God had given him."[28]

Nozick's Lockean proviso requires that this "privatization" of land not injure non-appropriators, either at the time of original acquisition or in future generations.[29] This condition is required to address at least the theoretical possibility that the institution of private property would produce an economy in which a portion of the population cannot find gainful employment. Accordingly, if this institution is responsible for innocent people suffering severe deprivation, then a condition of Lockean appropriation has not been satisfied. Under such circumstances, if voluntary efforts fail, individuals who benefit from stringent property rights may be forced to give up some of their wealth to ensure the survival of blameless members of their community.

Those who find themselves in peril through their own irresponsibility would not have an enforceable claim for such assistance because the system of individual ownership is not the cause of their problems. This does not mean that their plight should be ignored, just that it would be improper for the state to coerce us to assist them. Note further that Locke's "enough and as good" condition for just original appropriation is intended to leave others with an unemcumbered opportunity to provide for their own welfare, so a Lockean social safety net would aim to get the needy back on their feet, rather than paying a guaranteed stipend.

The second reason for assigning less than decisive weight to rights, including property rights, in all possible contexts is grounded in moral (or value) pluralism. John Kekes (a contemporary academic philosopher) helpfully describes this doctrine as holding that "there are no states of mind, values, or conceptions of the good life that should always override whatever comes in conflict with them."[30] This notion is not only a fixed part of our commonsense morality, but also prevalent in normative philosophy.

Thus, natural rights libertarianism must acknowledge the existence of values other than the preservation of rights. It seems intuitively obvious that the stringency of rights, including to property, would have to be relaxed if trivial impositions were the only way to save helpless members of our community from death or prolonged misery. In fact, even Nozick, widely regarded as a "hardcore" libertarian, held open the possibility that side constraints might be overridden to avert great tragedy.

Nozick did not elaborate on his understanding of the conditions under which this might occur, perhaps because this determination will always involve an element of human judgment that defies any hard and fast rule. However, as a rough approximation, we can say that it is permissible to override a right if upholding the right would cause harm to the innocent wildly out of proportion to the objective value of the interests served by it. One widely discussed, small-scale example (that surely qualifies), involves a hiker caught in a deadly blizzard who, in order to survive, must break into a remote, uninhabited cabin posted with a "No Trespassing, This Means You!!" sign.[31]

However, the acknowledgment that rights may be permissibly overridden in cases like the one just described does not open the door to the entire welfare state.[32] The coercion of rational agents is intrinsically wrong, and is to be countenanced only when the moral weight of some other good clearly overrides our reluctance to resort to threats of force. Accordingly, on the basis of respect for autonomy, we may limit the scope of positive welfare rights to assisting our deserving fellow citizens out of dire circumstances.[33]

CHAPTER TWO

Property rights, eminent domain, regulatory takings, and zoning

Few modern-day liberals deny that property rights are entitled to at least *some* weight in our deliberations regarding political morality. However, in order to justify the nonconsensual taxation required to fund the activist state, they generally contend that these rights have less stringency than their expressive and political counterparts, and thus may be set aside in order to accomplish important social goals.[1] This chapter briefly examines this view, and then critiques a type of state action that represents a direct and fundamental threat to private property, that is, the outright seizure of land through eminent domain, or the destruction of its economic value through onerous use regulation and zoning.

However, before proceeding further, it will be helpful to describe "property" in a more formal way. Tibor Machan, a contemporary libertarian theorist, has provided this useful definition: "property is anything tradable or exchangeable that may be of value to persons."[2] It includes our own bodies and our labor; land and other natural resources; improvements to real property (i.e., cultivating land or building on it); tangible personal property (cars, tools, gold, artwork, etc.); and intangible personal property such as financial instruments, cash, useful inventions, and so on. Accordingly, when I refer below to "property rights," I am using this term in its broadest sense, as a synonym for economic liberty generally, including freedom of contract.[3]

The stringency of property rights

Although libertarians derive their principles from a variety of distinct ethical foundations, they are united in recognizing that their political ideals cannot be instantiated without strong ownership rights (over justly held property).[4] Indeed, I believe it is fair to say that a hallmark of libertarianism is its affirmation that economic liberty has the same moral weight as all of our other freedoms. Thus, for Nozick, since the control and disposition of resources is an essential element of our rational agency, redistribution in the name of social justice substantially demeans us:

> This process whereby they take this decision from you makes them a *part-owner* of you; it gives them a property right in you. Just as having such partial control and power of decision, by right, over an animal or inanimate object would be to have a property right in it. (*ASU*, 172) (emphasis in original)

Another way to see the intimate connection between property rights and autonomy is simply to consider people's motivation for ownership. For most persons, accumulating wealth is not their ultimate goal, but simply a means of achieving it. As F. A. Hayek puts it:

> Strictly speaking, there is no "economic motive" but only economic factors conditioning our striving for other ends. What in ordinary language is misleadingly called the "economic motive" means merely the desire for general opportunity, the desire for power to achieve unspecified ends. If we strive for money, it is because it offers us the widest choice in enjoying the fruits of our labor.[5]

Thus, for instance, we don't work simply to have funds sitting in a bank account or invested in the stock market, but in order to eventually buy a home, to maintain our current lifestyle in retirement, to put our children through college, and so forth.

Because a secure right to property enables us to live as we choose, interference with it by other people or the state violates our autonomy in the same way as does the violation of our freedoms of expression, religion, and political participation. As acknowledged earlier, property rights do not have absolute stringency, and may be overridden in extraordinary circumstances, but this is a far cry from holding that they are generally inferior to others, or that they must always give way in order to realize what the authorities consider to be a more just distribution of wealth.

Egalitarians may object that this justification of economic liberty fails because it is fundamentally unfair to those who hold property of little value. In other words, since human rights are universal, what kind of right is it that disproportionately benefits the wealthy and is of little use to the poor?

My initial response to this challenge is simply to note that my defense of libertarian property rights relies on the ethical theory outlined in Chapter 1. Under Nozick's principles, political justice requires equality of opportunity, not equality of outcome. Thus, provided that the requirements of justice in acquisition and transfer are observed, great disparities in holdings are morally unobjectionable. If inequalities are the result of past institutional injustice, then (to the extent practical) rectification is in order. However, acknowledging this does not becloud property rights generally, rather it vindicates them.

It must be noted here that our society is not run on free market principles, and it is *this* failing that wrongs many citizens by denying them a fair opportunity to compete for desirable social goods. As shown in the remainder of this study, our state severely abridges economic liberty, which disproportionately harms those struggling to lift themselves out of poverty. To assist the poor, we should not weaken ownership rights, but neuter the state.

It is unsurprising that even in an equal-opportunity society some people will derive a more direct benefit from property rights than others, because this is true of *all* rights. For example, millions of citizens care nothing about politics; they remain completely ignorant of current affairs and never vote. Are we then to conclude that there is something suspect about political rights?

Similarly, many people never have a controversial and potentially inflammatory opinion that they desire to communicate publically, so they have no need for First Amendment protections. But this fact hardly diminishes the importance of freedom of expression. The basic point is that *all* rights are enabling. It must be left to the individual to use the moral space that they provide as he or she sees fit.

Libertarian theorists are also united in holding that secure property rights play a critical instrumental role in preserving liberty generally. Put most simply, individual freedom is severely threatened when the state has its grip firmly on both the political and economic levers of power. In an ironic twist of fate, Leon Trotsky, the exiled Russian revolutionary, learned too late the horrific consequences that can ensue from this overreach. Observing that Stalin was using food as a political weapon, he writes, "In a country where the sole employer is the state, this means death by slow starvation. The old principle: who does not work shall not eat, has been replaced with a new one: who does not obey shall not eat."[6]

Richard Pipes, a leading scholar of Russian history, articulates the logic behind this important idea:

> The right to property in and of itself does not guarantee civil rights and liberties. But historically speaking, it has been the single most effective device for ensuring both, because it creates an autonomous sphere in which, by mutual consent, neither the state nor society can encroach: by drawing a line between the public and the private, it makes the owner co-sovereign, as it were. Hence it is arguably more important than the right to vote (footnote omitted).[7]

Of course, every new regulation or tax will not instantly collapse a liberal democracy into outright tyranny. Societies rooted in classical liberal values, such as ours, can withstand a great deal of political mischief. But, we erode property rights at our own long-term peril.[8]

The abuse of eminent domain

I now turn to one of our state's most blatant and offensive assaults on property rights: its use of the power of eminent domain (often referred to as "condemnation") to take land from unwilling owners for purposes of economic development. The right of the state to seize private property was recognized in English common law, and is (implicitly) sanctioned here by the Fifth Amendment to the Constitution, which was then applied to the various states by the Supreme Court in its post-Civil War, Fourteenth Amendment jurisprudence. However, the Takings Clause limits such seizures to property taken for "public use," and requires the government to pay "just compensation" (which consistently has been interpreted as fair market value) to the owner. Today, this power is far more commonly exercised by states and localities than it is by the federal government.

Until relatively recently our courts understood "public use" to mean the condemned land would be (i) owned by the applicable jurisdiction (a road or public hospital, for example) or (ii) transferred to a private party for use by the general public (e.g., an easement for a railroad with common-carrier duties). However, a more expansive interpretation of public use was endorsed by the Supreme Court in *Berman v. Parker*, 348 US 26 (1954).

Here, for the first time, the Court approved the use of eminent domain to fight urban "blight," that is, it permitted the private redevelopment of a neighborhood that was, at least in the eyes of the authorities, severely overcrowded and generally uninhabitable. There was no claim in *Berman* that *plaintiff's* property was blighted, or somehow posed a threat to the community, but his department store simply didn't fit in with the District of Columbia's comprehensive plan. Nevertheless, the Court held that the District's interest in redeveloping this area was a legitimate public purpose, and thus qualified as a public use. Plaintiff was just collateral damage in the pursuit of the greater good.

Before going further, I should note that even the use of eminent domain for what would unquestionably qualify as a traditional public use is controversial among minimal state libertarians (of course, for anarcho-capitalists, this issue is moot because if we abolish the state no entity will exist to exercise this power). Some contend that without the power of eminent domain it will be impossible or prohibitively expensive, due to the problem of holdouts, to build roads and other infrastructure, while others dispute this.[9] I am not going to discuss this thorny issue further here because if we succeed in limiting the state to its core functions, which do not include economic development, the potential for mischief will drop precipitously.

Sadly, we are far from limiting eminent domain to its traditional purpose. In fact, *Berman* set the stage for a further expansion of the public use concept in the Court's infamous decision in *Kelo v. New London, Connecticut*, 545 US 469 (2005). *Kelo* upheld the exercise, pursuant to state statute, of eminent domain in favor of a commercial developer. This case involved no allegations of blight: at issue were 15 ordinary suburban residences whose only sin was that they stood in the path of a massive, mixed residential/commercial development planned by the named city. These residents did not wish to sell their properties for fair market value, and thus objected to the city's condemnation of their homes.

The Court's 5–4 decision held that the use of eminent domain to create employment opportunities and increase local tax revenues constitutes a legitimate public purpose, and thus satisfies the public use test. *Kelo* was properly met with widespread outrage across the nation because of the (accurate) perception that the Court was giving localities broad authority to harm completely innocent residents in the name of economic development. In this conflict, as in most other uses of eminent domain, the local government sided with powerful corporations and real estate promoters against ordinary homeowners.

It is especially outrageous that the properties taken in *Kelo* were family residences, and as such, intimately tied to the exercise of our personal autonomy. If rights—any right, not just those relating to property—are to have any meaningful value, they surely must be sufficiently stringent to preclude their infringement whenever some bureaucrat decides (often erroneously, as it turned out in *Kelo*) that the utilitarian gains justify it.

The injustice inherent in the use of eminent domain for private development is not redressed by the constitutional requirement that the victims receive compensation for their property. Obviously, if the subjects of an eminent domain proceeding desired to receive fair market value for their land, home, or business, they would already have this asset on the market. There are many reasons why a person would *not* wish to be forced to sell their property for a "fair" price, ranging from the purely financial to the entirely subjective.

Examples of the former would include the owner's judgment that the timing of the sale will produce a suboptimal price, or a mistrust of the valuation methodology used by the government. Of course, the owner might also feel deeply that the property is worth more to them than its fair market value due to their subjective preferences, that is, an emotional/sentimental attachment ("my children grew up here") or an all things considered desire to live in their present location relative to any other home they could purchase with the proceeds of the forced sale.

In either case, the use of eminent domain plainly violates the autonomy of the home or business owner by *forcing* them to sell and move against their will. The government is impermissibly using competent human beings solely as a means of achieving the putative greater good. If a forced exchange is absolutely necessary to achieve huge utilitarian gains for the public at large, simple justice demands that the person subject to this coercion have the opportunity to show that the asset is worth more *to them* than its fair market value.[10]

An indignant citizenry has pushed back against the outcome in *Kelo* through amendments to their state constitutions or eminent domain laws. Some 35 states now prohibit condemnation for private development of the sort approved in *Kelo*. Sadly, a majority still permit redevelopment for the eradication of blight, a convenient loophole for local politicians who wish to engage in massive revitalization projects to improve the local economy or to reward their political cronies.[11] Historically, "urban renewal" has often been used by municipal authorities to raze viable minority communities, displacing tens of thousands of residents and eradicating countless minority-owned businesses.[12] This fact explains the NAACP's decision to file an *amicus* brief in the Supreme Court on the side of the homeowners in *Kelo*, and its longstanding hostility to eminent domain.[13]

Even if blight is a serious problem in a particular community, there is no justification for the use of eminent domain to redevelop the neighborhood. Any condemnation should be on a case-by-case basis, and only as a last resort. If an individual property poses an unreasonable threat to the health or safety of local residents, the municipality should proceed under law to force its owner to repair or demolish it. Failing that, the authorities should simply condemn that property and immediately sell it off at public auction. There is no warrant for acting on a neighborhood-wide basis, except in the unlikely event that all the relevant properties meet the applicable standard.

While the use of eminent domain for economic development is odious to anyone with due regard for property rights, it has many defenders on the left. The editorial board of the *New York Times* spoke for them in defending the *Kelo* decision: "Connecticut is a rich state with poor cities, which must do everything they can to attract business and industry. New London's development plan may hurt a few small property owners, who will, in any case, be fully compensated. But many more residents are likely to benefit if the city can shore up its tax base and attract badly needed jobs."[14] So, to reiterate the theme struck earlier, this issue illustrates the gaping divide that separates libertarians from today's liberals: we are unalterably opposed to harming innocent persons for the benefit of others.

In conclusion, eminent domain should be limited to the purposes permitted under the traditional public use standard, and subject to the liberalized compensation rules described earlier. Ideally, Congress should protect the rights of all citizens by enforcing this rule by legislation or, better yet, constitutional amendment.

Regulatory takings

While eminent domain permits the state to seize title to real property, other laws, regulations, and administrative decisions may seriously damage or even completely destroy land values, while leaving nominal title in the hands of private owners. These include government actions regarding wetlands preservation, protection of wildlife habitat under the Endangered Species Act, building permits, designation of structures as historical landmarks, zoning (see the following section), and rent control. Interventions of this sort have come to be known as "regulatory takings."

If these restrictions were put in place after the affected landowner acquired the property, then their economic impact was not reflected in the purchase price, and the owner will, as a consequence, suffer a financial loss. However, regulatory takings are not sanitized in those cases where there is no harm of this sort, because liberty is diminished when the uses to which land may be put are dictated by the vagaries of the political process, rather than reflecting the "spontaneous order" generated by free markets; meaning, a harmonious, self-generating arrangement that in Hayek's words "is the result of human action but not human design."[15]

Sadly, as in the case of eminent domain, our courts have largely turned their backs on the rights of property owners. The prevailing constitutional interpretation of the Takings Clause sharply distinguishes a physical condemnation from the regulatory variety, permitting compensation (by means of "inverse condemnation" proceedings brought by the owner) only when the restriction in question eliminates all or substantially all profitable use of the property. See, for example, *Lucas v. South Carolina Coastal Council*, 505 US 1003 (1992). Accordingly, as Richard Epstein notes, "under current takings law, a physical occupation with trivial economic consequences gets full compensation, [while] . . . major regulatory initiatives rarely require a penny in compensation for millions of dollars in economic losses."[16]

The current law on regulatory takings is plainly unjust from the natural rights perspective. It permits the sacrifice of individual rights simply to satisfy the preferences of other citizens. If the political authorities are determined to (say) prevent the development of certain acreage in order to preserve it as wetlands, they should negotiate this restriction with the owner or purchase the site on a consensual basis; anything else amounts to the use of brute force.

A legal requirement that inverse condemnation be available to owners whenever the state substantially reduces the value of their property would still permit the state to abuse its regulatory authority. Nevertheless, this step would represent a distinct improvement over the status quo. At least the public would pay for any benefit it receives, which might slightly inhibit overregulation. Instead, under the current legal regime, the entire burden of providing this good (assuming it is one) is shifted to the hapless property owner, who is denied any compensation if his land retains even a sliver of economic value.

The *Kelo* decision sparked a widespread property rights movement, which included an ancillary focus on regulatory takings, but only Oregon and Arizona actually enacted reforms. Until Congress passes legislation that eliminates the distinction between physical and regulatory takings under the Constitution, our representatives will be unable to resist the temptation to pursue politically popular goals at the expense of a few unfortunate landowners.

Zoning laws

Generically, "zoning" is (as the name implies) the practice of designating, by district, the uses that may be made of real property, for example, providing that all structures within a particular area may only be single-family residences. As typically implemented, it is a complicated regulatory scheme that specifies for each zone the type of land use(s) allowed, intensity or density of development, height, maximum size and placement of structures (setbacks), amount and design of parking, signage, and so on.

Due to the obvious problems that arise from the inflexibility of this procedure, the authorities always reserve the right to grant exceptions ("variances") from the existing requirements. Such relief is generally granted if the zoning board concludes that denial would impose an undue hardship on the landowner. Moreover, the uses permitted in a neighborhood will often be modified over time (i.e., "rezoning") in response to changing demographics or developments in bordering communities. For example, a district designated as exclusively single-family residential may be rezoned to permit apartment units and light commercial activity.

Zoning in the United States was essentially unknown prior to New York City's pioneering ordinance of 1916. After the US Supreme Court upheld the constitutionality of this procedure in 1926, its popularity boomed, and by 1930 more than a thousand municipalities had adopted it in some form.[17] Even so, nearly half of our municipalities adopted their ordinances after 1950. Now, zoning is nearly universal, with Houston as the only major holdout.[18]

As should be evident, zoning laws are the central planning method of land use regulation, and embody all of the grave flaws inherent in this economic philosophy. Rather than let the voluntary decisions of buyers and sellers, guided by the price mechanism, determine the uses to which property is put, government officials presume to make these choices for us. Accordingly, the first thing to say about this practice is that it is inconsistent with our natural rights.

Zoning precludes perfectly innocent activities that pose no threat to the legitimate interests of area residents. For example, designation of a district as single-family residential will preclude not only duplexes, but also "granny flats" (small, separate-entrance apartments within larger residences) and home offices, even those that cause a *de minimis* level of noise and disturbance.

Moreover, zoning ordinances impose significant limits on how owners may develop their property. Such restrictions artificially limit the housing stock in affected areas, and thus exclude people from living where they like. Consider the following representative example.

Suppose a firm owns 5 acres of raw land in an affluent suburban setting. Under laissez faire, its profit maximizing strategy would be to build five town homes per acre, for a total of 25. It can sell each home for $200,000, making a net profit (after all expenses, including land acquisition) of $20,000 per unit, or $500,000 total.

In order to spur sales, the firm would have a strong incentive to place restrictive covenants in the deeds to these units that would preserve the residents' quiet enjoyment of their homes.[19] Similarly, the developer's profit motive would also prompt it to incorporate commercial elements in its plan that would increase the overall demand for these homes. This might include, for example, allocating leasable space for a cafe/restaurant, dry cleaner, convenience store, and so on.

In our actual world, the neighborhood in question would probably be designated exclusively as single-family residential, with (as is common) a 1 acre minimum lot size. Those living in proximity to this site will fight like hell against granting the developer a variance, believing that this would permit lower-income families entry to the neighborhood, driving down home values. Thus, the developer would quite likely be limited to five units. If local demand for residential housing permits a maximum selling price of only $500,000 per unit, the enterprise might only make $250,000 in net profit, and 20 families will be denied the opportunity to live in the location they regard as best suited to their employment and other needs.

This example illustrates the two ways in which zoning is fundamentally unjust. First, it violates the right of property owners to use their land as they see fit, subject only to the condition that they respect the equal rights of their neighbors, as judged by contemporary standards in the applicable community. Second, because zoning prevents developers and potential purchasers from entering into mutually beneficial agreements, it violates the freedom of contract that is the right of every competent adult.

Libertarians are willing to countenance the infringement of rights if necessary to prevent great harm. But zoning doesn't fit this bill, because even if the responsible administrators are well meaning, the entire enterprise is intellectually incoherent, akin to searching for unicorns. As Bernard Siegan, a prominent critic of the practice has written:

> Zoning has been a colossal flop because it supposed to do things it cannot do. What, for instance, is the "right" mix of homes and apartments? How much industry is "too much?" Where is business to be allowed, and what kinds? Is there some objective measurement available to determine the "best" use of some or all of the land, of growth and antagonistic proposals, and whether the land is better suited for open space, mobile homes, industry or the housing of people? Should the land be developed with one, two or four housing units per acre?[20]

Moreover, land use officials are not, in general, impartially trying to do the right thing. Such planners are subject to conflicting political pressure from constituents striving to preserve the status quo and developers. While the former may potentially vote them (or their superiors) out of office, the latter may offer tempting financial blandishments of both the legal and illegal kind. In short, this process is riddled with all of the pitfalls identified by public choice economists, and will therefore produce irrational and inefficient outcomes, often shaped to suit the needs of those administering the system and powerful special interests.

Thus, in addition to violating individual rights, zoning laws have been roundly criticized across the ideological spectrum for creating or exacerbating a wide variety of social ills.[21] These include raising the price of housing; environmental degradation (by wasting land, thus leaving less available for conservation as open space); denying parents educational choice by preventing them from moving to better school districts; promoting suburban sprawl, with longer, more polluting commutes; harming the economy generally by denying individuals the ability to live closest to their best employment opportunities; corrupting local politics; and segregating racial minorities and low income groups. As Bradley C.

Karkkainen, a legal scholar sympathetic to this institution (at least in principle) notes, from the 1970s onward, "academic literature has been almost uniformly critical of zoning."[22] Moreover, three presidential housing commissions appointed to study the practice have also condemned it.[23]

The popularity of this bureaucratic scheme in the face of such objections is primarily attributable to the widespread perception that it is necessary to preserve property values in middle-class and affluent neighborhoods by preventing the intrusion of lower-income residents and obnoxious uses. But zoning is not required to protect people's *legitimate* expectations for three reasons. First, the repeal of zoning would not lead to a chaotic free-for-all where major industrial operations and bustling commercial enterprises move into sleepy residential neighborhoods. This is because businesses are driven to site their activities by financial and operational considerations that will naturally segregate them from residential neighborhoods.

For example, even in the absence of zoning, Toyota will not locate a new assembly plant in a middle-class residential neighborhood because (among other things): the cost of land acquisition would be unnecessarily high; the plant would not (in all probability) be close enough to major transportation hubs, such as railroad terminals, interstate highways, ports, and airports; and it would be too distant from its pool of (primarily) blue-collar workers. Similarly, Siegan has observed, "gas stations and shopping centers will only locate on major thoroughfares because they require ready auto accessibility to succeed."[24] In other words, a spontaneous order will emerge.

Second, real property owners can often protect themselves against unwelcome land use(s) by entirely voluntary means.[25] To take a simple example, suppose neighbors A and B own adjoining homes somewhere in suburbia. Both owners strongly prefer to live next to another single-family residence and also believe that the resale value of their homes will be enhanced if potential purchasers can rely on this limitation remaining in force.

Accordingly, they agree to place restrictive covenants on the deeds of their respective properties, which will bind all future owners. Obviously, there is nothing to preclude A and B from attempting to widen the scope of their agreement to include neighbors C, D, and E before implementing it.[26] They could, for example, condition the covenant's effectiveness on getting these neighbors to agree to the same restriction. Moreover, as mentioned earlier, new developments will generally be accompanied by restrictive covenants designed to protect the quiet enjoyment of these residences, while allowing complementary commercial uses.

Finally, even if a homeowner is faced with an obnoxious land use that violates his rights, a laissez faire system would not leave him without recourse. Prior to the advent of zoning, disputes between neighbors regarding uses of real property were handled through the common law tort of nuisance, which dates back to medieval England. Most broadly, a "nuisance" consists of a "non-trespassory invasion of another's interest in the private use and enjoyment of land."[27] Accordingly, an aggrieved (typically residential) landholder could bring a private cause of action seeking compensation or an injunction against an allegedly unneighborly use, such as a gas station, factory, or funeral parlor.[28] While resort to this action for purposes of resolving such conflicts has largely been displaced by zoning ordinances (which supersede the common law), the tort of nuisance remains good law, and thus an available remedy if zoning ordinances were repealed.

Historically, in providing or denying relief from a claimed nuisance courts would balance the damage or inconvenience caused by the defendant against the economic cost of abatement.[29] Essentially, courts were reluctant to enjoin highly productive land uses in order to protect plaintiffs harmed in relatively minor ways. While this "balancing of utilities" approach would represent an advance over our current corrupt, central planning system, it is still unjust. Under libertarian principles, a landowner has the right to enjoin offensive uses of land by neighbors if they create a nuisance under the standards of his or her community, even if on balance this results in an overall loss of social welfare.

Importantly, "community standards" here refers to how the residents of particular neighborhoods *actually* behave with respect to claimed nuisances, not what they claim when in front of the town planning board. Thus, if members of a community generally do not, for example, object to a specific level of noise and traffic, a tribunal should not preclude the construction of duplex residences if they would impose no greater inconvenience in these matters than is currently tolerated.

While setting forth the procedures and the detailed legal standards that would govern such disputes is beyond the scope of this study, it would be desirable for litigants to have access to specialized adjudicatory bodies, including private arbitrators, to resolve nuisance claims. Ideally, this would include informal and user-friendly forums, as we now use to resolve traffic cases, for relatively simple and minor disputes. On the other hand, when the issues at hand are complex and involve great financial stakes, full due process, with appellate rights, should be available. Over time, as our experience with the common law has demonstrated, a body of precedent will develop that will substantially clarify the rights and responsibilities of neighbors with respect to their property.

In light of the arguments just presented, all zoning laws should be repealed immediately. I am sure that what I am proposing in place of this institution is an imperfect system of land use management, but the status quo is so flawed that it strains credulity that a system of private enforcement could be worse. And, what I am proposing has the decisive virtue of respecting our rights.

Of course, we may never live to see the abolition of zoning. In the meantime, there are useful reforms that, while not restoring our economic liberty, would reduce the harms stemming from its violation. These include: (i) reducing the number of local agencies involved in the regulation of land use and streamlining the approval process; (ii) simplifying the number and types of different zoning classifications, which in some cities now number in the dozens; (iii) replacing lot size, setback, and yard requirements with simple population density limits; (iv) eliminating all blanket prohibitions on duplex homes, granny flats, and home offices in residential zones; (v) showing far greater flexibility in permitting mixed commercial and residential uses; and (vi) zoning solely on the basis of environmental impact, not by type of housing, meaning that within the population density constraints specified for a particular community all housing options should be evaluated strictly on their consequences, not whether they are condos, apartment complexes, town homes, and so on.[30]

CHAPTER THREE

Rights of expression and association

This chapter first elucidates the libertarian defense of expressive rights, then compares it to a popular utilitarian justification that affords much less stringent protection. My focus then turns to the state's regulation of political campaign finance and commercial speech, which violates individual rights in both cases. I then analyze our antidiscrimination laws, which are also shown to be incompatible with libertarian principles, except in a narrow range of circumstances. Finally, I argue that the state should have no role in the right of association known as marriage.

The libertarian defense of free expression

The libertarian commitment to untrammeled freedom of expression, including what is known as hate speech, is an implication of the value we place on rational agency. As Thomas Nagel, a contemporary (left-leaning) philosopher, has written:

> The autonomy we value is defined not just by how we are treated, but by how we may be treated. To admit the right of the community to restrict expressions of convictions or attitudes on the basis of their content alone is to rob everyone of authority over his own mental life. It makes us all, equally, less free.[1]

The suppression of bigoted, malicious speech is wrong because it treats our rational agency as something that may be sacrificed to spare the feelings of others or to promote a supposedly higher good. The punishment of hate speech or other communication that most of us find highly offensive deters persons from expressing themselves. We thus limit their freedom, and rob others of the opportunity to be virtuous by rebutting these repellent ideas.

To endorse the censorship of expression because of the distress experienced by some (or even the vast majority of) listeners is to, in effect, recognize a moral right not to be pained by speech. But where does this purported right come from; in other words, what is its ethical foundation? After all, many other things that people do as a matter of right cause us pain.

For example, a popular entertainer might decide to retire young, depriving us all of the great pleasure we get from her work, yet few would claim that society may justly force her to keep performing. Why is offensive speech different? Questions of this sort have no satisfactory answers, and thus any claimed right not to be offended by speech is spurious.

One way to better understand the natural rights justification of free speech is to contrast it with a popular utilitarian defense of this right. I refer here to the value of an unfettered "marketplace of ideas" in the discovery of truth.[2] This idea appears to have originated with John Stuart Mill, and is an important element of our own constitutional jurisprudence.

But this logic can only be pushed so far. Much (perhaps the bulk) of the thought expressed by most people is demonstrably false, ill informed, redundant, malicious, poorly reasoned, or otherwise of manifestly inferior quality, and is quite unlikely to contribute, and may even detract, from the search for truth. Thus, even if the utilitarian starts with a rigid rule upholding free expression, since he regards unrestricted speech as only an *instrumentally* valuable means of discovering the truth, we may be able to admit exceptions.[3] In other words, we can improve the marketplace of ideas by excluding obviously false and misleading claims and opinions from the debate.

Our politicians, who should know better, are not immune from reasoning in this fashion. One well-publicized example may be found in an October, 2006 open letter written by two sitting US senators (Olympia Snowe and John D. Rockefeller IV) to Rex W.

Tillerson, the Chairman and CEO of ExxonMobil. Their missive objected to Exxon promoting its views regarding climate change: "ExxonMobil is responsible for much of this bogus scientific 'debate' and the demand for what the deniers cynically refer to as 'sound science.'" The senators went on to request that the company "end any further financial assistance or other support to groups or individuals whose public advocacy has contributed to the small, but unfortunately effective, climate change denial myth."[4] Here, Exxon's strong "public advocacy" was considered to be a serious problem, and not part of the process of discovering the truth.

Consider also in this regard the ubiquitous speech codes and harassment policies that have been adopted by our public colleges and universities. These vague rules and regulations prohibit any expression or conduct that mocks, insults, discomforts, harasses, or offends people on account of their race, ethnicity, religion, sexual orientation, and so on. As we might anticipate, these codes are primarily enforced against those expressing conservative political or traditional religious views, which are distinctly out of fashion on most campuses.[5] And, students and faculty are often disciplined and even expelled (or terminated) for violating them.

Many dozens of egregious speech codes are cataloged and quoted on the website of the Foundation for Individual Rights in Education, a nonprofit organization dedicated to protecting free speech on campus. For example, Oakland University (a public institution) has a regulation that provides: "No person shall use any telephone or other communications device to harass, offend, or disturb any other person, nor shall any person use threatening, obscene, immoral, or insulting language over any telephone or other communications device."[6] Assuming that they are acting in good faith, the officials responsible for such rules must sincerely believe that the perceived harm arising from offensive speech outweighs the intrinsic value of free expression.

Because libertarians respect property rights, we hold that private institutions, that is, those which receive no taxpayer funding, are entitled to establish and enforce whatever rules they wish regarding speech on their campuses, provided that these rules are clearly laid out and disseminated in advance.[7] However, those colleges and universities that enforce speech codes should not at the same time claim (as they typically do) to foster critical thinking and to promote the search for truth by means of rigorous analysis and debate, since this process may well "offend" or "disturb" many of the participants.

In additional to the moral argument just outlined, criminalizing *certain* speech based on its content is a classic example of the "slippery slope" or "line-drawing" problem. If we criminalize Holocaust denial, should we also ban speech claiming that the number of Jews killed by the Nazis has been exaggerated? Should we ban the denial of other Holocausts, suffered by the Armenians, Rwandans, Native Americans, Australian aboriginals, and so on? Should we also punish those who claim that AIDS is a holocaust deliberately perpetuated by whites against blacks? There simply is no *principled* way to distinguish between expression that is so lacking in "merit" that we can safely ban it, and all other speech. Once we start down this path, we are sure to end up with arbitrary and indefensible outcomes.

Campaign finance reform and commercial speech

Due to the excessive scope and power of the state, political influence has become of critical importance to corporate and other well-organized interest groups. If the state were limited to its few essential functions, the many constituencies that now stand to directly benefit from or be harmed by government interventions would have little reason to curry favor with the authorities.

Having first established this dependency relationship, Congress then took it upon itself to control the means that citizens may use to elect and influence their representatives. Within the last 40 years Congress has sought to redress the perceived corrupting influence of money in politics, by enactments that (in federal elections): (i) limit the amount of money that individuals can contribute directly to candidates; (ii) as a means of preventing people from circumventing "(i)" above, prohibit "soft money" contributions to political parties, meaning, funds that are used in coordination with the party's candidates; (iii) ban corporations and unions from directly contributing to political campaigns; (iv) forbid "outside" entities such as corporations (including nonprofits) and unions from running political ads that directly call for the election or defeat of any candidate; and (v) bar such "outside" entities from running political ads that even mention a candidate within a specified number of days prior to an election.[8] Not coincidentally, I think, such restrictions generally favor incumbents, who enjoy an inherent fund-raising advantage.

Thankfully, the last two restrictions were recently struck down on First Amendment grounds by the Supreme Court in *Citizens United v. Federal Election Commission*, 558 US 50 (2010). All of the remaining restrictions on campaign contributions identified earlier should also be repealed, as they contravene our right of free expression.

Persons are entitled to participate in the political process by either spending their own money on ads for the purpose of getting a candidate elected to office or by contributing funds to candidates (or parties) who will use them for the same purpose. The former is a direct exercise of self-expression in the political arena, and is both a self-evident moral right and an activity that is unquestionably protected by the First Amendment. The latter is an indirect exercise of the same right, pursuant to which the contributor, rather than speaking herself, facilitates political speech by others.

Of course, making a political contribution is not exactly the same act as personally running a campaign ad, but they both involve the use by individuals of their own resources to advance a cause that is important to them. And, critically, the exercise of either option cannot plausibly be said to constitute an act of force or fraud against other persons, who enjoy an equal right to political speech. Thus, the two choices are indistinguishable from the natural rights perspective, and so long as those directly funding candidates or parties publicly disclose this assistance—as a prophylactic against *actual* corruption—they are firmly within their rights.

On the other hand, if donors to so-called Super PACs, that is, organizations that have no connection to political candidates and are legally permitted to accept unlimited contributions, wish to remain anonymous, they should be allowed to do so. If our society is not prepared to recognize a zone of privacy with respect to its citizens' political views, then why do we utilize the secret ballot in our elections?

In addition, campaign finance laws are not self-enforcing, but must be administered by some governmental agency created and authorized for this purpose. Libertarians rightly fear that these laws will not be overseen in a fair and impartial way, but will be subverted either by the incompetence of the appointed officials or by political interference, as happened recently at the IRS in its review of applications for tax exempt status under 501(c)(4) of the Internal Revenue Code.[9]

The greatest controversy with respect to the private funding of political communications concerns corporations and unions. Both of these entities are creatures of the law and not natural persons, so it is frequently claimed that they should not enjoy the same speech rights as individuals. This view is based on the idea that it is unfair for corporations and unions to spend funds for political purposes without the approval of shareholders or members. However, the membership of these organizations can preclude such spending by simply electing officers who will not engage in it.

On the other hand, most shareholders and union members lack the resources as *individuals* to influence the authorities on matters vital to their finances and livelihoods. Therefore, the aggregation of their "voice" through corporate or union participation in the political process may be the only means they have of influencing policy. So, laws restricting the political speech of corporations and unions are antithetical to individual rights.

There is an important further argument against restricting corporate speech. It is entirely uncontroversial that media corporations, (i.e., firms that own newspapers, television and radio stations, internet news sites, and so on) have an unfettered legal and moral right to present the news and to communicate editorial content without government interference or censorship. These corporations do not need to make campaign contributions to protect their economic interests, as their leaders have substantial political influence by virtue of their ability to reach mass audiences with their views.

In contrast, corporations in other industries must rely on political speech, including issue-oriented advertising and campaign contributions, in order to protect the interests of their stakeholders, particularly when they are threatened by biased or slanted news coverage from media conglomerates. Therefore, it is manifestly unfair to grant media corporations unfettered expressive rights, while denying such rights to other firms.

The libertarian conception of free expression also requires that we abandon the distinction now made in our law between "commercial" and "noncommercial" speech. The disparate level of First Amendment protection afforded to these two (purportedly) different categories of expression was endorsed by our Supreme Court in *Central Hudson Gas & Elec. Corp. v. Pub. Serv. Comm'n*, 447 US 557 (1980), the governing precedent in this area of constitutional jurisprudence. There the Court held that while governmental regulation of noncommercial speech will always subject to the strictest scrutiny, meaning that it could be justified only under extreme and extraordinary circumstances, the regulation of commercial speech will be subject only to an "intermediate" standard of review, which entails that restrictions will be upheld if they "directly advance" a "substantial" public interest.

The effect of this distinction is that commercial advertising may be curtailed by the government in order to prevent potential harm to consumers even if the communication is not actually false, but merely incomplete, unsubstantiated, or likely to be misused. Examples include state laws that limit what attorneys may say about their services; the Federal Trade Commission's prohibition on health claims by herbal supplement companies about their products; and FDA regulations that prohibit pharmaceutical companies from providing physicians with truthful information regarding "off-label" uses of their drugs. Of course, the advertising of tobacco products on television has been prohibited altogether (our antismoking laws are examined in Chapter 4).

Individuals, groups of related persons (e.g., law firms), and corporations advertise their goods and services in order to convey their benefits to potential purchasers. Like other forms of expression, commercial speech may be false or misleading, but it typically advances an important and morally legitimate interest of the advertiser, and is an important element of economic liberty. Therefore, non-fraudulent commercial speech is entitled to the same protection from governmental meddling as any other form of expression.

Shouting "Fire!" in a crowded theater, and "time, place, and manner"

There is no space here to address all of the theoretical issues connected with the libertarian view that expression is entitled to a near-absolute level of protection. However, two important points should be made. It is often urged that the right to communicate must be balanced against other considerations because, as the saying goes, no one has the right to falsely yell "Fire!" in a crowded theater. But as constitutional law professor Alan Dershowitz has noted, such arguments completely misunderstand the nature of the "speech" at issue in this and other comparable cases.[10]

A prohibition on falsely and dangerously shouting, "Fire!" does not constitute the censorship of expression; it is simply the equivalent of a ban on pulling the fire alarm under the same conditions. The state is not acting wrongly when it punishes speech in such circumstances because it is clearly not regulating communication based on its *content*, but rather its effect.

Similarly, when a mugger sticks a gun in your back and demands "Your money or your life," he is not exercising his First Amendment rights, but committing a crime. Therefore, when we jail him we are not punishing his *speech*, but only his conduct. On this same logic, when the state criminalizes the incitement of violence against innocent persons, it is not acting to suppress speech because it disapproves of its content, but because the communication at hand is in furtherance of a violent crime.

Of course there are gray areas, and reasonable people will certainly disagree about particular, hard cases, but at least in principle it is possible to distinguish between censorship of speech based on its message, which is *always* wrong, and the permissible punishment of criminal acts or the redress of egregiously unethical conduct (e.g., libel, dissemination of stolen trade secrets, etc.) that is perpetrated *by means of* speech. In illustrating that individual rights are necessarily limited by the rights of others, Nozick quips that "My property rights in my knife allow me to leave it where I will, but not in your chest" (*ASU*, 171). Something similar might be said about free speech, but this hardly relaxes the stringency libertarians attach to this right.

It should also be clear that a near absolute protection for free speech is consistent with governmental regulation of its logistics, namely, its "time, place, and manner." Such regulation may be justified by the need to ensure that public demonstrations do not violate the rights of other innocent people. Thus, there is no "right" to hold political demonstrations that block rush hour traffic when there are other suitable venues for this purpose that are equally available to all interested groups.

However, if we ever get to the minimal state favored by libertarians, there will be much less need for governmental regulation of "time, place, and manner." Under such conditions there will be less public property and correspondingly more private property, and the owners of the latter would determine the uses to which it could be put. Parties wishing to stage demonstrations there could either obtain permission from the owners or rent property for that purpose. This would eliminate the inherent danger of governmental favoritism for some groups over others in the realm of political expression.

The right of free association

The libertarian defense of free expression applies equally to the prerogative persons have to associate with whom they please. Just as people have the right to express stupid and bigoted opinions, they have the right to interact exclusively with other stupid and bigoted people, or people of only a certain race, ethnicity, sexual orientation, and so on. A contrary position would empower the state to regulate our personal and social relationships, a view that cannot be defended under any plausible moral theory.

However, when we shift focus from personal associations to the economic sphere, the libertarian ideal of noninterference becomes highly controversial. In fact, the contrary perspective is the established legal order. Thus, under the Civil Rights Act of 1964 and subsequent statutes it is unlawful for any business engaged in interstate commerce that employs more than 15 persons to discriminate on the basis of race, religion, ethnicity, gender, age, and other characteristics in public accommodations (hotels, restaurants, etc.) and employment.[11] Given the Supreme Court's highly expansive interpretation of what "interstate commerce" means for purposes of the Commerce Clause, the federal antidiscrimination statutes now cover most of the economy.

I am about to argue that such laws violate our personal autonomy, and thus are unjust. However, this view in no way authorizes the *state* to operate in a manner that violates the rule of law. A state that denies equal protection to any group is morally bankrupt, and must be opposed. Moreover, past discrimination of this kind might require rectification, at least in the short run.

Accordingly, libertarians generally support the provisions of the civil rights laws that prohibit the authorities from engaging in *de jure* or *de facto* discrimination against any constituency. Moreover, in the Jim Crow South, the application of these laws to purely private conduct, for example, by innkeepers, restaurateurs, and employers, was justified by the need to remedy the effects of prior state discrimination.[12] In other words, the long history of state sanctioned oppression of African-Americans, including the denial of equal access to educational opportunities, employment, and investment capital, deprived them of a fair opportunity to compete in the marketplace. Thus, a temporary ban on private discrimination by white owners against blacks with respect to public accommodations, lending, and employment was required to rectify this prior injustice.

Subject to that qualification, antidiscrimination laws are morally indefensible. Prejudice is a bad thing, but those who harbor it are rational agents, and their choice of associates is a part of their character, even if an unseemly one. Prejudice falls far short of physical violence, theft, fraud, and the like, so using the law to enforce tolerance impermissibly treats persons solely as a means of achieving what the majority regards as the greater good.

If we accept this analysis with respect to personal relationships, then we must ask why owning a business should subject the proprietor to state coercion.[13] If the government has the moral right to enforce impartiality in a businessperson's selection of customers, where does this power end? Can the state also force the owner to hang a sign in her storefront window supporting its pet projects? Just as it is impossible to articulate a plausible ethical foundation for a purported right to be protected from insulting, even hurtful speech, so too is it impossible to make the case for a right not to have one's feeling hurt by a bigot's refusal to do business with you.

Due to the changing social attitudes that have expanded marriage equality under law, many of our states have begun to aggressively enforce their antidiscrimination statutes against business owners who, for reasons of conscience, do not wish to serve certain customers. The latest high-profile case involves a New Mexico commercial photographer who refused to memorialize the commitment ceremony of a same sex couple (a legal marriage being unavailable to them), because such relationships clashed with the owner's sincerely held religious convictions.[14]

The New Mexico Supreme Court held that the state's antidiscrimination law applied, and that the photographer may therefore be coerced into compliance by fines. Thus, dissenters from the "official" moral stance of the authorities may be put to a choice between adhering to their beliefs and earning a livelihood. This is by no means an isolated case.[15]

If antidiscrimination laws are grounded in sound moral principles, then they should apply to everyone, and not just to favored groups. If a commercial photographer with traditional Christian values must memorialize a gay couple's commitment ceremony, then why shouldn't an African-American photographer be forced to document a Klan rally? Obviously, the latter scenario is appalling, but the nature of the business owner's identity or beliefs shouldn't make a difference for purposes of testing the justice of a rigid antidiscrimination rule. Just as the right of free expression must apply equally to all content, the right of free association must protect even the bigot's right to discriminate.

In response, it is commonly argued that since corporations are not natural persons, but creatures of law, the state is entitled to impose whatever conditions it likes on the privilege of doing business. However, this claim fails to recognize that the benefits of the corporate form could just as easily be obtained by contract, in place of statute. In other words, if the laws authorizing corporations were repealed, those wishing to do business as a "corporation" would simply announce and widely publicize that they are only willing to transact business with those who agree that this entity enjoys limited liability and the other advantages of the corporate form. There is nothing unjust about such a proposition, and thus no good reason for a court not to enforce it. Accordingly, the state is not granting any special favors by authorizing corporations, and therefore is not entitled to impose any special obligations.[16]

The claim that corporate statutes entitle the authorities to bend these entities to their will also clearly proves too much. Because limited liability entities are legal fictions, can the state then justly demand that they discriminate against blacks or other minorities? Obviously not. Why, then, are the authorities licensed to coerce proprietors to do business with those they do not wish to serve?

Under free market capitalism discrimination by private businesses will rarely if ever inflict serious harm on disfavored minorities both because there will usually be other firms eager for this business and because those enterprises that discriminate will lose not only the patronage of the target group but all members of the community offended by this practice. Thus, discrimination by a firm would work to the advantage of its competitors, providing a strong financial incentive not to do so.[17]

In a worst case scenario, where a large majority of a particular community is biased against a minority, the affected group could open businesses that cater to its members. If private discrimination did somehow threaten grave injury, this would justify overriding the right of free association, but I believe this risk is very low in our society.

Marriage equality under law

The rule of law demands strict impartiality by the state in its treatment of married and unmarried persons. But, if a political community elects to confer certain benefits only on the married, then it equally violates the rule of law to deny any member of society the right to this status. Until recently, the various states restricted this privilege to heterosexual couples. This discrimination is rapidly eroding, as more and more states have enacted marriage equality. Libertarians should welcome this development, but our ultimate goal must be to end all state involvement in defining, regulating, or promoting marriage.

Our laws confer certain rights only on spouses, such as intestate inheritance, various tax breaks, survivor benefits under social security, the authority to make medical decisions in the absence of a living will, and so on. As things now stand, the state's definition of marriage effectively determines who can be a "spouse" for purposes of enforcing these rights. Under libertarian principles, the state has no warrant to favor married people over the unmarried, or to discriminate in marriage against any arrangement voluntarily entered into by competent adults. Polygamous relationships do not harm other people under libertarian standards, and there is consequently no justification for denying consensual participants whatever legal rights and status are conferred under law by marriage.

There is clearly no need for state involvement in this institution because all of the reciprocal legal rights that spouses enjoy could be established by contract, for example, alimony and child support, intestate inheritance, and so on. Moreover, our laws could easily be changed so that the rights spouses now have with respect to third parties (health care decisions, survivor benefits, etc.) would instead vest as designated in writing by the person holding that right.

Despite the fact that marriage equality does nothing to get the government out of the marriage business, nor to ending discrimination against single persons, it does bring us closer to the rule of law by making marriage available to a larger portion of the population. Accordingly, it deserves libertarian support, although it should not distract us from the ultimate goal of divorcing the state and the institution of marriage entirely. This is the only outcome consistent with libertarian principles.

CHAPTER FOUR

Paternalism

Paternalism has a bad name. Therefore, it should not surprise us that the legislative histories of our statutes are not rife with declarations that the electorate is simply not smart or responsible enough to manage various things for themselves, such as saving for retirement, purchasing health care services and insurance, deciding whether to smoke and to use recreational drugs, and so on.

To be sure, some governmental policies that reek of paternalism have other effects, such as redistributing wealth and erecting barriers to competition, so that it is not always apparent how we should characterize them. This chapter identifies and examines a variety of important societal institutions that seem *primarily* motivated by paternalism. My analysis also includes certain interesting, related issues.

Specifically, I focus on the proper application of libertarian principles in a distinctly non-libertarian world where people do not suffer the consequences of their freely chosen actions, and I examine the supposedly more benign form of intervention known as "soft" or "libertarian" paternalism. I leave to the following chapter those laws that, while perfectly congenial to the Nanny State, may well be motivated by the perceived need to prevent the exploitation of vulnerable members of society by the more powerful.

The libertarian objection

Gerald Dworkin, an academic philosopher, defines paternalism as "the interference of a state or an individual with another person, against their will, and defended or motivated by a claim that the person interfered with will be better off or protected from harm."[1] This practice is perhaps the most blatant possible insult to our rational agency, in effect treating competent adults like children, unfit to make important decisions for themselves. It is a grossly disrespectful response to the attribute that gives persons their special moral status.

Paternalism not only violates the right of persons to decide things for themselves, but also erodes the citizenry's sense of personal responsibility and self-reliance so as to make further political assaults on freedom inevitable. Over 170 years ago, Tocqueville observed that in democracies, paternalism

> does not destroy, but it prevents existence; it does not tyrannize, but it compresses, enervates, extinguishes, and stupefies a people, till each nation is reduced to nothing better than a flock of timid and industrious animals, of which the government is the shepherd.[2]

He was prescient. As the liberal democratic state has assumed an ever greater role in providing goods that were formerly the province of individual citizens or private organizations, including retirement savings, health care, and poverty relief, our society has become increasingly dependent on it, and willing to accept further intrusions into our private spheres.

Consider in this light the seemingly inexorable expansion of the state's role in health care, an industry that represents one-sixth of our economy. Prior to the enactment of Medicare and Medicaid in 1965, this was limited to the relatively minor task of providing care to military veterans, which was rightly regarded as the payment of a special debt owed to those who had sacrificed much for their country. However, outlays for these programs have steadily grown, so that by 2012 the combined federal and state (primarily on Medicaid) spending on health care had reached 44 percent of the nation's total.[3]

This trend shows no sign of abating. The Clinton Administration's ambitious effort to remake the US health care system, the Health Security Act of 1993, never made it out of a Democratically controlled Congress. However, less than two decades later, the even more costly and intrusive Affordable Care Act of 2010 was enacted. When this legislation fails to achieve its goals (see Chapter 9), federally provided universal health care ("single payer") is the logical progression.

Social Security

The Social Security system is one of the oldest and most consequential examples of paternalism. It affects virtually all wage earners, and even the self-employed are required to pay into the system. President Roosevelt promoted the program in the mid-1930s as a government enforced self-insurance program, whereby the worker would be protected against disability and poverty in old age. Even apart from what should be fatal rights-based objections, it is apparent that its implementation has gone badly awry and that it must be restructured (again) in order to pay the benefits previously promised.

This program obviously violates libertarian values because it *forces* unwilling people to contribute their wages into the system. There is no justification for this, because workers can appreciate the need for retirement savings and disability insurance and protect themselves as they deem necessary. If they elect *not* to save or insure, they should be prepared to live with the consequences.

The Social Security payroll tax violates the workers' right to invest these funds as they like, or from using them *now*, to start a small business, pay for their children's education, care for a sick parent, take that once-in-a-lifetime adventure vacation while they are still physically fit, and so on. Or, for that matter, from exercising their God-given right to be stupid. As Milton Friedman has put it, "Those of us who believe in freedom must believe also in the freedom of individuals to make their own mistakes."[4]

Moreover, Social Security cannot be defended as a means of providing a minimal safety net for the elderly. If our concern is to keep innocent retirees from severe want, why don't we provide assistance directly to the relatively small percentage actually facing this danger? Why must *everyone* be compelled to participate in the government's retirement system? Even assuming that coercion is justified to save people from dire straits, there is simply no warrant for this wholesale violation of liberty when less intrusive means are available.

At this point, we should consider F. A. Hayek's suggested alternative. He observes that in advanced industrial societies the needy, regardless of the cause of their poverty, will receive assistance from the state. Knowing this, some people will rely on the existence of this safety net and neglect to save for retirement or insure themselves against disability. Accordingly, he argues that, "It seems only logical, then, that those who will have a claim to assistance in circumstances for which they could have made provision should be required to make such provision themselves."[5]

Of course, Hayek does not have in mind the massive redistributive bureaucracy of the Social Security Administration, but he contemplates instead a statutory mandate to purchase private insurance against disability and to save for retirement. Just as those who wish to obtain a driver's license must show proof of insurance, the state could, he suggests, compel us to address these risks, or face a fine or other penalty. According to Hayek, a requirement to self-insure is justified because it will shield those who conscientiously save for their own retirement from being forced to provide for those who don't.

Even granting Hayek the controversial assumption that the existence of a bare bones safety net induces widespread financial recklessness, his argument is not persuasive from the natural rights perspective. Our commitment to side constraints precludes the state from coercing innocent people even if doing so would prevent greater coercion overall. Such a step still involves sacrificing individuals for the greater good, which Nozick rightly condemns as a mere "utilitarianism of rights" (*ASU*, 28). The libertarian ideal would be simply to allow able-bodied people to provide (or not) for their retirement and insure (or not) against disability as they see fit and, critically, enjoy or suffer the consequences. I note that one hardly needs to be an investing wizard to beat the paltry returns provided by the low-yield governmental bonds that the Social Security trustees are required to purchase.

Nevertheless, political realities will probably put the libertarian solution out of reach for the foreseeable future. So the best practical alternative is probably compulsory private pensions and disability insurance, which would be far superior to our current system. Even apart from its evident paternalism, the status quo violates rights on a wholesale basis.

First, payments under the system are heavily redistributive, in more than a single dimension. It is redistributive in the conventional sense in that high-income employees, who have over the course of their careers three times the amount of withholdings as low-wage workers, do not receive anything like three times the retirement benefits. Also, benefits count as "income" for purposes of the income tax, which is then taxed progressively.[6]

Furthermore, it is arbitrarily and irrationally redistributive between generations.[7] Payments to current retirees come not out of any trust fund created from their own withholdings, but from payroll taxes paid by current employees and their employers. Thus, those fortunate enough to retire in the years immediately following the initiation of the program in 1937 received generous benefits even though they had only trivial withholdings. Subsequent generations also did exceedingly well. In real (inflation adjusted) terms, a typical (male) worker who retired in 1960 received *six times* more in benefits than they paid in Social Security taxes (assuming average life expectancy).[8]

As a result of this structure, and the program's faulty demographic and actuarial assumptions, the imbalance between contributions into the Social Security system and payments to beneficiaries has continued over time. According to the economist Jagadeesh Gokhale, as of 2010 there was a $17.4 trillion gap between what the system has (and will) pay out to past (and current) retirees and the value of all related withholdings (plus imputed interest).[9] So, from the inception of this system through 2010, retirees did what economists say is impossible, at least in the private sector, that is, they got a $17.4 trillion free lunch. It is this fact that explains the popularity of the system.

At some point, this Ponzi scheme will inevitably end badly. The withholding rate has gradually but inexorably increased from 2 percent at inception to the present 12.4 percent (up to the $117,000 income cutoff, as of 2014). Even these dramatic tax increases have proven insufficient to stabilize the program, as retirees are still living (and drawing benefits) longer than expected, and are being supported by a smaller than anticipated (and still shrinking) base of current employees.[10]

Clearly, baby boomers and future generations of retirees will have to have their benefits cut significantly and/or the retirement age raised and/or payroll taxes increased even further.[11] Alternatively, our politicians can attempt to evade this painful reality (with the Fed's cooperation) by paying the promised benefits with dollars that have lost, as a result of inflation, much of their purchasing power.

The fact that the system is structured to enforce the redistribution of wealth makes it ripe for political manipulation. As Hayek observed more than 50 years ago, "It is easy to see how such a complete abandonment of the insurance character of the arrangement . . . must turn the whole system into a tool of politics, a play ball for vote-catching demagogues."[12] The coercion inherent in this program is morally offensive, as is its treatment of future generations of employees, who will face onerous financial obligations to which they did not consent.

This program should be terminated in an orderly and fair way. Younger workers should receive back what they have contributed into the system, plus imputed interest, but no surplus of the sort enjoyed by earlier generations.[13] In order to protect their expectation interests, those at or near retirement should receive the promised benefits, but on a means tested, sliding-scale basis. In terms of what is politically practical, we should aim for a system of mandatory individual retirement accounts and disability insurance, a version of which has been law in Chile since 1981.[14]

Medicare

Medicare is also a centrally planned, paternalistic, beggar-the-next-generation creature that is doomed to collapse under its own weight, and most of what was said earlier applies equally to it. Sadly, Medicare's unfunded liabilities dwarf those of the social security system. However, it will be more productive to analyze it in the context of our entire dysfunctional health care system, so we will postpone this discussion until Chapter 9.

Motorcycle helmet and seat belt laws

In a society founded on libertarian principles, people would be free to decide for themselves whether to wear motorcycle helmets or to fasten their seat belts when riding in an automobile. The flip side of this freedom, however, is that individuals would be held accountable for the foreseeable consequences of their decisions. Accordingly, if you crash your cycle and scramble your brains because you like to feel the wind in your hair, others would not be required to pay the neurosurgeon, the hospital and for long-term care, and so on, if you cannot.

However, it goes without saying that it will be impossible to realize this ideal here. In our society, medical costs resulting from motorcycle riders' refusal to wear helmets (and motorists refusal to wear seat belts) will be passed on to others, in the form of either increased insurance premiums or taxes. I strongly suspect that it is the perceived existence of these negative externalities that has given rise to state laws mandating helmets for cyclists (and seat belts for motorists).[15] Unfortunately, these rules plainly violate the rights of many if not most of those affected, including those who have the financial means to pay for any needed medical care and those who never get into an accident involving a preventable injury. On this basis, these laws plainly offend libertarian principles.

On the other hand, as we have seen, libertarians are equally committed to the view that it is wrong for the state to tax person *A* for the benefit of *B*. Since the rest of society is, in the absence of helmet and seat belt laws, forced to subsidize those individuals who suffer avoidable harm, this situation should (arguably) be governed by the standard libertarian opposition to redistributive taxation. Thus, from this standpoint, helmet and seat belt laws may be regarded as necessary to vindicate the property rights of those who object to paying taxes (or higher insurance premiums) for the medical care of the irresponsible.

One rights-preserving solution would be the issuance of a special license for helmetless riding or seat belt-less motoring to those who have proven that they have either sufficient net worth or medical insurance to pay the cost of care should an accident occur. In the absence of such a program, there seems to be no acceptable way to resolve this conflict that is consistent with libertarianism. But, this judgment is incorrect because upon further reflection would-be helmetless cyclists and seat belt-free motorists have no standing to object to these paternalistic laws.

This conclusion follows from the simple fact that under the most basic libertarian principles property owners, absent special circumstances not relevant here, get to set the terms of use for their property. So, the homeowner decides whether smoking is permitted in his/her residence and so on. If you are invited to a person's home, you are free to make requests about such matters, but if the homeowner rejects your suggestions, your only remedy is to decline the invitation.

In the present case, the public highways and roads are "owned," morally if not legally, by those who paid to build them. There are different funding sources for our various public highways and byways, but in all cases they are paid for by taxes or tolls, with the nature of the levy depending on the jurisdiction (federal, state, local) under whose authority they were constructed. Ideally, those paying for the roads would collectively determine the rules governing them, but it is impossible under current circumstances to poll them as a distinct group.

Accordingly, the democratic process may reasonably be seen as a fair proxy for the wishes of the owners. In this regard, I note that most road/highway tax and toll payers are also eligible voters, and most voters have paid at least some taxes and tolls, so the two groups are roughly coextensive. Thus, if the political process generates a law requiring the use of motorcycle helmets, this is a tolerably just outcome.[16]

Note that this reasoning does not countenance arbitrary governmental decision making with respect to roads or public property generally, such as granting permits for political demonstrations only to those groups favored by the authorities. The state has a stringent moral obligation not to discriminate against any of its citizens, either in the formulation or enforcement of legislation. Doing so plainly violates the rule of law. Nor does the earlier argument justify mandating helmets (or other safety rules) for sky diving, skiing, or other recreational activities, because the sky and the mountains were not built with public funds.

Antismoking laws

Tobacco companies and their customers are clearly one of the favorite whipping boys of the Nanny State. Extremely heavy and discriminatory taxes are levied on tobacco products, their public advertisement has been severely restricted, scary health warnings are dictated on their packaging, public service announcements decry their use, and smoking in or near public buildings has been banned, and even outdoors in public parks. However, nowhere in this country does the law ban smoking or other tobacco usage in private homes, and very rarely in the private areas of apartments or condos.

Thus, it is not clear that paternalism is the only or even the primary motivation for this antismoking campaign, since it is frequently justified on other grounds, discussed below, such as the need to limit associated health care costs and the effect of ETS (environmental tobacco smoke, also known as "second-hand smoke") on those who must live or work in close proximity to smokers. Nevertheless, it seems inescapable that the paternalistic impulse is heavily at work here, both because of the views expressed by those leading the war against tobacco and because the other rationales are so unconvincing.

I do not dispute that cigarettes and chewing tobacco are harmful to those who consume them, but under libertarian principles competent adults are entitled to assume this risk so long as they do not harm others. Thus, if we reject paternalism as an adequate reason for regulation, I can conceive of only two arguments that might justify our current war on smoking: (i) the necessity of addressing negative externalities in the form of increased health care costs that are passed on to nonsmokers and (ii) the need to prevent harm from ETS.

The first rationale is based on the notion that, as expressed by economist Jane Gravelle, there are "financial spillover costs from smoking that are incurred because we have social and medical insurance systems that charge uniform premiums and don't differentiate those premiums according to whether or not you smoke."[17] As everyone knows, smokers have a greater likelihood of premature death from lung cancer, heart disease, stroke, and so on.

Naturally, it is expensive to treat these conditions, and the studies that conclude that smoking imposes massive costs on society are typically based on a methodology that simply estimates and adds up all the various expenditures involved. But this approach assumes that those smokers who died from their habit otherwise would have lived forever! In reality, because smokers are more likely to die of tobacco-related diseases, they are less likely to die of *other* causes, and the treatment of these ailments *also* consumes vast amounts of medical resources.

In fact, convincing scientific evidence exists that smokers do *not* create negative externalities, although as one would expect the evidence is not conclusive.[18] Our society's effort to offset what we incorrectly assume to be the disproportionate health care utilization by tobacco consumers takes the form of heavy, discriminatory taxes on this product. These consist primarily of a federal tax of $1.01 per pack and state excise taxes that vary widely, but average $1.49 per pack (as of January 1, 2013).[19] For the reasons stated earlier, it is almost certain that the huge tax revenues collected from cigarette smokers far exceed the extra costs, if any, that they impose on our health care system.

Thus, taxes on tobacco are simply an expedient way for politicians to finance a larger public sector, since few nonsmokers will feel any sympathy for users. However, if it should turn out that smokers *do* impose additional medical costs on nonsmokers, this would still not justify paternalistic legislation and taxes. Rather, it would merely provide good cause for smokers to pay a premium for health insurance sufficient to offset this externality, a surcharge already collected by private carriers.

The fact that private health insurers charge smokers more for coverage is consistent with my prior claim that smoking does not produce negative externalities, since these firms need only concern themselves with the medical costs incurred by their customers until Medicare takes over at the age of 65. Smokers have a tendency to get ill and die while relatively young, and thus tend to incur heavy medical expenses while covered by private insurance, but this does not imply that they incur excess costs relative to nonsmokers over their entire respective lifetimes.

Therefore, insofar as we are considering only their self-regarding behavior, meaning, what smokers decide to do with their own bodies, far from earning their status of social pariahs, smokers are actually more like a persecuted minority. In light of the obvious flaws in the health care externalities argument, antismoking crusaders also typically invoke the dangers of ETS.

Without attempting to wade through the mountain of studies that have been done on this subject, suffice it to say that the evidence purporting to show that ETS poses a *serious* health threat is manifestly weak.[20] However, my argument against legal prohibitions on smoking in privately owned buildings based on the danger of ETS does not rest on this assumption, but is rights-based.

Just as a property owner has the right to control the color and interior design of her space, so too does she have the right to set smoking policy, or to delegate this decision to others, specifically, her tenants. The state has no justification for regulating private property unless the owner is conducting or permitting some activity on it that harms innocent others. Smoking, when allowed by the owner, does not harm those who object to being exposed to ETS because they can shop at other stores, restrict their job search to smoke-free workplaces, and live in condos and apartments where smoking is prohibited. Thus, from the libertarian perspective, this case is closed.

Having said this, it turns out that by respecting property rights we would also reach more rational decisions about smoking from a cost/benefit perspective. First, smokers obviously enjoy this activity, and this pleasure should be incorporated in any utilitarian calculation. At the same time, many people find ETS objectionable, and think it adversely affects their health. The obvious advantage of the laissez faire solution over an inflexible legislative one is that since potential customers and employees can "vote with their feet," the profit motive should cause owners to carefully weigh these groups' preferences (and their intensity), yielding close to the optimal mix of smoking and nonsmoking establishments.

The patrons of certain businesses (art galleries, fine restaurants, expensive boutiques, etc.) will usually demand entirely smoke-free environments, which the proprietor will surely accommodate. In other cases, such as commercial office space or shopping malls, it might make sense from the perspective of the owner (or his tenant) to have special smoking rooms. Finally, for certain bars and restaurants it might maximize profit to allow smoking throughout the establishment. In each case, the profit-maximizing owner will tailor his policy to the preferences of his employees and customers, which will tend to maximize utility overall.

Recreational drugs and prostitution

The natural rights libertarian position on recreational drugs is straightforward and probably therefore the least interesting of the topics we will consider in this chapter. Here again, it may be that the paternalistic impulse is not the only motivating factor in our ongoing "war on drugs," but the status quo is so irrational from the standpoint of any fair cost/benefit analysis, that we may strongly infer its overbearing presence. Not only is it incredibly costly to prosecute this war and incarcerate its prisoners, but it also produces a host of harmful side effects, including the funding and empowerment of gangs that spread their tentacles outside of the drug trade; violent crime committed by addicts struggling to pay the artificially high prices created by prohibition and by gangs protecting their "turf"; breaking up families; saddling many young men with criminal records; chasing lawful businesses out of affected neighborhoods; and reducing the incentive for employment outside of the drug trade.[21]

It is difficult to imagine that in the event of legalization the negative externalities from recreational drugs could be worse than they are under the current system, or those caused by the consumption of alcohol. Since we are willing to tolerate the consequences of alcohol abuse, intellectual consistency demands the legalization of cocaine, marijuana, heroin, and other proscribed substances. The potential harm to adult users should not factor into our policy making because, as argued earlier, rational agents have a right to decide what kind of life they will lead, provided that their choices do not infringe on the equal right of others to do the same.

Finally, nothing said earlier should be understood to forbid the prohibition of the sale of recreational drugs to, or their use by, minors. Parents are presumptively the appropriate guardian of the interests of their immature offspring. However, no responsible parent could approve the use of heroin by their 8-year-old. Therefore, the state is justified in acting in those circumstances where parents fail to protect the interests of their children.

Libertarian objections to antiprostitution laws are very similar to those against the criminalization of recreational drugs. This conduct, when between consenting adults, is the quintessential victimless crime, and other individuals or the state have no moral warrant to interfere. It is difficult to even articulate a nonpaternalistic argument against legalization, since this step would, in the words of economist Jeffrey A. Miron, "help the women who serve as prostitutes by reducing the violence they suffer from johns and pimps," who now have little fear of prosecution.[22]

Soft paternalism

Recently, certain scholars have proposed and defended the use of what is known as "soft" or "libertarian" paternalism, most famously by Richard H. Thaler and Cass R. Sunstein in their book *Nudge: Improving Decisions About Health, Wealth, and Happiness*.[23] It is supposedly distinguished from the traditional kind by its requirement that the choice made by the governing authority be ratified by those affected, meaning that they are informed of it and offered an easy way to reverse it. It turns out, however, that much of what its proponents claim for soft paternalism is entirely consistent with libertarian principles, and thus offers us nothing new, while the balance remains morally offensive.

One well-known suggestion offered by Thaler and Sunstein involves the selection of a default option with respect to worker enrollment in employer 401(k) programs. In most firms, if employees do not affirmatively request enrollment they are left out of the plan. Alternatively, under soft paternalism, the employer should, in the absence of a response, automatically enroll the employees up to the point where their contributions take maximum advantage of the company's matching payments. This decision would be coupled with the employees' right to withdraw from the plan or modify one's contribution with a couple of mouse clicks.

But, such a policy is not paternalism, soft or otherwise, but simply the exercise of a *right* held by the entity sponsoring the plan. Because the employer is using its resources to fund this benefit, the selection of a default option is rightfully its alone. At most, workers have an enforceable expectation interest of *participating* in a 401(k) plan, if this was offered as an inducement to accept employment.

It is analogous to the choice facing a person who gratuitously decides to knit sweaters for a few of her coworkers as Christmas gifts. She would be acting benevolently if she makes them in colors she believes the recipients will like, and spitefully if she knowingly selects those they will hate, but she is not acting paternalistically either way. Neither choice makes the recipients worse off than if she never knit the garments, so it cannot constitute an objectionable "interference . . . with another person," as required by Dworkin's definition.

Similarly, other purported examples of the soft variety turn out not to be revisionary. As discussed earlier, it would not be objectionably paternalistic under libertarian principles for bureaucrats to employ CBA, *assuming* that the government has the right to regulate the activity in question (see Chapter 5). However, once we move beyond the uncontroversial cases, we are back in the world of old-school, coercive regulation, whereby the government *forces* restaurant owners to post dietary information on their walls, sell only soft drinks of less than a certain size, and so on. Hence, I agree wholeheartedly with libertarian journalist Will Wilkerson that "The whiff of paradox in 'libertarian paternalism' may have set up hopes for a category-defying revolution, but *Nudge* is the book where those hopes, and the tiny monster of an idea, prove flightless."[24]

CHAPTER FIVE

The regulatory state

In our society, regulation envelops us like water does a fish, but with less salutary effects. Virtually everything we do and touch is affected in one way or the other by the dictates of our various administrative agencies. Consider in this regard that as of year-end 2013 the Code of Federal Regulations consisted of a mind-boggling 175,496 pages, up from a "mere" 71,244 pages in 1975.[1] State and local rules add substantially to this thicket.

Broadly speaking, our regulatory efforts can be divided into two categories. The first consists of those measures commonly justified as necessary to protect society from predatory employers and producers, that is, health and safety regulations. I include here our federal and state laws regulating the bargaining process between capital and labor over compensation and other terms of employment.

The libertarian case for the abolition of such administrative controls is that they impermissibly preempt the right of rational agents to decide these important matters for themselves. This position presupposes reasonably free markets. For example, if the government grants a monopoly to one of its cronies, then the ability of the public to protect itself against corporate abuse by patronizing competitors has been vitiated. In such circumstances, regulation might be preferable to the "free market."

Defenders of health and safety regulations typically argue that in their absence great societal harm will occur due to asymmetries of information, inequalities in the respective bargaining position of market participants, lack of competition, and so on. But, as we shall see, their repeal would not (at a minimum) produce the sort of devastation that should make libertarians reconsider their principles.

The second category of governmental rule making is distinguished from the first in that it is not paternalistic in the sense just described, but is designed to prevent parties from imposing negative externalities on other members of the community. Classic examples are air and water pollution. Because libertarians uniformly hold that pollution may unjustly injure others, some constraint on this activity is necessary, but it is not clear that governmental regulation is the optimal means. Here I argue that, at the very least, the techniques now employed should be radically reformed.

Health and safety regulations

If regulation were the only way to prevent grave, large-scale harm to the innocent, meaning that without it many more consumers would be killed by unsafe products, many additional workers would die in easily avoidable on-the-job accidents, and so on, we might ignore libertarian niceties. But this is not the case.

Notice first that free markets have certain built-in incentives that promote the welfare of consumers and workers. Consider, for example, the question of workplace safety. The Occupational Safety and Health Administration ("OSHA") was formed in 1971 for the purpose of reducing industrial accidents, but as Charles Murray writes,

> in the twenty before [OSHA] was established, on-the-job deaths dropped from 27 to 17 per 100,000 workers; in the twenty years after OSHA was established, it dropped from 17 to 8 per 100,000 workers. Matters didn't get worse after OSHA was established; neither is it easy to make a case that OSHA made much positive difference.[2]

A variety of causes likely contributed to this result. But surely an important part of the picture is the business owners' profit motive. When workers are lost to injury or death, production slows down, litigation ensues, and higher compensation is demanded. Regulations might have an incremental positive effect, but they certainly come with a hefty price tag that must be included in any fair CBA.

Moreover, workers and consumers can protect themselves. Were the regulatory tide to recede, it would be replaced by a flood of information from private sources that would enable individuals to make rational decisions about the pros and cons of consumer products and employment opportunities. These include good old-fashioned word of mouth, now powerfully amplified by social media.

Additional information is available on a subscription basis from sources such as *Consumer Reports*, *Consumers' Research*, and *Angie's List*. More commonly these days, independent ratings/evaluations are provided for free online as an inducement to visit a particular website, which will then "monetize" such traffic, as for example, *Amazon*, *Yelp*, *Glassdoor*, *Kelly Blue Book*, *CNET*, and *Vitals* among countless others.

In a myriad of other cases, producers or vendors find it commercially advantageous to obtain, at their expense, an independent stamp of quality. Accordingly, even though the government is in theory regulating the safety of such devices, many electrical products available in the marketplace include a visible UL certification, representing that the product meets the standards establish by Underwriters Laboratory. For dental products, there is the approval of the American Dental Association. Those who keep kosher, or wish to purchase food that is, will look for *hechshers* (little symbols) on packaging that evidences a certification by the Orthodox Union (or a similar organization) that the product was produced in accordance with Jewish law. If you buy a diamond, it has probably been graded by the Gemological Institute of America or a competing company, and so forth.

Case study: the FDA

One way to test the claim that we could repeal all of our health and safety regulations without disastrous consequences (and perhaps even with positive ones) is to imagine a world without the Food and Drug Administration ("FDA"), which most people regard as an indispensible guardian of our welfare. As things now stand, before a new pharmaceutical (or medical device) can be marketed in the

United States the agency must determine that is safe and effective for its intended use. On average it now takes almost 10 years for the agency to approve a new drug,[3] and—largely as a result—the cost of development now exceeds $1 billion.[4] Most of the expense and time involved is attributable to the requirement for clinical trials, especially the demonstration of efficacy.[5] The nature of this process has substantial negative repercussions for public health.

I note initially that were the FDA to be shuttered tomorrow, most consumers would still be vitally interested in ensuring that the medicines they take are benign. Thus, instead of relying on the FDA, they would search for alternative sources of information, which would present an obvious business opportunity for ambitious entrepreneurs. Since most consumers would be willing to pay a premium to have the producer's claims for a pharmaceutical independently verified, these companies would have a powerful incentive to submit their products for safety testing, and potentially for efficacy as well.[6]

Unlike the FDA, which is a government imposed monopoly and thus immune from market discipline, private agencies that elect to perform drug evaluation would view their reputation for accuracy as their primary asset.[7] Their *imprimatur* will only have value, and pharmaceutical companies will only pay for it, if consumers trust it. Accordingly, if such an organization were proven guilty of serious corruption or gross negligence, it would almost certainly go out of business.

Depending on the commercial potential of a new drug, including the availability of competitive products, pharmaceutical firms might, under laissez faire, forego the costly, large-scale efficacy testing now demanded by the FDA. Instead, they might opt for less extensive, and thus less definitive, trials than are now required. Or, for therapeutics designed to treat rare diseases, and thus with limited commercial potential, they might refrain entirely from such testing.

However, it is critical to understand that the absence of clinical trials *prior* to the sale of a new medicine does not mean that physicians and patients will forever be left in the dark regarding its efficacy. For marketing purposes, pharmaceutical companies themselves have reason to monitor the performance of their products after introduction. In addition, research universities, health care networks, nonprofit organizations like the ECRI

Institute, and medical insurance companies are motivated to undertake performance studies.[8]

It is even possible that in some cases a drug company would release a new compound with little or no testing for safety. This might occur because the drug has great potential benefits for patients with otherwise untreatable conditions and/or because it appears to have a similar molecular structure to other safe drugs or to substances that occur naturally in the human body. So long as the producer does not fraudulently misrepresent the benefits or risks associated with this therapy, it should be permitted to sell it and competent adults should be free to decide for themselves whether or not to take it.

Accordingly, from the rights-based perspective, there are two fundamental differences between the current paternalistic system and a purely private one. First, pharmaceutical firms—as the owners of this property—would decide how much and what sort of clinical testing is cost effective for particular compounds. However, they do have long-term economic incentives that should influence their decision making in a way that is sensitive to the needs of their customers.

Secondly, an entirely private system would not so severely limit consumer choice. Patients would have the option to purchase drugs not blessed by governmental officials, or even private testing labs, if they thought the benefits were sufficiently great.[9] No prescription would be necessary, since this requirement is simply another paternalistic intervention of the sort condemned in the previous chapter. Rational agents are entitled to decide such things for themselves.[10]

Would the libertarian alternative be perfect? Of course not. Some companies, out of incompetence or greed, will overstate the virtues or understate the potential dangers of their products. However, the probability of expensive, time-consuming, and reputation-damaging litigation should have a significant deterrent effect. This threat would also provide drug companies with an additional reason to submit their compounds for safety evaluation prior to sale.[11] Nevertheless, some consumers will exercise their newfound discretion to make unwise purchase decisions, and suffer the consequences.

However, the status quo is also far from ideal. Just to start, the enormous cost and time that must be invested to bring a new treatment to market forces companies to restrict their focus to "blockbuster" drugs, meaning, those that achieve more than $1 billion in annual sales. Therefore, many valuable potential therapies for relatively rare conditions are abandoned before they are even submitted to the FDA.[12]

Furthermore, the FDA's onerous efficacy requirement substantially delays the introduction of new compounds, costing many lives, and prolonging sickness and suffering during this waiting period. A number of credible studies have confirmed this commonsense inference.[13]

The agency's preference for delay and even rejection exists because, as many commentators have noticed, these officials face asymmetrical incentives that warp their decision making.[14] The introduction of a seriously harmful drug will likely destroy the careers of those responsible and rain down political scandal on their agency. Conversely, delays in the introduction of badly needed medicines will largely go unnoticed, and can be defended as the unavoidable price we pay for protecting public safety and ensuring that drug companies do not market useless medications.

Even with such twisted incentives, the FDA has still approved many dozens of pharmaceuticals that subsequently had to be either withdrawn or sold only with a "black box" warning.[15] The best-known recent examples are probably the diabetes drug Rezulin, the obesity drug fenfluramine/phentermine ("fen-phen"), and the painkiller Vioxx. Critics have, with some justification, accused the FDA of relying too heavily on consultants whose ties to "Big Pharma" present an apparent conflict of interest.[16]

When an administrative agency is "captured" by those it regulates, its directives will tend to favor established competitors over new entrants and to advance the industry's interests at the expense of consumers.[17] This is a well-known phenomenon in our governance, and occurs because of the political influence of the regulated firms and the "revolving door" that permits easy transition from one camp to the other. It is yet another reason for skepticism that the FDA in particular and regulation in general promotes the public good.

Another unintended consequence of the FDA's operations is industry consolidation. Given the inevitably high ratio of misses to hits, few companies have the resources to absorb the massive costs imposed by the existing testing requirements. As a result, mergers are consummated in order to achieve the economies of scale required to absorb these expenses.[18] Competition is thereby reduced, to the detriment of consumers.

The activities of the FDA present a textbook example of what Fredric Bastiat, the great mid-nineteenth-century French liberal, labeled the problem of the "seen and the unseen."[19] The benefits of preventing unsafe and ineffective drugs from being sold are highly visible to the public, but the massive costs associated with this activity are largely hidden from view: the treatments for rare diseases abandoned because the regulatory burden makes them unprofitable; the lives lost because the introduction of breakthrough drugs is unduly delayed; and the uses that otherwise would have been made of the resources dedicated to compliance.

In light of earlier arguments, there is no reason to think that deregulating the sale of pharmaceuticals and medical devices would produce a level of harm that would require us to disregard the moral imperative of respecting human autonomy. Indeed, common sense and the available evidence strongly suggest the exact opposite. The analysis presented here regarding the FDA can be generalized to encompass all health/safety agencies and their regulations.

In each case, application of the seen/unseen framework will show that our polity can happily live under laissez faire because there are consensual mechanisms that can substitute for administrative control, and we would avoid the unintended negative consequences arising from it. Furthermore, the costs of compliance (*estimated at $1.7 trillion annually* at the federal level)[20] would be better spent on other things, even under a utilitarian standard.

While the figure just cited represents about 12 percent of our annual economic output, it captures only the direct burden of compliance, and excludes the indirect effects of the sort noted earlier, for example, negative effects on competition, reduced economic growth, and inability to adapt to changes in consumer demand. There is reason to believe that these costs equal or even exceed the direct ones.[21]

Laws and regulations affecting the workplace

All health and safety regulations are morally pernicious, but minimum wages laws, licensure mandates, and our labor code deserve special scorn. These laws are not just rights violating, but the harms fall disproportionately on those struggling to lift themselves and their families out of poverty. I will discuss each in turn.

Minimum wage laws

The federal minimum wage is now set at $7.25/hour, and applies to almost all US workers, subject to certain exceptions for tipped employees, workers under 20 (for their first 90 days of employment), full-time students, and the disabled.[22] As of January 1, 2014, 21 states and the District of Columbia, led by Washington ($9.32/hour) and Oregon ($9.10), mandate minimum rates for their workers in excess of the federal requirement, often substantially so.[23] A few cities and municipalities—including Seattle, Santa Fe, San Francisco, and San Jose—have gone farther still, with minimum wages topping $10/hour (Seattle leads the pack with a $15 floor, phased in over the next several years).

Quite obviously, minimum wage laws interfere with freedom of contract, but they are typically defended on the basis that the harm caused by the loss of a "few" low-wage jobs is more than offset by the benefit of lifting a greater number of people out of poverty.[24] Even granting proponents of the minimum wage this highly controversial premise,[25] these laws plainly prevent persons from deciding for themselves whether to accept employment at below the mandatory rate, and are therefore unjust.

Untrained workers and those with little work experience greatly benefit from employment, even if below the prevailing minimum wage, because it lays the groundwork for a promotion or for a better-paid job elsewhere. Minimum wage laws deny workers with fewer perceived skills the opportunity to compete for employment in the only way they can, namely, on price.

In other words, at anything less than full employment, companies will hire the workers they believe to be the most productive, leaving the others behind. As is frequently the case, Milton Friedman (writing here with his coauthor, wife Rose) says it best:

> The government first provides schools in which many young people, disproportionately black, are educated so poorly that they do not have the skills that would enable them to get good

wages. It then penalizes them a second time by preventing them from offering to work for low wages as a means of inducing employers to give them on-the-job training. All this in the name of helping the poor.[26]

Society is not entitled to violate the rights of even a few persons for the so-called greater good, particularly when the alleged benefits are both marginal and speculative.

Licensure

Our occupational licensing laws should also be repealed. While dressed up as necessary to protect the public from unqualified or even dangerous tradesmen and other service providers, the actual effect of these laws is simply to erect barriers to entry that keep people (mostly those with lower incomes) from gainful employment. A recent study by the Institute for Justice ("IJ") identified 102 (!) different "blue-collar" vocations (i.e., *excluding* doctors, attorneys, aircraft pilots, architects, etc.) that are licensed by one or more of our states.[27] Louisiana ranks first, with 71.

The 102 occupations include, in addition to all of the building trades, barbers, cosmetologists, cat groomers, tattoo artists, taxi drivers, tree trimmers, locksmiths, caterers, massage therapists, bartenders, interior designers, and florists. While in 1950 only one in 20 US workers were subject to licensure, the number now approaches one in three. The IJ study reveals that on average a license costs the aspiring worker $209, requires one exam, and 9 months of education and training.

Licensing laws are unnecessary because people can determine for themselves whether businesses and trades people are reputable. Private companies already supply, either on a free or subscription basis, voluminous pertinent information. In addition, service providers can assure potential customers of their *bona fides* by voluntary means.

Interested persons may earn certificates of competency from a wide variety of independent, private organizations. A very small sample of such credentials would include those issued to: plumbers (conferred by the American Society of Sanitary Engineering); property managers (Institute of Real Estate Management); automotive repair and maintenance technicians (National Institute for Automotive

Service Excellence); and hotel managers/administrators (American Hotel and Lodging Association).

These programs exist because consumers perceive there to be a benefit in doing business with individuals holding these credentials and/or employers prefer to hire them. If there is, under laissez faire, little or no demand for *certified* interior designers, bartenders, or florists, then people working in these occupations will not make the effort to obtain such a credential. This would prove that they serve no useful purpose, and the absence of government-mandated versions should be welcomed, not mourned.

Plainly, the purpose and effect of our licensure fetish is not to protect the public against (say) incompetent interior designers, but to restrict competition, thus boosting the incomes of those already licensed. This harms consumers by reducing their available choices and raising prices, and aspiring careerists by imposing unnecessary burdens on them. Most importantly, the elimination of all such mandates would vindicate our freedom of contract.

Although no doubt more controversial, precisely the same rationale applies to the elite occupations. State laws that make it a crime to practice law or medicine without a license simply rob rational agents of their right to choose for themselves whether retaining a *licensed* professional is worth the incremental cost associated with the credential. We will return to this subject in Chapter 9.

Labor laws

This brings us to another important element of the regulatory state, our labor code. These statutes, like their minimum wage and licensure counterparts, are justified by abstract appeals to the greater good, while ignoring the rights of particular individuals, especially the less well-off. I will first critique our labor laws as they relate to private firms, and then describe libertarian objections to those governing the public sector.

Before going further, let me state clearly that libertarians have no objection to labor unions as voluntary associations of employees, and recognize the right of private sector workers to bargain as a group and to elect representatives to negotiate the resolution of disputes with employers. Unfortunately, the laws regulating collective bargaining do not simply protect this right, but instead impose a tyranny of the majority.

Consider initially that under the National Labor Relations Act (the New Deal legislation also known as the Wagner Act), as amended in 1947 by the Taft-Hartley Act, a union need only secure the consent of a bare majority of workers to be recognized under the law as the *exclusive* employee representative. The organizing union is thereby authorized to negotiate a collective bargaining agreement with the employer that binds *all* workers, and the employer is obligated to bargain in good faith with the union on a number of specified subjects, including wages, hours, and other terms and conditions of employment.[28] If an employee—for whatever reason—prefers to negotiate her own terms, she is simply denied this right, which is manifestly unjust.

Moreover, in the 26 states that enforce so-called agency shop arrangements, the collective bargaining agreement may require all employees, current and future, covered by the agreement to pay union dues, except for the portion used for political contributions and organizing activities.[29] Conversely, in the 24 states with "right-to-work" ("RTW") laws (expressly authorized by Taft-Hartley), employers and unions are prohibited from including in any collective bargaining agreement the requirement of union membership or payment of union dues.[30]

Unions have a much harder time organizing in RTW states because of what their sympathizers call a free rider problem, that is, employees can accept the "benefit" of any collective bargaining agreement without paying dues. This discourages unions from putting in the time and money required to win exclusive bargaining rights. Accordingly, in RTW states only a very small percentage of private sector workplaces are subject to collective bargaining agreements.[31]

The existence of free riders on union contracts cannot justify the coercion present in our labor code. First, given the vast number of jobs lost because of unrealistic wage demands by organized labor, their representation is at best a mixed blessing.[32] Much more fundamentally, the mere receipt of an unrequested benefit does not establish an obligation on the part of the recipient. If I am away on vacation and a contractor takes it upon himself to remodel my home, am I obligated to pay him for his work? I think the answer is obvious.

Under libertarian principles, the state should neither favor nor disfavor unions in the workplace. Business owners would be permitted to attach whatever conditions they like to employment, including a prohibition on union membership. By the same token, organized labor could start or purchase businesses, and require membership and dues as a condition of employment. The free market would determine the prevalence of union representation.

Therefore, except for the standard prohibition on the use of force or fraud, our labor code should repealed in its entirety. In the meantime, RTW laws are necessary to preserve the rights of those workers who do not wish to be represented by unions or to pay union dues.[33]

That RTW laws prohibit employers from agreeing to agency shop arrangements is used by certain "left libertarians" as an argument against them.[34] But, this ignores the plain fact that in non-RTW states the coercion of workers to pay dues invariably comes from the union, not from employers, who have no apparent motive to insist on this. Moreover, RTW laws do not prevent collective bargaining, nor the collection of dues as a condition of (voluntary) union membership, and therefore do not violate the associative or economic rights of workers.

Agency shop arrangements also unjustly harm workers not covered by collective bargaining agreements. Consider the following example: a real estate developer enters into a collective bargaining agreement with a local carpenters union, pursuant to which it pays these tradesmen a minimum of $40/hour. Clearly, a less experienced and skilled nonunion carpenter, worth hiring only at the rate of $30/hour, will be shut out of this market.

Of course, libertarians would not object to this outcome if it were the product of a free and fair process, but in non-RTW states there is no assurance that this is true. Most probably this contract only exists because at its inception the employer was prohibited by federal law from negotiating individual arrangements with dissenters, or from dismissing disgruntled workers and offering their jobs to the public during the mandatory bargaining process. Rather than face a costly and disruptive strike, most employers simply accede to the union's demands.[35]

Somewhat different considerations apply to government workers. Obviously, in a society organized under libertarian principles entire federal cabinet level departments would be eliminated or consolidated. Similar reductions would occur at the state and local levels, and these jurisdictions would no longer provide many services that they do now, or they would be outsourced to private contractors under a competitive process. However, in the meantime, the laws regarding public sector labor relations should be reformed to ensure that taxpayers are not unjustly forced to pay exorbitant compensation to government employees.

Government employment is unlike its private sector counterpart in two fundamental ways, and these differences militate against collective bargaining rights. Just to be clear, this means that not only would unions be prohibited from collecting dues on a nonconsensual basis, but they would also be barred from acting as the nonexclusive bargaining agent for workers. However, this would not prevent public employees from forming voluntary associations to articulate and present their views and concerns to their agency heads and public officials.

First, when collective bargaining is permitted, the public officials nominally representing the taxpayers typically receive generous campaign contributions from the union representatives sitting across the table from them (paid out of their members' dues).[36] This all-too-cozy relationship has led to cronyism and gross abuse, particularly with respect to retirement benefits.[37] Therefore, the usual arguments for freedom of contract do not apply to such agreements.[38]

Additionally, unlike their private sector counterparts, government workers are employed by *monopoly* suppliers of goods or services. If private sector consumers don't like a vendor's price or performance, they can take their business elsewhere. In contrast, citizens dissatisfied with public services cannot hire an alternative set of public school teachers, police department, district attorney's office, department of motor vehicles, and so on.[39] This fact gives public sector employees enormous and unwarranted economic leverage through the threat of strikes or informal job actions such as "sick-outs." Thus, a prohibition on collective bargaining for public employees is necessary to protect the rights of taxpayers.

In recognition of the important dissimilarities in public and private sector employment, federal workers are denied the privilege of collective bargaining with respect to compensation and benefits.[40] Unfortunately, this is generally not the case at the state and local level. Thirty-one states and the District of Columbia authorize collective bargaining for public sector workers, although only 12 permit strikes (and generally not by public safety workers).[41] In states that authorize collective bargaining, this power will be abused until it is eliminated.

Environmental laws and regulations

The air that we breathe and the water in our great rivers, lakes, and oceans are not privately owned. Accordingly, the free market cannot price their use. In the absence of a market mechanism, there are powerful incentives for economic actors to exploit these resources as free dumping grounds for the by-products of their commercial operations.

Thus, pollution control stands on a different moral footing than health and safety regulations, which seek to paternalistically protect individuals from their own foolish choices. While persons have an inherent right to decide how they wish to live, they do not have an unconditional right to impose negative externalities on innocent others. But what constitutes a rights violation in the environmental context?

Recall from Chapter 1 that libertarians may consistently use community standards to resolve conflicting claims of right with respect to land use, including pollution and the imposition of nonconsensual risk. Accordingly, emissions that contravene such norms may permissibly be enjoined. Local environmental standards can be identified using the tools employed in CBA. Only they are able to differentiate between people's *expressed* preferences, which reflect their political and moral views, and the values revealed by their actual behavior.[42]

However, the state cannot be relied upon to apply CBA in a fair and neutral manner. Given the nature of public choice, environmental decisions will inevitably be driven by politics rather than by any defensible theoretical framework. This raises the distinct possibility that regulation will produce greater injustice than unfettered free markets.

Indeed, administrative control has the potential to violate property rights on a wholesale basis either by imposing unjustified burdens on owners or (less likely here) by allowing polluters to violate the rights of the public at large. In fact, our current top-down regulatory approach unduly restricts the freedom of property owners and imposes costs on the economy that many experts regard as grossly disproportionate to the benefits achieved.[43]

Accordingly, it is plausible that the use of the tort system (including class actions) might, despite its obvious flaws, be preferable to bureaucratic control as a means of arbitrating the competing rights of those whose activities impact the environment and those affected thereby.[44] The threat of liability could be amplified by consumer boycotts of large-scale polluters, and the preferential purchasing of products regarded as environmentally friendly. Toyota Motors' development of the popular Prius line of automobiles might reasonably be seen as an example of a corporation cleverly exploiting this market potential. I know of no way to determine with confidence whether a tort-based system or the regulatory approach would be superior in this regard.

Obviously, the state is, for better or worse, in the pollution control business, and regulates in a way that pays little heed to individual rights. Accordingly, at a bare minimum, it must be fundamentally reformed. We should start by repealing all paternalistic laws and regulations. For example, pursuant to the authority granted by the Toxic Substances Control Act ("TSCA"), the EPA is given virtually a blank check to ban or regulate the use of all chemicals, even those used exclusively in manufacturing, and thus not sold to the public or released into the environment.[45] Competent adults are both able and entitled to make up their own minds about whether or not to use potentially dangerous chemicals.

With respect to those activities that create negative externalities, we should heed David Boaz's commonsense recommendation that environmental policy "should be handled at the most local level possible."[46] This would—contrary to our existing regulatory scheme—permit each county, state, or even region (as appropriate) to control pollution in the way that most accurately reflects its values regarding the trade-offs that must be made between economic growth and an absolutely pristine environment. As Boaz expresses it, "We lose the benefits of decentralization and experimentation when we impose one solution on the whole country."[47]

Once we have started down the path of administrative controls, there probably are sources of pollution, such as from motor vehicles and fertilizer runoff, that are best handled at the federal level. In such cases CBA, based on the observed preferences of all citizens, should be employed to determine if regulation is warranted, and if so, to ensure that it is implemented in the most efficient way possible. Unfortunately, neither of the two major pillars of our regulatory scheme, the Clean Air Act of 1970 (as amended) and the Clean Water Act of 1972 (as amended), require the EPA to employ

CBA in formulating its regulations, and the agency has expressly found its use to be inconsistent with its legislative mandate.[48]

More recently, the agency has been forced to incorporate CBA analysis into its rule making in response to political pressure and judicial precedent requiring "rational" decision making. However, this methodology is enormously sensitive to the assumptions and the quality of the data used; it is a classic example of "garbage in/garbage out." Unfortunately, there is clear and convincing evidence that the EPA's use of CBA has been both technically inept and highly politicized.[49]

A neutral and competent application of CBA would force the EPA to abandon its current micromanagement of the specific means and technologies that firms must employ in their manufacturing processes or incorporate in their products. Instead, for point-source pollution, the agency should set permissible emission levels, and then let each business meet the standard in the most efficient possible way. In other cases, the EPA should set an overall environmental target for a particular pollutant, and then pursue this goal in the most cost-effective way. In specific cases, this might be accomplished by a "cap-and-trade" system or a tax on the activity giving rise to the pollution.[50]

CHAPTER SIX

The federal income tax and the federal reserve system

It is not entirely coincidental that the first peacetime personal income tax and the Federal Reserve System (the "Fed") were both established in 1913.[1] They are equally products of the Progressive Era zeitgeist that placed great stock in scientific and expert knowledge, and in the capacity of the state to use it to enhance the lives of ordinary citizens, including affording them protection against the ill effects of concentrated economic power. A larger public sector could only be financed with additional tax revenues, and the private sector could not be trusted to manage the nation's supply of money and credit.

Both the federal income tax and the Fed fund the state, albeit one more directly and overtly than the other. The former is the primary means by which the national government raises revenue,[2] while our central bank can reduce the government's real cost of borrowing by policies that lower interest rates or produce inflation, rightly called a hidden tax.[3] Accordingly, it is fitting that they be discussed together.

I show that these institutions violate our natural rights in significant ways, and are thus unjust. After outlining these objections, I present the libertarian alternatives, taking into account the current political environment. I start with the income tax and then turn my attention to the Fed.

The federal income tax

No sane person defends our existing tax code. It includes a seemingly infinite number of deductions, credits, and inviting loopholes, all inserted to satisfy the demands of powerful political constituencies (e.g., homeowners, parents, student borrowers, etc.) and corporate lobbyists.[4] However, the design of a suitable replacement serves as a virtual "Rorschach test" of our ideological preconceptions, with "liberals" clamoring for a steeply progressive structure, conservatives pushing family friendly versions, and economists of various stripes advocating plans they claim to be the cheapest to administer, least distort economic behavior, minimize the misallocation of resources, and so on.

I should also note before going further that I focus here only on questions of justice, and put aside issues relating to economic efficiency of the sort just mentioned. Such considerations would be relevant only in the event that a rights-based scheme would inflict disastrous utilitarian costs. As discussed in more detail below, my proposal calls for the elimination of all tax breaks, and the imposition of a proportional or "flat" tax (meaning, all taxpayers pay a uniform percentage), which would be assessed on all income, however derived, beyond that required for mere subsistence.[5]

Although there is no certainty that this scheme would be the most efficient possibility, there is absolutely no reason to think that it would inflict substantial harm, either. Eliminating all tax breaks would permit the nominal rate to be lower, without any loss of revenue, thereby reducing the incentive for tax shelters and other wasteful schemes. Academic studies have consistently found a measurable correlation between lower marginal rates and economic growth, which should enhance prosperity generally.[6]

When the personal income tax was enacted in 1913, the "basic" rate, paid by the overwhelming majority of taxpayers, was 1 percent.[7] The tax was progressive in theory, but the rate increased only for incomes in excess of what would be $450,000 in today's dollars, and it topped out at 7 percent for ultrahigh earners. The one-page tax form was accompanied by three pages of instructions, and the law itself was only 14 pages long.[8]

However, even then the statute contained numerous exclusions, including interest received on state and local bonds and corporate dividend income.⁹ The huge increase since then in the tax "bite," applicable regulations, and the number and complexity of the forms required to prepare a return testify to the explosive growth of our government and the pervasiveness of political favoritism and rent seeking in our laws.

Argument for the flat tax

From the libertarian perspective, the sole morally legitimate purpose of the state is to provide those *essential* goods that cannot be supplied by voluntary means, or will only be produced if some citizens shoulder an unfair burden.[10] The only clear-cut cases are defense against foreign aggressors and domestic criminals, and the adjudication of civil disputes ("classic public goods").[11]

As previously discussed, it is *possible* that use of the state's eminent domain power would prove necessary for the construction of infrastructure (roads, bridges, etc.), and that suitable environmental protection could only be achieved through regulation. Also, *if* private relief proves inadequate, coercive taxation to fund a social safety net for the truly helpless is consistent with libertarian principles (see Chapter 1). Thus, it is conceivable that additional levies might justly be imposed in order to provide these goods ("non-classic goods").

The key principle governing a rights-based tax system is that the benefit and burden of taxation should be distributed equitably, which is to say that they should be linked as tightly as possible (the "benefit principle"). This basic idea is widely accepted across the ideological spectrum, but its application is highly controversial.[12]

This principle, properly understood, requires proportional taxation. Critically, it is the nature of classic public goods that they benefit *all* rational agents. An effective national defense deters or preempts attacks by foreign aggressors or mega-terrorists. Its absence would leave the members of a relatively just and peaceful nation vulnerable to enslavement, or to being held hostage to the dictates of aggressor states.

By the same token, in a society with tolerably decent values, delegating to the government responsibility for domestic security, meaning, the enforcement and adjudication of the criminal law, enables the citizenry to dodge the risks inherent in the private supply of this good. Specifically, that it would create violent chaos or lead to the formation of abusive and oppressive cartels.[13] A similar outcome might eventuate if citizens did not have access to a reasonably fair and efficient means of resolving contractual and other civil disputes.

If taxes were levied only to protect expressive and associative rights, it might seem just even to egalitarians that the burden should be proportional and not progressive, since all citizens appear to benefit to the same relative extent in having the freedom to say what they wish, worship (or not) as they please, and so forth. However, the provision of security also quite clearly protects property, and egalitarians argue that the wealthy benefit disproportionately from this public good, and therefore should pay a higher percentage of their resources in taxes. On this view, paying taxes is analogous to purchasing property insurance.

But, as tax expert Kip Hagopian rightly notes, this logic supports at best a proportional scheme, because,

> To argue otherwise requires a belief that the price of property insurance increases faster than the value of the property (in this case, income), which is observably untrue. If the insurance analogy were applied, those with two times as much income or property would pay two times as much tax, which would be proportionate, not progressive. It's no accident that "historically almost all exponents of benefit theory employed it to support proportion as against progression."[14]

Put slightly differently, the rich and poor *value* their property in equal measure. A person of little means may live in a single-wide, dive a "beater," and have personal possessions of minimal market value, but these assets are as vital to the pursuit of her projects and plans as the luxurious counterparts held by the rich. Accordingly, as economist James Rolph Edwards holds, "taxes properly should be proportional rather than progressive because people benefit from the provision of public goods in proportion to their income and assets protected."[15]

Interestingly, there is a respectable argument that at least a portion of the tax burden, representing noneconomic rights, should be a fixed amount, rather than proportionate; because all citizens benefit *equally* from freedom of expression, association, religion, and so on, they should pay the same *amount* to safeguard them.[16]

In other words, just as rich and poor alike pay the same price for a can of tomato sauce at the grocery store, so too should they pay the same price for the defense of these rights.

However, I reject this argument because the ability of individuals to *exploit* their noneconomic rights is proportionate to their resources. For example, a wealthy person cannot only freely express his opinions, but can widely disseminate them, contribute meaningful amounts to political candidates and think tanks that will articulate them, and so forth. Therefore, a flat tax is appropriate even here.

Libertarian principles, then, rule out both the capitation tax pursuant to which all persons pay an equal amount, and all forms of progressive taxation. Although many economists consider consumption taxes, such as the sales tax or value-added tax, to be more efficient than the flat tax, they too are excluded on moral grounds because they allocate the tax burden based on people's propensity to consume, rather than the benefit received from the state.

The arguments in favor of a proportionate tax scheme also apply to the provision of non-classic goods.[17] If it turns out that a coercive subsidy to the poor is required to prevent a moral catastrophe, this responsibility falls on all members of society, and there is no reason why some should pay disproportionately to discharge it. Similarly, if environmental regulations or the assertion of eminent domain prove to be unavoidable, taxes to fund these services should, on the logic outlined earlier, be allocated on a proportional basis, since the benefits are universal and everyone gains on the same relative basis.[18]

Implications of the proportionality principle

Assuming, then, that a proportionate tax is the only one that passes muster from a rights-based perspective, there seem to be only two goods that could, as a practical matter, serve as proxies for the benefits conferred by the minimal state, namely, wealth and income. The choice between these alternatives depends on two important considerations: (i) whether the stock or flow of resources best measures the value received[19] and (ii) which levy is more congenial to libertarian principles.

With respect to the first question, I see nothing to choose between the taxation of wealth and income. After all, wealth does not magically spring into existence, but is produced by labor and capital investment. Accordingly, we can either tax such income once, when earned, or we can periodically tax its accumulation. In both cases, we are taxing an imperfect proxy for the benefits of the minimal state, and both mechanisms can raise the required revenues.[20]

However, with respect to the second criterion, the income tax is clearly the better choice because it is less coercive and intrusive. Property is not an end in itself but merely facilitates the pursuit of our real objectives. A person who chooses to hold wealth in an illiquid form or who is unable or uninterested in generating earned income will see the means available to her shrink continuously by force of law. In contrast, income arises as a result of a conscious decision to labor or invest, and is thus more compatible with free choice.

Moreover, a wealth tax implies that we never own property "free and clear," meaning, that the state is our eternal partner, and that what is ours is never really ours. This overbearing presence is inconsistent with the respect due rational agents. In the words of UK newspaper columnist Allister Heath, it "drastically alters the relationship between citizen and state: we become leaseholders rather than freeholders, with accumulated taxes over long periods of time eventually 'returning' our wealth to the state."[21]

Assuming, then, that income is the most appropriate measure of the value conferred by the state, justice requires that the government not tax the same income twice. Because corporate dividends are paid out of after-tax dollars, the state may permissibly tax either a corporation's income or its distributions to shareholders, but not both. If we elect to retain the corporate tax, the shareholders would be entitled to a credit for the tax they have indirectly paid at the corporate level. Therefore, on the basis of administrative efficiency we should favor a single tax, collected from individuals.

Before leaving the subject, I should note that our corporate income tax serves as a splendid example of the utter irrationality of our code. We tax the earnings of public corporations, but not those of other large, for-profit enterprises that are functionally equivalent, including master-limited partnerships and real estate investment trusts.[22]

It also follows from the proportionality principle that the *nature* of one's income should not matter for tax purposes. All forms of income, whether from labor, capital, intellectual property, and so on, should be taxed at the same rate, because they all register the benefits received from the state. And, in a horrible blow to venal politicians everywhere, justice requires that there be no deductions or credits available to offset taxable income.[23]

The almost innumerable tax breaks enshrined in our tax code, for both individuals and corporations, plainly violate both the benefit principle and the rule of law. For example, homeowners receive valuable tax breaks under our system, specifically, the deduction of mortgage interest (up to specified limits) and, upon sale, the exclusion of the home's appreciation from the capital gains tax (up to $500,000 for married couples).[24] These shift the burden of paying for the government's operations onto renters. But, both groups receive the same benefits from the state, and therefore they should pay the same taxes, all other things being equal.

The proportionality principle also rules out a tax on the inheritance of property. Death does not generate new income, and inheritance is simply the legally prescribed means by which resources are *transferred* from the testator to her designated beneficiary (which, in the absence of a will, happens by operation of law). Accordingly, inheritance stands on exactly the same moral footing as gift giving.[25] Thus, just as a person who has acquired property in a morally innocent way has the right to give his property to others without incurring any special obligation to the state, so too does the person making a bequest.[26]

A truly flat tax of the sort proposed here seems so radical to majority opinion that its enactment is quite improbable for the foreseeable future. However, while the two major parties have serious disagreements with respect to specifics, there appears to be a growing bipartisan awareness that our high nominal rates on both individual and corporate income, coupled with a crazy-quilt of tax favors for powerful constituencies, retard economic growth, harming all.[27] So, it is possible that there will be some modest movement toward, in wonk-speak, "lowering the rate and broadening the base," which should make the system slightly more proportionate in the way advocated earlier. Libertarians should support this idea as the best politically practical outcome.

The Fed: a brief history

To understand libertarian objections to this institution, it is helpful to briefly review the Fed's history, starting with its predecessor, the "national banking system" created under the National Banking Act of 1863 (heavily amended in the following 2 years). This arrangement, as modified from time to time, was in place until the Fed commenced operations in 1914.[28]

The backbone of this system consisted of three tiers of federally chartered ("national") banks, corresponding to the populations of the cities where located. These consisted of country, reserve city, and central reserve city banks, totaling 638 by the end of 1864. National banks were commercial banks that were permitted to accept demand deposits (i.e., checking accounts) and to issue uniform currency ("notes"), meaning, paper dollars that each bank in the system was required to accept at par.

However, for each note issued these banks were legally required to have an equal dollar value of government bonds on deposit with the Comptroller of the Currency. This was the *only* note collateral permitted by the Act. This provision and the prohibition of branch banking were largely responsible for the ultimate failure of the system.[29] During the national banking era, the notes issued by the chartered banks circulated as hand-to-hand money alongside, and at par, with gold and silver coins, and paper notes (redeemable into gold or silver), issued by the Treasury.

National banks were subject to stringent capital requirements, and initially had to hold substantial reserves in "lawful money" ("greenbacks") to back up their demand deposits, and from 1879 onward, had to redeem their notes on demand for gold at the rate of 23.22 grains of pure gold per dollar (inversely, gold was valued at $20.67 per ounce). The three-tier structure encouraged the "pyramiding of reserves," meaning that, as described by monetary economist Bruce Champ, "a significant fraction of reserves tended to accumulate in banks located in the reserve and central reserve cities, with a large proportion of bankers' balances concentrated in New York, where deposits were often lent in the form of call loans."[30]

The national banking system proved to have two persistent flaws: first, there was a shortage of currency and credit, particularly in rural areas not served by a reserve national bank. Because the quantity of currency issued was limited to the value of the bonds placed as collateral with the Comptroller, as described by historian Roger Johnson, "the national bank note currency . . . grew or contracted in response to the realities of the bond market rather than in response to the requirements of American business."[31] Since demand deposits at banks were the source of commercial loans, a scarcity of currency affected the availability of credit as well. This was known as the problem of "inelastic" money.

This was troublesome because during harvest season farmers desperately needed currency to pay workers and agricultural buyers needed money to purchase crops, so deposits at local national banks would be depleted. They in turn would obtain currency by drawing down their reserves at the city banks, who would then obtain currency from the central reserve banks. Depending on the intensity of demand in any given year, the money center banks could be forced to abruptly call existing loans and to curtain lending, damaging the economy.[32]

These seasonal problems might have been tolerated by the politicians and the public generally, but the system was also widely blamed for the banking panics of the late nineteenth and early twentieth century, triggered by various external economic shocks. The most severe of these occurred in 1907, and was caused by the collapse of a speculative bubble in a major corporation's stock, which in turn led to a loss of depositor confidence in a number of large New York banks that had lent to the speculators. The ban on branch banking meant that individual banks could not head off "runs" by shifting reserves to where they were most needed, contributing to widespread bank failures, and a recession.

The 1907 crisis fed the perception that far too much power and control over credit was concentrated in the hands of money center bankers and their clients in the large Eastern cities. This feeling was particularly intense in agricultural regions that had long felt starved of credit on liberal terms. Thus, there was a perceived need for a "lender of last resort" during bank panics and for a more elastic currency generally.

Although substantial political sentiment existed for reforming the banking system within the bounds of private ownership (the "Aldrich plan"), this was seen by the progressives as leaving too much control in the hands of the big bankers. The legislation establishing the Federal Reserve was a messy compromise, incorporating elements designed to appease the competing constituencies (big-city bankers, small business owners, agrarian interests, etc.).[33] As stated in the enabling legislation, the intent was: "to provide for the establishment of Federal reserve banks, to furnish an elastic currency, to afford means of rediscounting commercial paper, to establish a more effective supervision of banking in the United States, and for other purposes."

Congress sought to accomplish this by replacing the national banking system with a new structure consisting of 12 quasi-private, regional Federal Reserve Banks overseen by a presidentially appointed Board of Governors.[34] The Banking Act of 1935 created the Federal Open Market Committee (consisting of the seven Fed governors, the New York Fed president, and three other rotating members, drawn from the presidents of the regional banks), through which most monetary policy is conducted.

The Federal Reserve Act gave the national banks 22 years (until 1935) to retire their outstanding notes.[35] As a replacement, the Fed was authorized to issue its notes as currency and to inject liquidity into the system by now familiar means (adjusting bank reserve requirements, setting the interest rate on loans from the Fed to member banks, and most importantly, through open market operations). The Act required that the Fed have gold reserves equal to 40 percent of the value of the paper currency it issued and 35 percent of its demand deposits.

Because the Fed's notes are, by law, legal tender for all obligations owed to the government (including taxes of course) and for all contracts that fail to specify an alternative medium of payment,[36] the Fed enjoys a practical monopoly on note issuance. However, neither the currency nor the Fed's powers were infinitely elastic because the nation remained on the gold standard, with the dollar still convertible into gold at the rate of $20.67 per ounce.

Moreover, the nation remained on an international gold standard. Specifically, most major industrialized nations had currency convertible to gold, which by implication meant that they had fixed exchange rates. This disciplined Fed policy by means of what is known as the "price-specie-flow mechanism."[37]

Very briefly, an overly expansive monetary policy by the Fed would, through trade and investment flows, result in foreign central banks holding a surplus of dollars. They would opt to exchange them for US gold reserves, thereby reducing the supply available for domestic dollar conversion. The Fed would then have to dial back its easy money regime or risk running out of gold. Accordingly, while the Fed had been granted substantial legal authority and powers in order to combat bank runs, and to ensure a more elastic money supply, in the words of Milton and Rose Friedman, "It was taken for granted that it would operate within a world gold standard, reacting to external events but not shaping them."[38]

The constraint on monetary policy enforced by domestic convertibility ended when the US abandoned its internal gold standard in 1933 during the throes of the Great Depression. Not only was convertibility terminated, but by executive order 6102 (subsequently ratified by Congress) President Roosevelt criminalized the private ownership of gold stocks (subject to exceptions for collectible coins, commercial inventory, etc.), requiring owners to sell their holding to the government at the (now) bargain price of $20.67/oz. Soon thereafter, the price of gold for international convertibility was raised to $35/oz. The Fed's discretion over monetary policy expanded further when our adherence to the international gold standard was suspended in 1968, and then officially terminated by statute in 1976.[39]

In the late 1970s, some economists still believed in the existence of a predictable trade-off between full employment and price stability (the "Phillips Curve"), such that the former could be achieved only at the expense of the latter. Contemporaneously, a new generation of Keynesian economists had come to accept monetary policy as a useful tool in stimulating aggregate demand via the mechanism of interest rates. Congress did not wish to let the Fed's fear of inflation stand in the way of Keynesian-engineered full employment, and so in 1977 it amended the Fed's charter to direct it to "promote effectively the goals of maximum employment, stable prices, and moderate long-term interest rates" (i.e., the Fed's "dual mandate").[40]

As monetary economist Steven Horwitz writes, the Fed has come to interpret this directive "to mean the maximum employment compatible with stable prices, but since 2008, more people associated with the Fed have simply been using the term 'full employment.'"[41] There are both practical problems with this formula, and larger concerns regarding the discretion it implies. The two obvious "technical" issues are, very briefly: (i) given the number of variables at work in the economy, the impact of which fluctuate over time, it is impossible for policymakers to know what constitutes "full employment" and (ii) assuming for purposes of argument that monetary policy *can* be effectively used to reduce long-term unemployment, there is no *principled* way to arbitrate any trade-off that exists between this objective and price stability.[42]

Whatever the force of these objections, the dual mandate clearly delegates broad authority to the Fed. This has spurred critics to claim, in the words of economist Marc Labonte, that it frees the Fed "to offer any systematic rationale for its policy decisions, and therefore [allows it to] pursue any policy direction it desires without effective accountability."[43] Whether emboldened by its dual mandate or not, in its efforts to mitigate the severe economic downturn that began in 2007 the Fed undertook a series of unprecedented interventions of dubious statutory authority.[44] These include bailouts of Bear Stearns and AIG, direct lending to investment banks and money-market funds, and massive "quantitative easing," pursuant to which it purchases Treasury bonds and mortgage-backed securities ("MBS") to reduce interest rates and increase bank reserves, with the goal of boosting the economy.

QE purchases have totaled more than $3 trillion as of the end of 2013, a truly astonishing figure.[45] This program has unfolded in stages, with the most recent version (commonly referred to as "QE3") committing the Fed to monthly purchases of $85 billion a *month* in Treasury bonds and MBS until certain specific economic targets are achieved.[46] In very late 2013, the Fed announced that it would begin to reduce its purchases, and as of February, 2014, the volume has been eased to $65 billion/month.[47] The Fed will continue to ease, unless it changes course, as it has once already.[48]

This level of asset purchases by the Fed is novel, and thus untested. Richard Fisher, a member of the Federal Reserve Board, has acknowledged that this strategy carries unforeseen risks:

> I believe that with each program we undertake to venture further in that direction [monetary accommodation], we are sailing deeper into uncharted waters . . . And nobody—in fact no central bank on the planet—has the experience of successfully navigating a return home from the place we now find ourselves.[49]

So significant and unconventional are these new policies that it is hard to argue with economic historian Jeffrey Hummel's assessment that "the Fed that emerged from the crisis is no longer the same as the Fed before the crisis."[50]

Monetary discretion and the rule of law

The rule of law exists when citizens are required to obey only clear and unambiguous rules, applied in a predictable and fair way, and not the arbitrary whims of the political authorities. In the introduction I adopted Hayek's particular gloss on this subject, which adds the condition that a society's laws not arbitrarily favor any particular constituency at the expense of others. As just seen, the history of our monetary policy is the steady and inexorable march toward virtually unconstrained discretion on the part of Fed officials.[51]

As noted earlier, property is the necessary means by which individuals pursue their plans and projects. Because citizens, particularly the less well off, have no alternative but to hold a substantial portion of their assets in dollars, they are *entitled* to sound money—a medium of exchange that retains its value over time—and to monetary policy that does not sacrifice the interests of innocent people in the name of the "greater good." If there remained any doubt on this score, the Fed's recent history shows that its charter is incompatible with the rule of law.

The Fed, through its admittedly ad hoc policy interventions from 2008 until the present, has knowingly produced financial winners and losers in ways that could not reasonably be anticipated by the typical American. To start with, the Fed's decision to bail out Bear Stearns and AIG, but not Lehman Brothers, seems completely arbitrary, and probably misled many in the marketplace. More generally, even if this is not its primary purpose, its policies have favored the wealthy and those with a sophisticated knowledge of financial markets, while harming other segments of society.

This is not an unintended consequence of Fed policy. To the contrary, its governors are deliberately trying to harness the so-called wealth effect. In the words of Chairman Bernanke, "if people feel that their financial situation is better because their 401(k) looks better or for whatever reason, their house is worth more, they are more willing to go out and spend, and that's going to provide the demand that firms need in order to be willing to hire and to invest."[52]

In line with this strategy, the Fed's massive purchases of Treasury bonds and MBS has driven up the prices of these assets, while depressing long-term interest rates generally. Because equity securities and bonds are competing investment options, lower bond yields make stocks relatively more attractive. Additionally, lower long-term rates make it easier for people to qualify for mortgages, thus pushing up home prices.

Accordingly, QE clearly helps those heavily invested in equity securities, and the owners of high-end homes of interest to them.[53] By the same token, it hurts those looking to purchase a residence at a bargain price. Also benefiting are people and companies associated with the housing industry, such as residential construction firms, realtors, and mortgage lenders. For example, bank profits rise when there is an increase in the number of mortgages issued, and when there is a larger "spread" between their cost of funds and the rates charged consumers.[54]

The biggest losers under QE have been the millions of savers looking for secure income. For substantial periods over the last 5 years the real rate of return on 1, 2, and 5-year Treasury notes (among the safest investments) has been negative, meaning that expected future inflation over the term of the security is higher than its nominal yield.[55] And, even real returns on 10-year Treasuries have been at best marginally positive during this period. Thus, in order to get a meaningful inflation-adjusted yield, fixed-income investors are forced to loan to much less creditworthy borrowers or to accept serious interest rate risk, meaning, the potential loss of principle arising from an unexpected rise in rates.

Many economists believe that massive QE will eventually lead to unacceptably high levels of inflation, damaging the economy generally and especially those not sophisticated enough to anticipate it. Thus, as Bill Gross, one of the nation's leading managers of fixed-income mutual funds, notes "they [the Fed] are robbing savers and taking money surreptitiously from longer-term asset holders whose assets don't anticipate future inflation."[56] Even if those predicting a harmful spike in prices are wrong, it is still true that we are sailing into uncharted and dangerous waters. Accordingly, it is far from clear that in the long run the Fed's activist approach will prove successful, even from a utilitarian perspective.

Bernanke has candidly acknowledged that his seemingly never-ending QE has created both financial winners and losers. However, he claims that this should not trouble us:

> We are quite aware that very low interest rates, particularly for a protracted period, do have costs for a lot of people. They have costs for savers . . . I think the response is, though, that there is a greater good here, which is the health and recovery of the U.S. economy, and for that purpose we've been keeping monetary policy conditions accommodative, trying to support the recovery, trying to support job creation.[57]

But this answer is wholly unsatisfactory. The Chairman is in effect "playing God" with innocent people's financial security. This attitude would only be morally acceptable if he and the other Fed governors were omniscient and infallible. But, these are the very same folks who missed the collapse of the housing bubble, and its significance, as it was unfolding before them.

Thus, in January 2007, as housing prices were about to plunge, and as the nation was on the verge of a major recession, Bernanke opined that "We're not seeing anything out of the ordinary or a persistent pattern, and that gives me more confidence that nothing really bad is going to happen here."[58] At the end of that year, he doubled down: "I do not expect insolvency or near insolvency among major financial institutions."[59] His predecessor, Alan Greenspan, was no more prescient, and has admitted that he completely missed the formation of the housing bubble.[60]

If economics qualifies as a "science" it is not, to put it mildly, an exact one.[61] Once we move beyond the most basic observations, such as "all things being equal, consumers will purchase more of a commodity when prices fall, and less when they rise," virtually every claim in this discipline is beset by intense, unresolved controversy. Thus, it is unsurprising that the economists at the Fed were slow in appreciating the housing collapse and its implications, but therefore imperative that it not violate the rule of law based on the false promise that it knows all. If a pilot isn't instrument-rated, he shouldn't take passengers up in bad weather.[62]

The libertarian alternatives to the Fed

The rule of law demands that interested citizens know in advance the path the Fed will follow in its monetary policy. Or, better yet, that the stock of money, interest rates, and other economic variables now set or influenced by the Fed be determined by market forces, without the need for any external management.

There are an impressive number of different proposals formulated by economists to reign in the Fed's unfettered discretion. As outlined by Horwitz, these fall into four main categories (with numerous subvariations):

1   constraining the central bank by making the money it creates redeemable in a commodity such as gold,
2   ending the Fed's dual mandate and imposing a price-level or inflation rate target,
3   closing the central bank and allowing banks to competitively create money and evolve their own processes for coordinating their reserve flows,
4   targeting nominal gross domestic product.[63]

I wish I could be more decisive in selecting one of these alternatives, but as Horwitz cautions, each of these "has its own costs and benefits, and each should be the subject of serious consideration as a replacement for the discretionary monetary policy of central banks both here and elsewhere."[64] I can say that while option no. 2 might incrementally enhance the predictability of the Fed's policy, it would still fall substantially short of adherence to the rule of law. The reason is that virtually any intervention by the Fed can be justified as required to maintain price stability. In fact, as Labonte has observed, the Fed has expressly justified QE "in terms of the need to avoid deflation to achieve price stability under the dual mandate."[65]

Choices nos. 1 and 4 attempt to bring the Fed back within the ambit of the rule of law by committing it to a preannounced and essentially mechanical rule for regulating the money supply.[66] Option no. 3 (known as "free banking") has the greatest theoretical appeal for libertarians, as the quantity of money and the interest rates charged for its use would be determined by supply and demand, like any other commodity. As economists Donald Wells and L. S. Scruggs describe it:

> any firm can enter the banking business by acquiring funds in any non-fraudulent manner and can put those funds to any legal use it wants. A bank may attract funds by offering banknotes (currency) or deposits convertible on demand to specie (gold and silver coin). The bank's success would depend upon its gaining public confidence for holding its banknotes and other bank liabilities, and on the probability that it can use its funds profitably. No bank would have any special privileges, like those currently enjoyed by central banks, such as a monopoly of the note issue or the protection of a legal tender law, giving its notes forced currency. There would be no government agency or central bank on which the bank could rely as a lender of last resort, it would have to borrow in the private market at a rate consistent with the risk involved.[67]

The banks issuing currency would, like their current counterparts, join clearinghouse associations to simplify the exchange of checks, drafts, and notes, as well as to settle balances. This process would discipline reckless or corrupt banks, because, as monetary economist Lawrence White notes, when one member of the association receives another's notes or checks "it returns them to the issuer . . . for redemption in basic money or in claims on the clearinghouse. An issuing bank knows that it would suffer adverse clearings and a costly loss of reserves if too many of its liabilities came into the hands of its rivals."[68]

Sparked by Hayek's 1976 book, *Denationalization of Money*,[69] there is now a quite a substantial literature on the history and economics of free banking. This system is not novel, and its advocates point to what they claim were successful episodes in Australia, Scotland, Canada, Sweden, and other nations.[70] A form of it was even in place here between 1837 and 1863 (after Congress failed to renew the charter of the Second National Bank and before the national banking system).

During this era, banks were unregulated by the federal government. Some states abandoned the practice of requiring their legislatures to charter a bank before it could operate, and allowed anyone to enter this business provided that they followed certain rules, including: depositing specified capital with the state; publishing prescribed financial information; and committing to redeem any of their banknotes for specie.[71] This system ended with the advent of the national banking system, which imposed a prohibitive 10 percent tax on state banknotes in 1865.[72]

Free banking is subject to a number of criticisms even from economists with some libertarian sympathies, including familiar objections to gold or other commodity standards, and the concern that absence of a lender of last resort would replicate the failure of the national banking system.[73] Monetary economics is incredibly complex, and there are a number of competing theoretical models, the respective virtues of which are hotly disputed. The success of failure of this system would obviously depend on whether the theoretical and empirical assumptions of its proponents are well founded.

Because I am not qualified to untangle these controversies, my endorsement of free banking is qualified. It assumes that its performance, relative to the alternatives, is not so inferior as to inflict grave harm on those who must rely on it. Apart from this constraint, however, utilitarian considerations should come into play only if two or more systems are equally respectful of the rule of law.

The problem of calculating the likely success of free banking is compounded by weighty public choice considerations. Not only may public opinion, right or wrong, limit the feasible solutions, but there is a real chance that should a (perceived) free market monetary policy fail, the experiment would actually be counterproductive.[74] Accordingly, an incremental approach may be prudent in this arena.

CHAPTER SEVEN

Corporate welfare and the welfare state

Libertarians share an unshakable commitment to free markets, and not simply to private property. Accordingly, we are unalterably opposed to any interference by the state in the economy in order to benefit certain competitors or industries, or to protect producers at the expense of consumers, a practice that critics call (with appropriate scorn) "corporate welfare." Sadly, according to the Cato Institute, in fiscal year ("FY") 2012 the federal government spent almost $100 billion on corporate subsidies,[1] a figure that *excludes* the many tax breaks embedded in the Internal Revenue Code, trade restrictions, state and local business subsidies, and the benefits conferred by government-sponsored enterprises such as Fannie Mae and Freddie Mac. This chapter briefly catalogs this spending and shows that in all cases it is morally reprehensible.

The cost of our corporate subsidies pales, however, in comparison to the expense of our welfare state, which amounts to almost $1 trillion annually.[2] The use of state coercion (as a last resort) to fund a minimal safety net for those truly unable to care for themselves is consistent with libertarian principles. However, this conclusion hardly commits us to public assistance as now financed and administered. Indeed, the means by which we deliver publicly funded social services should be radically reformed in order to vindicate the rights of taxpayers and to better serve the disadvantaged.

Corporate welfare

Corporate welfare spending is liberally sprinkled throughout the entire federal budget, reflecting political favors granted on both a large and small scale. Some of the big ticket items include (as of FY 2012): more than $20 billion in direct and indirect subsidies paid to farmers (and even nonfarmers who own arable land) from the Department of Agriculture's budget; more than $17 billion spent by the Department of Energy to improve existing energy technologies and to develop new ones; approximately $16 billion in subsidies for mortgage insurance provided by the Department of Housing and Human Development (which benefits mortgage lenders, and the housing industry generally); and almost $14 billion spent on applied research and development by the National Institutes of Health (the fruits of which are commercially exploited by the pharmaceutical industry).[3] There are also many relatively miniscule items, like the $10 million in subsidies to fisheries by the Department of Commerce.

Many of these payments (e.g., those going to agricultural interests) are such pure political pork that no one even attempts to defend them apart from the politicians who dole them out and the privileged constituencies that benefit. These programs continue, seemingly forever, because of one of the glaring flaws in the democratic process: the asymmetry of incentives between the taxpayers and the recipients. Since these favors matter a great deal to the latter, they fight tooth and nail to maintain them with professional lobbying, campaign contributions, public advertising, and so on.

Conversely, about 43 percent of households, constituting a huge electoral block, pay no federal income tax at all, and therefore do not bear the cost of corporate welfare.[4] Moreover, the electorate understands that their *individual* votes will have no impact on these programs. Thus, most citizens are not motivated to inform themselves about this spending, or to invest the time, energy, and resources necessary to combat it.[5] Also, even if they are appropriately outraged, this is but one of many issues that influence their vote. Unfortunately, there is never a referendum on corporate pork generally, or its subcomponents.

In contrast, there are some subsidies, such as those for green energy and medical research, that are politically popular, and have mainstream advocates. This support is typically based on some version of the "market failure" argument. In the words of economist John Ledyard, according to standard economic theory, this occurs when "competitive markets [fail] to achieve an equilibrium allocation of resources which is Pareto optimal," meaning that there exists a possible alternative outcome where one or more market participants are made better off without another party being made worse off.[6] Classic causes of such failures include the absence of competitive markets, externalities, or the potential undersupply of public goods.

Clearly, the claim that market failures should be corrected is utilitarian. Ledyard describes the logic this way: "if market allocations are inefficient, everyone can and should be made better-off."[7] Even if we were to concede, against the weight of the evidence, that corporate handouts are necessary to correct flaws in market outcomes, *and* that government intervention will not make matters worse, this concession would not justify corporate welfare.[8] The efficiency rationale fails in this case because the state can correct such purported failures only by the morally impermissible means of coercive taxation.

Such compulsion is justified when necessary to ensure an adequate supply of those public goods, specifically national defense and law enforcement, that are essential to the exercise of our rational agency, or to prevent severe harm to innocent people. But, no one can seriously argue that ending green energy subsidies or government-funded research would cripple autonomy, or inflict such huge utilitarian losses that we should abandon our moral principles. Accordingly, all corporate welfare should cease immediately.

Because national defense is a legitimate state function, none of our huge (and often wasteful) military spending is included in Cato's $100 billion corporate welfare calculation (I am leaving until Chapter 10 questions regarding the proper size and scope of our military's mission). Nevertheless, in certain important respects the defense procurement process is badly infected with crony capitalism. That is, high ranking congressmen and women feel an irresistible urge to disregard considerations of military need and efficiency when they conflict with the interests of powerful constituencies.[9]

This dynamic is on display in Congress's inability to decide on the number and location of our domestic military installations using conventional legislative procedures. Since the political pressure is so intense, our representatives have been forced to delegate the task to an independent commission (the "Base Realignment and Closure Commission") appointed by the President. The Commission submits its recommendations to him or her, and if approved, go into effect unless rejected by a joint Congressional resolution adopted within 45 days (no amendments are permitted).[10]

Congress also regularly meddles in the weapon systems procurement process. One recent example is its mandate, adamantly opposed by the Pentagon, that a second (interchangeable) engine be produced for the F35 Joint Strike Fighter. A second instance is Congress's veto of the Air Force's 2008 award of its refueling tanker contract to a primarily foreign-owned consortium. Both these examples resulted in costly delays and wasteful spending.[11]

With respect to corporate welfare generally, our best hope for dealing with this destructive addiction is the use of something akin to the military base-closing commission.[12] A panel of respected outside figures would be selected by the President and bipartisan leaders from both houses of the legislature. This commission would agree on a recommendation for ending, or at least reducing, these illegitimate subsidies, and our representatives would be required to cast an up or down vote on the entire package, without amendment.

The welfare state

According to Robert Rector, an expert on government antipoverty efforts at the Heritage Foundation, in FY 2011 we spent $717 billion on 79 overlapping means-tested programs at the federal level and $927 billion overall.[13] A separate study by Michael Tanner of the Cato Institute found that in this same FY the federal government spent more than $668 billion on at least 126 different antipoverty programs, which when combined with state and local spending amounted to nearly $1 trillion.[14]

To put this figure in perspective, Rector has calculated that we spend on average some $33,000 per lower-income family with children (including medical care). Factoring in these families' earned income, the average total resources available to each of them exceeds $40,000 per year, well above the government's own official poverty rate of $23,492 in annual income for a family of four (as of 2012).[15] For my purposes, the exact sum we devote to poverty relief is irrelevant; what matters is that we spend an enormous amount, and do so in ways that violate libertarian principles.[16]

Because welfare is supplied by coercive means, taxpayers have a *right* that their resources be spent efficiently, and to the greatest possible extent, on the truly helpless. In other words, such assistance should be *conditional*, meaning, in the words of libertarian philosopher Daniel Shapiro, that "able-bodied or nondisabled adult recipients must, in a fairly short period of time, work or take serious steps to enter the work force."[17] Given this premise, antipoverty programs should aim at removing the barriers, such as the absence of marketable skills, mental illness, and substance abuse, that stand in the way of gainful employment.

On the other hand, children, the disabled, and others unable to fend for themselves should not be treated as second-class citizens, confined to programs, such as Medicaid and many other forms of public assistance, that provide substandard services. Nor should the children of those receiving aid suffer the harms that often arise as a result of their parents' dependence on welfare. Our current antipoverty programs violate the rights of taxpayers and fail to meet the needs of recipients, and accordingly should be replaced by a more just and effective strategy, that is, one that relies to a far greater extent on free market principles.

When President Lyndon B. Johnson declared "war on poverty" in his January 1964 State of the Union address, he was quite clear that his goal was not simply to enrich the needy by means of transfer payments. Instead, he spoke of "our failure to give our fellow citizens a fair chance to develop their own capacities" and proclaimed that "Our aim is not only to relieve the symptom of poverty, but to cure it and, above all, to prevent it."[18] Despite spending more than $20.7 trillion (in 2013 dollars) to date in prosecuting this war, we have made little progress in reducing statistical measures of poverty.[19] We have certainly not even begun to "cure" or "prevent" it.

The federal government's estimate of the percentage of Americans with incomes low enough to constitute "poverty" was 19.0 percent in 1964. It reached a nadir of 11.1 percent in 1971, increased to as high as 15.2 percent (in 1983), and stands at 15.0 percent in 2012 (the most recent available year).[20] Putting aside quite serious problems of definition and measurement,[21] and using the government's own yardstick, it's hard to conclude that we are spending our resources wisely.

The government first began calculating the poverty rate in 1959, and the official rate then stood at 22.4 percent, so in the 5 years preceding the start of LBJ's war, it had already dropped 3.4 percent.[22] In fact, because of a constant parade of scientific advances and technological progress, our standard of living has steadily increased and poverty has decreased in this country since its founding.[23] Thus, to attribute any material part of this to governmental programs is to confuse correlation with causation. As Charles Murray observes:

> Using retrospective calculations of poverty, the trendline shows a regular drop in poverty from World War II through the 1960s, with the Johnson years accounting for their fair share, no more. Counting by the decades, the steepest drop in poverty occurred during the 1950s, not the 1960s.[24]

A more granular analysis of our state's antipoverty effort should still leave us intensely dissatisfied. By far the largest line item in our current antipoverty spending is Medicaid, which in FY 2013 consumed approximately $283 billion in federal funds, with matching state contributions of around $158 billion.[25] The cost of this program has rapidly escalated, rising from "only" $118 billion (at the federal level) in FY 2001 (inflation adjusted).

The Patient Protection and Affordable Care Act of 2010 substantially expands Medicaid eligibility, and annual total spending on this program is projected to reach an astonishing $795 billion in FY 2021.[26] Unfortunately, study after study has shown that Medicaid provides an inferior quality of medical care relative to that received by individuals with private health insurance, and some indicate that outcomes are no better than being uninsured.[27]

Other important elements of the government's poverty relief strategy include direct-cash assistance, totaling approximately $163 billion at the federal level (e.g., the earned income tax credit, or "EITC" and the Supplemental Security Income program) and $19 billion by the states (all figures are for FY 2011); the Temporary Assistance for Needy Families ("TANF") program, which replaced the old "AFDC" (about $30 billion when all related benefits are included);[28] food aid of various sorts (about $102 billion in federal spending and $7 billion in matching state expenditures); housing assistance ($54 billion at the federal level and $2.1 billion from the states); and means-tested educational spending ($60.1 billion, all at the federal level).[29]

Unfortunately, because of the statutory criteria used to determine "poverty," these programs fail to focus on the truly destitute, and are thus wasteful. Typically, eligibility is tested by comparing the applicants' income to some ratio of the government's standard for poverty. For example, Medicaid is generally available to all people under the age of 65 with incomes below 133 percent of the poverty level, and for food stamps the cutoff is 130 percent.[30]

But, eligibility based solely on annual income does not accurately register need because it obviously fails to take into account savings and actual consumption. Also, as Nicholas Eberstadt of the American Enterprise Institute has observed, "the surfeit of spending over income among poorer US households has increased dramatically since the 1970s—making income an ever less dependable predictor of living standards for the disadvantaged."[31] Since households with substantial assets are still able to qualify for welfare benefits under existing standards, we must presume that an unknown, but significant, portion of our antipoverty spending goes to people who are not in dire need.

Moreover, the bureaucratic nature of our public poverty relief effort inevitably gives rise to high overhead and massive fraud. Note initially that qualification for most welfare programs occurs on the basis of information submitted via multiple forms and, after review, face-to-face interviews (in the best case). Eligibility is then assessed and periodically reassessed according to the complicated standards and formulas mandated by law.

Naturally, this process generates many millions of individual files that must be maintained and periodically updated, which is done by a veritable army of federal and state workers, with multiple layers of supervision. And, these employees are, by most measures, well compensated, particularly when benefits are considered. Accordingly, it is very costly to administer these programs, often exceeding 10 percent of the budget.[32]

On the other hand, administrative costs are typically low for programs that involve little more than the electronic transfer of cash or in-kind benefits to recipients, based on self-reported data, such as the Earned Income Tax Credit or the food stamp program. However, in these circumstances fraud is prevalent, if not endemic. For example, there is credible evidence that about one-third of the funds disbursed under the EITC program are fraudulently obtained or unauthorized.[33]

Perhaps the most important reason for this waste and inefficiency is simply the lack of powerful incentives on the part of governmental agencies to manage resources frugally. Private charities must compete for scarce resources, and any mismanagement of donations will prompt many contributors to switch to organizations that will deliver more "bang for the buck." In contrast, taxpayers have no effective remedy if HHS squanders their dollars.

But the most troubling of all the flaws in our public safety net is that it operates in a way that encourages dependency, often over multiple generations, thus harming recipients, their children, and taxpayers. We are adept at giving the needy fish, but inept at teaching them how to fish. As Tanner correctly observes: "The vast majority of current programs are focused on making poverty more comfortable—giving poor people more food, better shelter, health care, and so forth—rather than giving people the tools that will help them escape poverty."[34]

Paradoxically, our success at ameliorating the pain of poverty inhibits many individuals from breaking free of it. Since our welfare state provides a plethora of valuable benefits to the needy, and because entry-level jobs for unskilled labor generally do not pay well, transitioning from public assistance to work (or to better paying employment) may not improve the recipient's standard of living in a meaningful way, at least in the short run. Put in more technical terms, families on welfare, particularly those with dependent children, face a high marginal tax rate, in some cases as high as 80 percent.[35]

It is impossible to quantify the exact effect of this disincentive to work, but there is evidence that it is significant.[36] This conclusion is supported by data from analogous choice situations. For example, economists have found a strong relationship between the duration of unemployment insurance payments and the period of time that recipients remain unemployed.[37] It seems reasonable to infer that a similar preference for benefits relative to low-paying jobs might motivate many on public aid to remain unemployed or in part-time work. This factor may also explain why businesses often have difficulty filling demanding entry-level jobs that become vacant following crackdowns on undocumented workers.[38]

Welfare dependency and a variety of social ills are strongly correlated with single-parent households, yet our system seems to ignore this relationship. Among families headed by two married parents, only 7.5 percent live in poverty, while the number skyrockets to 33.9 percent for families headed by a single mother (based on 2012 Census Bureau data).[39] Yet, our poverty-relief programs still contain perverse incentives in this regard.

Although two-parent households are not automatically denied benefits under TANF (as they routinely were under AFDC), there it is still a substantial "marriage penalty" imposed by the welfare system. In some circumstances, their combined income may disqualify the couple from Medicaid or materially reduce their total after-tax income (relative to filing separately as unmarried persons), because they now qualify for a smaller EITC payment.[40]

Moreover, from the perspective of a single mother, the existence of a fairly generous safety net makes matrimony less urgent as a matter of economic survival. Accordingly, the overall incentive structure of public assistance still discourages marriage. This is an important failing because, as just seen, households headed by a married couple are far less likely to be impoverished.

When public aid becomes a way of life, rather than emergency assistance, it harms the children of recipients, including elevated levels of criminal behavior, out-of-wedlock births, lower incomes, and (thus) a greater probability of welfare reliance.[41] The widespread and accurate perception that the AFDC program was dysfunctional in just this way led to reform in 1996 by means of the Personal Responsibility and Work Opportunity Reconciliation Act ("PRWORA").

PRWORA replaced AFDC's entitlement structure, which had led to ever-increasing costs, with a system of fixed block grants from the federal government to the individual states. Furthermore, the states were given the flexibility to design their own programs, rather than having eligibility and benefits determined at the federal level, but were required to continue spending at least 80 percent of the amount they previously had on AFDC. Perhaps most controversially, PRWORA imposed a 5-year limit on benefits (for adults) and required the states to meet certain targets with respect to adult participation in "work activities" (a much more flexible requirement than actual gainful employment).[42]

The block grant strategy radically altered state financial incentives, since they would now bear the full cost of increased caseloads, and conversely would benefit from reductions. Thus, in the 5 years following PRWORA's enactment, caseloads fell by half, and employment rates and earnings by single mothers improved.[43] Rector points out that this caseload reduction was accomplished as much by discouraging unnecessary new enrollment as by moving existing families off the rolls.[44]

Although PRWORA has been at least a modest success, the 5-year benefit limitation included a variety of "loopholes" and exceptions that made it, in Rector's words, "almost entirely symbolic."[45] Perhaps as a result of having this fallback, as well as inherent bureaucratic inefficiency, state agencies are still struggling to move program participants into the workforce. Thus, as of March 2011, 58 percent of TANF families included an adult subject to the work requirement, but over half of these individuals performed no "work activity" at all, while about another quarter performed some, but failed to meet the federal standard.[46]

Moreover, most other welfare programs do not have even nominal time limits, and many do not have work requirements.[47] For example, one in seven Americans (about 47 million) received food stamps in 2012, and half of the massive resources spent on this benefit went toward individuals who had been on the program for 8 or more years.[48] Sadly, the statement made by President Clinton upon signing PRWORA remains true today: "the current welfare system undermines the basic value of work, responsibility, and family, trapping generation after generation in dependency and hurting the very people it was designed to help."[49]

The libertarian alternative to the welfare state

Before going further, I must reiterate my confidence that if the libertarian policy prescriptions outlined elsewhere in this study were implemented, we would greatly reduce if not eliminate the need for public assistance. Repealing costly and unnecessary governmental regulations would spur the creation of new businesses and enhance economic growth, substantially increasing the demand for labor. Similarly, removing state-created barriers to entry, such as zoning, licensure, and minimum wage laws, would make it much easier for people to find jobs or to self-employ. Closing the public schools would result in a more skilled and productive workforce, and ending the federal government's control of health care would greatly reduce waste, thereby freeing up enormous resources that would be employed elsewhere to better effect.

Dismantling the welfare state would also increase the availability of private assistance. The provision of a public safety net induces the popular belief that citizens satisfy their moral obligation to the unfortunate simply by paying taxes. If we terminate coercive "charity," there is at least some empirical evidence that private efforts would prove adequate to the task.[50]

However, the rosy scenario just described is an empirical prediction, and as such cannot be used to exclude *philosophical* challenges regarding the sufficiency of the libertarian response if things don't go as planned. If a public safety net proves necessary, we should start by eliminating all federal welfare programs, and the taxes that fund them, and shifting this responsibility entirely to the states. They, in turn, may wish to delegate this function to more local levels of government.

By definition, a public safety net will have to be funded by nonconsensual taxation, but this does not imply that the government should play any active role in the delivery of assistance. Just as in the case of school vouchers, the state should simply provide the intended beneficiaries with the means to obtain private services. In contrast to the failed bureaucratic approach that offers a patchwork of one-size-fits-all programs, private organizations can offer a personalized, holistic strategy, based on the specific needs of the individual. They would not only do a better job in prioritizing aid, but can more effectively identify and address the underlying causes that prevent people from finding work.

This is not a theoretical claim, but a verifiable fact. Existing private organization, of both a secular and religious orientation, such as Goodwill Industries, Feeding America, The Lighthouse for the Blind, Habitat for Humanity, the Salvation Army, Catholic Charities USA, and the Union Gospel Missions, are already doing much of the same work performed by the state, but with greater success and less overhead, waste, and fraud.[51]

These private charities don't assess the vocational strengths and weaknesses of their clients through forms and occasional interviews, but observe and mentor them on an ongoing basis. Their personnel don't outsource the assistance and training duties to others, but can provide them in-house, often in residential or workplace settings tailored to the participant's individual circumstances. They can also refuse service to those who won't play by the rules.

A rights-based approach to poverty alleviation would leverage the caring and expertise of those who lead and serve in such organizations by delegating to them, with appropriate supervision, the provision of the social safety net. This could be achieved by soliciting grant proposals on a nondiscriminatory basis from all reputable local charities, including religious and secular entities, profits and nonprofits, and so on. These entities would bid for this "business," introducing a healthy competition for taxpayer dollars, and fostering experimentation with new and creative strategies for getting people back on their feet. Those in need would have the freedom to choose the charity that he/she thought could best serve them.

The jurisdictions funding this activity would audit the performance of recipients in meeting objective criteria, such as employment rates, criminality, and substance abuse. Contracts would be periodically rebid, and the authorities would give preference to those organizations achieving the best results. Medical care could either be incorporated into the package of services offered by these entities, or could be provided by means of subsidies that would enable the destitute to purchase health care and private insurance.

A strategy that exploits, to the greatest possible extent, the efficiency and responsiveness of the private sector can offer a humane level of social services, including medical care, for those unable to care for themselves, and do so at a cost substantially less than we now pay. This would vindicate the rights of taxpayers by ensuring that coercive taxation is minimized and that assistance is better prioritized. By the same token, those unable to support themselves would be served more effectively, and multigenerational dependency and related pathologies would be reduced.

I am under no illusion that my proposal is a perfect solution to the problem of unmet human need. I am sure that political factors will influence the selection of providers, and I acknowledge the great difficulties involved in evaluating their performance. Nevertheless, I cannot see how a proposal along these general lines could possibly be worse than the incredibly costly and ineffective status quo.

Admittedly, such radical surgery is not in the political cards anytime soon. Accordingly, the most realistic reform is something like what was accomplished in morphing AFDC into TANF, that is, consolidating the federal funding of our many antipoverty programs, and providing it to the states as block grants, along with the authority to experiment with different designs and strategies. Perhaps, certain of our more entrepreneurial states will eventually try out the sort of privatization approach just outlined.

In fact, Florida has since 2007 run a pilot program that exploits the advantages of free markets in delivering medical services to the indigent. This experiment covers five of its counties, with a total of 290,000 Medicaid recipients, and employs federal and state funds to subsidize the purchase of a wide variety of different private insurance policies. It allows recipients to choose coverage that best suits their specific requirements, and forces providers to compete for this business.

According to the analysis of the responsible Florida officials, the program has saved the state $161 million annually, improved the health of enrolled patients, and achieved high patient satisfaction.[52] The legislature has passed and the governor has signed legislation to expand the program statewide. In February 2013, this proposal was approved by the responsible federal agency "in principle," subject to a number of conditions that may prove to be deal killers.[53] If expanded to cover Florida's entire Medicaid population, it is estimated that the state would save $901 million annually. If replicated nationally, saving could reach an additional $28.5 billion annually.[54]

CHAPTER EIGHT

Public education

Our system of public education is remarkable, although not in a way that should make us proud. Not only does it violate the rights of virtually all participants, but contrives to do so in a way that favors the affluent at the expense of the less well-off. I first describe the moral principles that guide my policy recommendations, then outline the various injustices present in our existing system of K-12 education. Next I present what I regard as the ideal solution, as well as the most practical reform option. I then turn briefly to the libertarian prescription for postsecondary education.

First principles

Education is first and foremost a parental responsibility, and this obliges them to equip their children with the tools required for gainful employment and to function as citizens in a democratic polity. Because they have this mandate, parents must have the freedom to discharge it as they see fit. Except in those cases where they are unable to do so, the state should have no involvement in the educational process.

The moral basis for this position is straightforward. Bringing children into the world is a voluntary decision, and just as we expect parents to provide their offspring with food, clothing, housing, and health care, so too should we expect them to fulfill their educational responsibility. Put somewhat differently, why should adults who for various reasons elect not to have children subsidize the expenses of those who make the opposite choice?

Defenders of the status quo typically rely on the public good argument. In other words, they claim that the education of children to a minimum standard provides non-excludable benefits that are enjoyed by all. Without nonconsensual taxation to finance this good, it will be seriously undersupplied due to the problem of free riders, that is, taxpayers without children or whose offspring have already been educated will underfund this good.[1] But this argument clearly fails on two distinct grounds.

First, the chief beneficiary of an adequate education is the child receiving it. Society at large profits in only an indirect and secondary way. Thus, this good is largely excludable, in that schools can simply deny enrollment to the children of parents who refuse to pay tuition. Accordingly, there is no realistic threat of widespread free riding that can only be addressed by the coercion now used to fund our public schools.

Second, even if education satisfies the technical definition of a public good, this does not imply that the state must *provide* it by means of nonconsensual taxation. Parents typically love their children and strongly desire to give them a decent education, and in our affluent society most parents can afford to do so, particularly if relieved of the taxes imposed to fund the current system. Thus, as John Stuart Mill advised over 150 years ago, society's interest in an adequately prepared work force and electorate would largely be vindicated by a legal requirement that parents educate their children to a specified standard.[2] Parents who elect to home school already face this mandate in many states.

However, government intervention may be appropriate in the case of parents who are simply incapable, for financial or other reasons, of educating their children. These youngsters did not ask to be born into such circumstances, and the negative impact of this deprivation would be so great as to justify relaxing the side constraints against coercion that usually apply. Therefore, if voluntary efforts prove unavailing, nonconsensual taxation to fund the education of such children would be permissible.

But, here again, the potential need for state action in these narrow circumstances does not provide a rationale for a government-administered system. As Milton Friedman advocated at least as early as 1962, a system of school vouchers would be far more effective in advancing the interests of children from disadvantaged backgrounds (see discussion below).[3]

In addition to the public good argument, another commonly heard defense of government run schools is the need to assure the existence of a common set of core, "liberal" values, including a tolerance of diverse cultures and views necessary for maintaining social stability. But this argument assumes, without justification, that the vast majority of parents do not already wish to inculcate these values in their children and that in contrary cases the state could, in the face of parental hostility, successfully promote them through public schooling. Furthermore, it is doubtful that the public schools do generally promote tolerance, but in fact are at least as likely to indoctrinate students with contempt for any political and social perspective that conflicts with those held by the teachers and administrators running this system.

Finally, this argument clearly proves too much. If it were true, parents should not be allowed to send their children to private schools (including those affiliated with religious institutions) or to home school them. We as a society allow these options because we rightly embrace the principle that parents are the most reliable and trustworthy guardians of their children's interests, including the transmission of cultural values.

K-12 Education: the morally illegitimate status quo

Libertarians view our current K-12 educational system as morally illegitimate for a number of distinct reasons. First, is the labor code that governs it: as we have seen, in a majority of states collective bargaining by teachers is legally permitted. A second element is the near universal requirement that would-be teachers obtain a certificate before they are allowed to practice their profession. As previously argued, collective bargaining for public sector employees should be outlawed, and all licensure requirements abolished.

Additional objections center on two closely related features: the method by which our schools are funded and their monopolistic character. In fact, it is the former that is the cause of the latter. Parents who do not wish to send their children to the nearest taxpayer-funded institution must pay for the privilege twice; once through their taxes and a second time in the form of tuition.

It is as if the government imposed a special tax of $25,000 on all households in a particular jurisdiction and then delivered the *same* car to each one, without regard to their individual needs and preferences. Since the families in my imaginary example have already paid for the state-supplied car, relatively few will be able to afford the vehicle they really want.[4] Of course, in my example those receiving the government automobile could at least trade it in for the car they prefer, but no such option is available for the hapless consumers of public education.

I note that parents do not generally have freedom of choice even *within* the public school system.[5] Accordingly, for most of the middle class and the poor, the school in their district operates as a monopoly. If the quality of the education provided by that particular institution is substandard, or if its instructional philosophy is a poor fit with their child's preferred style of learning, there is nothing the parents can do about it. Most of them must work for a living, so home schooling is simply not an option.

History shows that in the private sector monopolies cannot long endure (with the possible exception of so-called natural monopolies, like utility services) because entrepreneurs will use their ingenuity to devise new technologies and business models to displace even the most firmly entrenched firms. Thus, at various times over the last 50 years IBM, Microsoft and Google were thought to have achieved lasting dominance in key markets. However, in each case new competitors rendered this threat moot.

In stark contrast, except for parents who can afford to pay twice for their children's education, our public education system is a *permanent* monopoly because it has the force of law. It will endure until we repeal the statutes enforcing it. Interestingly, the affluent are generally among the staunchest defenders of this perverse arrangement. If you are fortunate enough to live in Beverly Hills, Brookline, Scarsdale, or some other tony suburb, your children will have access to excellent public schools.

The staff there doesn't have to worry nearly so much about getting mugged on the way to or from school, and their students will generally be better socialized than those in rougher neighborhoods. Thus, these districts will have their choice of the best and brightest instructors. Moreover, if these parents happen to prefer private school, the additional cost will not pinch too badly. If I were cynical, I would say that the affluent prefer the current system because it ensures that their children enjoy a lasting competitive advantage over the offspring of the *hoi polloi*.

Children from impoverished backgrounds are the real victims of our present system, and would benefit greatly from its radical transformation. By any objective measure, the schools that serve these students are an abject failure. First, according to a detailed study by the nonprofit organization America's Promise Alliance, as of the 2010 school year, the 4-year high-school graduation rate was 78.2 percent overall, but only 66.1 percent for African-Americans and 72.4 percent for Hispanics. This study also identifies over 1,400 high schools, labeled "dropout factories" by the authors, where the graduation rate was less than 60 percent. These schools disproportionately serve minority communities.[6]

The 78.2 percent overall graduation rate just mentioned represents a 5 percent improvement compared to 2006, with even greater gains made by Hispanic and African-American students. However, it is not clear to what extent this improvement actually reflects better educational outcomes, rather than a mere relaxation of standards for graduation.

Second, the performance of students in our public schools generally and among minorities in particular lag behind their peers in other developed nations. In the 2012 international PISA (Program for International Student Assessment) study, conducted by the Organization for Economic Cooperation and Development, US 15-year-olds ranked 17th out of 34 developed countries in reading skills, 21st in science and 26th in mathematics.[7]

But not to worry says the National Education Association, the largest of the unions representing public school teachers and administrators; the problem is poverty, not pedagogy. Dennis Van Roekel, the NEA's president, dismisses the OECD data, claiming that while students from affluent homes do well on the PISA assessments, "socioeconomic factors influence students' performance in the United States more than they do in all but few of the other PISA countries."[8]

The NEA apparently believes that *our* poor kids, compared to those of other nations, simply *can't* learn, and thus are a far greater drag on our standardized test results. Their solution: greater expenditures, particularly on the salaries of teachers and administrators. But, as Jay Greene, an academic authority on education notes, "the vast majority of studies have found no sustained positive relationship between spending and classroom results."⁹ In fact, over the four decades between 1970 and 2009 we have *tripled* our real per pupil spending on the public schools (i.e., adjusted for inflation), yet standardized test scores of high school seniors in math, science, and reading have remained flat.[10]

Even indulging in the extravagant hypothesis that funding levels determine educational outcomes in some straightforward way, we already spend generously on our government schools. According to another OECD data set, in 2010 (the most recent year for which information is available) the United States spent $11,193/student in public elementary schools and $12,464/student in public secondary schools. These expenditures placed us in fourth place among all nations for elementary education and fifth place for secondary.[11]

Does this broad average conceal miserly spending for inner city schools? This is simply not the case. A study by the Third Way (a Democratic think tank that according to its own website "creates and advances moderate policy and political ideas") found "that average [nationwide] per-pupil spending in the public schools in 2011 was $11,925 in affluent school districts, $10,349 in middle class school districts, and $11,799 in low-income districts."[12] This study is consistent with the OECD data cited immediately above, and shows that generally speaking there is no great disparity in educational spending by socioeconomic status, and that in any case the pattern of funding does not discriminate against the poor.

Many educational reformers have embraced charter schools as an important means of raising the quality of the education received by disadvantaged children. Charter schools are public institutions, financed entirely by tax dollars. However, their faculties are generally not unionized, and their administrators are thereby freed of work rules and discipline rights laid down in collective bargaining agreements. While a step in the right direction, charters are no substitute for vouchers that would enable poor parents to freely choose the best educational option for their children. If a modest degree of school choice is good, unrestricted choice is much better still.

The most glaring limitation on the effectiveness of charter schools is that as of this writing seven states do not authorize them at all. Of at least equal importance, many of the remaining states do so pursuant to laws that severely limit their effectiveness. These provisions include stringent limitations on the number of authorized charter schools (or total student enrollment), failure to exempt charters from collective bargaining laws, and dramatically inferior funding levels relative to conventional public schools. Indeed, the Center for Education Reform, a pro-charter advocacy group, in its most recent (2012) evaluation of states on their treatment of charters, gave only 4 states an "A" grade; 9 a "B"; 19 a "C"; and 11 a "D" or "F" (the seven states not authorizing charters were not graded).[13]

There is a great deal of controversy regarding whether private and charter schools produce better educational outcomes than traditional public ones. I believe they do, but as with almost all social science data, there are almost insurmountable problems of measurement and interpretation. Since we don't identify cohorts of children when they enter preschool who are alike in all relevant ways (IQ, motivation to learn, parental involvement, etc.) and then track them through their academic careers, we are left to interpret data that does not fully control for these factors.[14]

Fortunately, I need not enter into this debate. Nobody seriously denies that *many* private and charter schools outperform their public counterparts in districts throughout the country and, in any case, statistical averages obscure the qualitative benefits experienced by students whose parents are able to enroll them in a school where they are happier, socialize with a better peer group, develop greater self-confidence, and the like. Most fundamentally, as a society we have properly decided that parents are the most reliable guardian of their children's interests, and there is no reason that this authority should not extend to choices regarding their education. In short, parents have a *right* to make these decisions, and this prerogative is clearly offended by the current quasi-monopoly arrangement.

The solution

In light of the above, all local property, state income, and all other taxes used to finance the public schools should be eliminated, and these institutions should be closed. Obviously, this would dramatically expand the demand for private schooling, which now accounts for only about 10 percent of all K-12 students, with an additional 2–3 percent being home schooled.[15] With this would come even more intense competition and innovation, including greater use of "distance learning." Those administrators now running charter and conventional public schools could reopen them as private schools, with the same staff (if they choose), and compete for these dollars.

Importantly, tuition at private schools is typically substantially less than what we spend per pupil in the pubic system. A 2010 study by Adam Schaeffer of the Cato Institute found that in our five largest metropolitan school districts, plus the District of Columbia, median private school tuition was $7,728, compared with reported average public school expenditures of $12,663/student in these same districts.[16] Freed of their existing tax burden, most parents would be able to afford a suitable education for their children.

Even so, some will be unable to fully or even partially discharge their educational obligations. Voluntary efforts to educate these children through private scholarships and subsidies should be explored and encouraged, but if this fails then state intervention is justified. This assistance should take the form of vouchers (the equivalent of cash that can be used only for tuition), with amounts based on a means-tested sliding scale, and financed out of general tax revenues. Parents with special needs children, whose education consumes more resources, should receive vouchers representing greater monetary value.

Since the ideal system may be politically unrealistic for the foreseeable future, libertarians should press for an end to all legal discrimination against charter schools, including artificial limits on their growth, and the creation of voucher programs for low-income children in failing public schools. I believe that as the virtues of the small number of existing voucher programs become apparent, political pressure will grow for expanded use.[17]

Higher education

Our elite colleges and universities are generally considered to be the finest in the world. Many tens of thousands of foreign-born applicants from around the globe vie for admission to US schools. Private schools—from major universities to small colleges—occupy most of the top spots in the popular rankings of our institutions of higher learning. The self-evident success of privately funded and administered institutions invites the question of what role if any remains for state involvement in higher education.

Because the coercion of innocent persons is justified only in extreme situations, the answer is "none." There are a wide variety of employment opportunities available to individuals with a high school degree, including self-employment or starting a business. Moreover, they can pursue further academic studies or vocational training on their own. Accordingly, the absence of publicly funded postsecondary institutions will not destroy the life prospects of those high school graduates who cannot afford to immediately pay for additional private education.

We spend lavishly on our public colleges and universities. Federal financial aid to students totaled almost $170 billion in the 2012–3 fiscal year, while state-level aid amounted to $9.7 billion.[18] In addition, a recent study by Illinois State University estimates that in 2014 the various states will spend $72.1 billion on general operating expenses for their colleges and universities.[19] This largess is provided on a nonconsensual basis, and is thus morally impermissible.

While there is every reason to believe that these subsidies enable many students to attend college who wouldn't otherwise, this fact should not be celebrated. First, just as in the case of our state-run K-12 system, a large percentage of students drop out before graduation—only 56 percent of those who enroll in 4-year college ever earn a bachelor's degree.[20] Clearly, these students either were not prepared to do college level work or finally realized that their tuition represented a poor investment of their and/or their parents' resources.

In fact, we now face a shortage of workers with key vocational skills, and this training is not available in traditional 4-year colleges.[21] It can be acquired either on the job or through specialized instruction at community colleges and for-profit schools. The overall welfare of our society will likely be enhanced if we graduate fewer individuals with BA degrees of questionable relevance to gainful employment, and replace them with more small business owners, skilled trades people, machinists, health care workers, and so on. In short, the status quo has encouraged a huge misallocation of resources.

Moreover, it is reasonable to infer that the easy availability of government grants and loans is partially responsible for the astronomical rate of increase in college tuition and fees, which for the last three decades is running at least three times general price inflation.[22] As then Secretary of Education William Bennett wrote in 1987: "increases in financial aid . . . have enabled colleges and universities blithely to raise tuition, confident that Federal loan subsidies would help cushion the increase."[23] This inflation harms everyone who must pay for higher education.

As tuition rises, so too must the level of student debt required to pay it. As of late 2011 there was over $1 trillion in outstanding student debt, the vast majority of which was financed by the federal government (rather than from private sources).[24] For the 60 percent of students who had to assume loans in order to pay for their college education, the average balance upon graduation was $26,500 (as of 2012).[25]

Since this is an average, there are clearly millions of graduates with much higher levels of debt, and their career options are limited to those that will enable them to service it. Here again, the unwelcome side effects of our educational policies fall disproportionately on students from middle and working class families, whose parents lack the means to simply pay tuition out of savings.

In light of the above, the rights-based libertarian prescription for higher education is simple. The supply of educational services should be allocated by the intersection of the supply and demand curves in a free market. The federal government and the states should end all taxpayer-financed support of postsecondary education, including all grants, loans, guarantees, tax credits, and direct assistance.

I understand that this prescription is wildly unrealistic in the present political environment, so that all this is left to us is to chip away at the edges of this monstrosity. However, this effort may prove more efficacious than seems possible at first sight, since in my judgment we will eventually be forced to undergo fiscal austerity as a result of out-of-control governmental spending and borrowing. In such circumstances, the political class may be amenable to budget cuts that were unthinkable in more affluent (and profligate) times.

CHAPTER NINE

Health care

Our state intrudes into nearly every aspect of medicine, and thereby displaces the voluntary arrangements that providers and patients would otherwise make for themselves. In fact, perhaps the defining characteristic of our system is the extent to which freedom of choice and accountability have been eliminated. Instead, the health care we receive is predominantly paid for by our employer or the government, covering services that we did not select, at prices we did not negotiate.

This governmental interference not only violates rights on a grand scale, but also produces an inefficient, wasteful, and substandard health care system. This chapter explains why the status quo is failing, describes what free market medicine would look like, and shows that it would not be materially worse than what we have, and would almost certainly be better. My argument here is not utilitarian, but the fact that unjust laws and regulations are directly responsible for the system's poor performance is surely relevant for purposes of demonstrating that we could get along quite nicely under competitive capitalism, with the possible exception of financing care for the truly helpless.

The status quo

Our existing laws and regulations impermissibly limit in various ways people's right to enter and practice the different health care professions.[1] First, and most obviously, all of our 50 states license doctors, nurses, EMTs, and so on. Rather than allow consumers to decide for themselves whether they wish to patronize a provider preapproved by the state, the authorities make this decision for us, enforcing this monopoly with laws criminalizing the "unauthorized practice of medicine."

Clearly, licensing represents a barrier to employment in these occupations, thereby reducing supply. To receive a license, candidates must graduate from accredited schools, as determined by organizations designated by the state, and must pass special examinations. Accreditation committees are susceptible to regulatory capture (see Chapter 5) by the AMA and other trade groups that have a financial interest in limiting the number of "qualified" professionals, thereby increasing compensation for those holding the requisite credential.[2]

Moreover, the states tightly regulate the services that each of these clinicians may provide, so that, for example, in a majority of states only physicians are permitted to prescribe pharmaceuticals without supervision, and only registered nurses may perform certain types of examinations.[3] And, there are substantial regulatory barriers that prevent health care workers from practicing across state lines.[4] Our regulatory reflex has also led many states to require hospitals, nursing homes, and other medical facilities to obtain a "certificate of need" from a state planning board before opening.

All of these regulations, as well as the operations of the FDA, violate the rights of every competent adult. Subject to the standard libertarian prohibition on fraud, if a person, for example, wishes to be treated by an unaccredited physician, or by a nurse operating beyond her "scope of practice," that is, entirely his or her business. The adverse consequence of our administrative controls is to create shortages of and higher prices for medical services.

Our federal tax code also profoundly influences the delivery of medical services in this country. The vast majority of working Americans receive health insurance through their employer, as part of their benefits package. This phenomenon is largely a historical accident, arising as a means by which firms circumvented the wage and price controls imposed during the Second World War. Tight labor markets induced employers to compete for workers by offering health insurance, which was not subject to these controls, and was not counted as compensation for purposes of the federal income tax.[5] To this day, our law treats the employer's cost of providing health care insurance as a deductible business expense, and workers are not taxed on the value of this benefit.[6]

In contrast, except for individuals with health savings accounts ("HSAs"), those who directly purchase insurance policies get no tax break, and must use after-tax dollars. Accordingly, our tax code violates the rule of law by unfairly discriminating against working-age Americans who do not have employer-sponsored coverage available to them. This disparity has had profound, detrimental ramifications for our medical system.

The effect of employer-sponsored insurance, and enrollment in federal health care programs (Medicare, Medicaid, and care provided by the Veterans Administration), is that, despite having approximately 48 million uninsured living here, only 11.4 percent of health care spending in the United States is out-of-pocket, meaning paid by the person receiving the service directly to the provider. Surprisingly, this represents the fourth lowest percentage among the 20 largest industrialized economies.[7] By way of contrast, the figure is 30 percent in Switzerland, which has universal health care coverage.[8]

The dominance of third-party payment for health care causes both price insensitivity and significant overutilization. If consumers had to pay the full cost of a test, procedure, devise, or examination, they would more carefully assess its worth relative to other uses of their scarce resources. Moreover, they would be motivated to shop around for the best price/value proposition, and providers would be more inclined to compete by publishing data regarding their prices and outcomes. As *Wall Street Journal* columnist Holman Jenkins has observed, "Such information doesn't exist in health care because consumers don't demand it, because somebody else is almost always paying for our health care."[9]

In fact, it is reasonable to conclude that if we collectively paid much more of our medical care out-of-pocket, our system would be radically transformed. Consider the fact that automobile insurance does not reimburse maintenance costs, and most policies have meaningful deductibles. The essential feature of this coverage is the protection it affords against low-probability, devastating events, such as a major injury accident.

Automobile insurance doesn't reimburse minor expenses because the administrative burden would raise premiums to the point where coverage would not be cost effective. Moreover, most car owners are more than capable of paying these items out-of-pocket. When they do purchase such things as oil changes, brake-pad replacements, and minor dent repairs, they are likely to look closely for the best deal (notice the number of businesses fiercely competing to provide it). The same points could be made about homeowner's insurance.

Naturally, if you compile a horrible driving record, car insurance will get more-and-more expensive, and ultimately unobtainable. This feature of free markets provides a significant financial incentive for responsible behavior. In contrast, if you are one of a large group of employees covered at work, your health-related lifestyle choices will have an immaterial impact on your insurance premiums, and if you are on Medicare or Medicaid, none at all.

As one would expect, then, when consumers purchase health insurance as individuals, they predominately purchase "major medical" (also known as "catastrophic") policies. Unfortunately, each state has its own regulatory apparatus and coverage mandates, preventing companies from freely selling policies across state lines.[10] This substantially reduces competition in each of these 50 discrete submarkets, thereby significantly raising prices.

As should be clear by now, what is usually called health insurance here lacks the most fundamental characteristic of *insurance*, namely, the mitigation of *risk*, and is more accurately described as a prepaid medical care, funded mostly by private employers or by the federal government. Recall Nozick's description of the virtues of private property, which includes the claim that "private property enables people to decide on the pattern and types of risks they wish to bear." This presupposes that individuals live with the consequences of their choices. Our health care system has completely abandoned this concept. It is metaphorically like an all-you-can-eat Vegas-style buffet, where the casino has "comped" the meal: beneficiaries have every incentive to "get their money's worth."

Of course, upon reaching the age of 65, Americans are covered by Medicare, which, if anything, represents an even more pervasive (and harmful) interference with free market medicine. This program is blatantly coercive in that it imposes a nonconsensual 1.45 percent payroll tax on *all* workers, matched by an equal tax on the employer.[11] The Affordable Care Act of 2010 (the "ACA" or ObamaCare) raises this tax to 2.35 percent on incomes exceeding $200,000. If the worker would prefer to purchase private health insurance with their withholdings, or use them for some other purpose, they are simply denied this option.

The taxpayers forced into Medicare participate in a one-size-fits-all program that, like Medicaid, is rife with waste, fraud, and abuse. It is credibly estimated that each year Medicare is defrauded to the tune of between $60 and $90 billion, which represents more than 10 percent of the program's total budget.[12] In comparison, fraud committed against private sector health insurers is estimated at 1.5 percent of expenditures.[13]

Medicare also violates the freedom of contract of consumers on one side, and clinicians, hospitals, and pharmaceutical companies on the other, to reach mutually advantageous agreements; instead, bureaucrats dictate to participants what they will pay for the various goods and services covered by the program. For physicians whose practices center on the elderly, this program closely resembles a monopsony, meaning, a market dominated by a single buyer.[14] However, for the same reason that monopolies are rare and fleeting in the private sector, that is, new entrants, monopsonies are too. In the public sector, they can endure as long as the laws establishing them remain on the books.

Medicare providers have money and political influence. They use trade associations and lobbyists to turn the reimbursement system to their advantage. On the other side are groups like AARP, that attempt to hold prices down. But outcomes derived in this manner are unacceptable from the moral perspective because they do not reflect the *voluntary* choices of market participants, but rather the arbitrary decisions of regulators sailing with the prevailing political wind.

If the bureaucrats administering Medicare set reimbursement at rates above what would prevail under free market conditions, they unjustly penalize taxpayers (who partially fund the system) and program beneficiaries (through higher co-pays and premiums).[15] Conversely, if they are set at less than what would prevail in a free market, they violate the rights of providers.

Moreover, reimbursement rates indirectly determine the *availability* of certain types of care, implicating the rights of patients. Thus, while no one seems to complain about shortages of surgeons, dermatologists, and radiologists, there appears to be a genuine shortage of primary care physicians relative to what we would expect to find in a free market.[16] There is good reason to attribute this undersupply at least in part to the fee levels set under Medicare (and Medicaid), which are skewed against family doctors.

For example, a 2010 online survey of Medicare-accepting physicians by the AMA found that 17 percent are currently restricting the number of these patients in their practice. That number rises to 31 percent among primary care physicians. The two most frequently cited reasons are that the payment rate is too low, and the threat of future payment cuts.[17] In addition, a relatively small but growing segment of primary care physicians have opted out of Medicare entirely.[18] Since payments from federal health care programs represent a substantial portion of many clinicians' compensation, a reimbursement schedule tilted against general practitioners will discourage medical students from entering this field.

Under free market conditions, an undersupply of family doctors or an oversupply of certain specialists should self-correct over time, as the incomes of these professionals would rise or fall to equilibrate the demand for such services with the existing supply, which is largely fixed in the short and intermediate terms. This would in turn tend to steer medical students to or away from these practice areas. However, since Medicare reimbursement rates are set by program administrators, this process is inhibited. Accordingly, innocent persons may be denied access to appropriate medical care, or forced to endure long delays.

Medicare, despite all its deficiencies, has remained politically untouchable because it seems to offer what is impossible outside of the realm of governmental largess, namely, something for nothing or the proverbial "free lunch." As in the case of social security, payroll withholdings are not held by the government in an account dedicated to the workers' future health care expenses, but are instead used to pay benefits to an earlier, now-retired generation. Each generation has, courtesy of servile politicians, helped itself to ever more generous benefits, far in excess of their payroll withholdings.[19]

Indeed, the very structure of entitlement programs grants current recipients a license to steal from future generations of workers, who may be saddled with taxes and debts that they had no opportunity to oppose. In the case of Medicare, its trustees estimated in May 2013 that we have made *unfunded* promises of benefits, coming due over the next 75 years, totaling *at least* $34 trillion.[20] While democratic approval cannot sanitize arbitrary and nonconsensual redistributions of resources, our entitlement programs makes such abuse almost certain.

Because its expenses rise automatically with the number of retirees, and since politicians are unwilling to materially trim the benefits they receive, Medicare annual spending is projected to grow from $592 million in 2013 to $1.1 trillion in 2023. Even under optimistic assumptions, expenditures as a percentage of GDP would grow from 3.7 percent in 2013 to 7.7 percent in 2050.[21] As economists genteelly say, such growth is "unsustainable," and there will inevitably be substantial increases in taxes and major benefit cuts.[22] Even politicians eventually run out of other people's money.

As a result of the third-party payment (for most everything) model adopted in both Medicare and employer-based "insurance," the salutary discipline of individual choice and personal responsibility has largely been eliminated. For decades our spending on medical goods and services has risen faster than the general rate of inflation, thus consuming an ever-increasing share of our GDP, and this trend shows no sign of abating. Thus, in 1980, health care spending represented 9 percent of GDP; in 2010, this was 17.9 percent, and is projected by the Congressional Budget Office to increase to 19.6 percent in 2021.[23] In 2012, we spent about $2.7 trillion on health care (equal to roughly one-sixth of the size of our entire economy), 50 percent more on a per capita basis than any other country, without noticeably better outcomes.[24]

Not surprisingly, much of the care provided here is unneeded or of marginal value. The respected Institute of Medicine, an arm of the National Academy of Sciences, estimates that (as of 2012) we waste $750 billion a year, roughly 30 percent of every medical dollar spent. The Institute identified six major categories: unnecessary services ($210 billion); inefficient delivery ($130 billion); excess administrative costs ($190 billion); inflated prices ($105 billion); prevention failures ($55 billion); and fraud ($75 billion).[25]

The affordable care act

The response of the political authorities to the glaring inadequacies of our existing health care system is the Affordable Care Act, enacted in 2010, but which becomes effective in stages stretching out to 2020. This legislative and regulatory behemoth greatly expands the state's authority over a vast range of health care decisions that belong properly to each individual or family. It packages popular "reforms" designed to address perceived flaws in the current system—the large number of uninsured Americans, the unwillingness of some insurers to cover preexisting conditions, and lifetime caps on the amount of benefits—with massive and costly structural changes.

As discussed below, these flaws can be addressed more effectively within a free market framework, thereby avoiding the use of morally illegitimate coercion on a grand scale. Sadly, the ADA ignores the *systemic* problem of wasteful, ineffective, and costly care, the causes of which has been previously identified. Furthermore, its reach, complexity, and reliance on bureaucratic discretion provide fertile ground in which crony capitalism may flourish.

Taxes, subsidies, regulations, and peverse incentives

For funding, the legislation relies on a variety of new or increased taxes, totaling about $1 trillion over the 2013–22 decade.[26] During this same period, the ACA also authorizes up to $1.2 trillion in subsidies (tax credits) for the purchase of insurance on government-run health insurance "exchanges."[27] These subsidies are not just for the truly poor, but extend to individuals and families, not offered qualifying employer-based coverage, earning up to four times the federal poverty rate. So, a family of four that includes two dependent children, and that earns as much as $94,000, can receive a tax credit of up to $8,000 toward the purchase of a mid-level ("silver") policy.[28]

Subject to an exception for the impoverished, who will be relegated to the awful Medicaid program, all uninsured individuals were required to purchase coverage on these exchanges by March 31, 2014. This is enforced by a penal tax on those who fail to comply, which is minor at first, but escalates to the greater of $695 per individual ($2,085 family) or 2.5 percent of income, by 2016.

In setting the premiums for these policies, insurers cannot discriminate by gender or medical condition, and are limited in their ability to price by age. Accordingly younger, relatively healthy individuals will generally pay more than they would under free market conditions, subsidizing the middle-aged. Whether or not purchasers desire to pay for these benefits, all individual plans (other than those "grandfathered") must now provide a range of "essential health benefits" ("EHBs"), including full, first-dollar coverage of many types of preventive care (including contraception and surgical sterilization), mental health care, and substance abuse treatments.[29]

Some 15 million Americans were, prior to the enrollment deadline, covered by individual (nonemployer-based) plans. Only some two percent of these policies offer all EHB benefits, and a majority are not grandfathered in under the ACA. Accordingly, roughly 7 million Americans have to date received cancellation notices from their current insurers.[30] Those receiving such cancellations should be able to obtain new insurance, but most will find that they face increased premiums, higher deductibles, or a more restricted list of providers.[31] Since ObamaCare was sold with the assurance that everyone would get to keep their existing plan and doctors if they so desired, we can add this one to the long list of broken government promises.

Moreover, the continuing viability of this coercive scheme rests on whether the "young invincibles" will participate in large enough numbers to generate the necessary subsidies for the older, less healthy participants. If this doesn't occur, prices will increase the next year and more people in the insurance pool—generally the healthiest—will elect to self-insure, further driving up premiums, sparking more withdrawals, and so on. This set of incentives can produce the dreaded insurance "death spiral," and crater the entire marketplace for individual insurance.[32]

The ACA also mandates that employers with more than 50 *full-time* employees (those working at least 30 hours/week) provide health care insurance to their workforce by January 2015 that meets federal standards for coverage and affordability, or pay a $2,000 fine per employee. And, importantly, deductibles are limited to $2,000/year per individual and $4,000/year per family. There are also caps on annual out-of-pocket expenses.[33]

The employer mandate is already provoking many firms to find ways to stay beneath the statutory 50 employee threshold, that is, by putting expansion plans on hold, turning some employees into part-timers, or reducing the firm's head-count. Those persons harmed in this way are further collateral damage inflicted by the ACA's command and control philosophy.

Moreover, since the $2,000/per employee fine is substantially less than the cost of providing federally approved coverage, and given the availability of the subsidies described earlier, companies now have a powerful incentive to drop health care insurance for their workforce, especially for part-time employees. In early 2013, the Congressional Budget Office estimated that 7 million people will be dropped from employer-sponsored coverage; other estimates are much higher.[34]

There is nothing sacred or even desirable about employer-based health insurance, but companies at least have a financial incentive to hold the line on costs since they enjoy only a deduction for this expense and not a dollar-for-dollar credit. Also, insurers share this motivation since they must compete for customers. Thus, over the last decade the trend has been for employers to offer plans that require more out-of-pocket payments from employees, by requiring higher deductibles and by paying only a set amount for certain goods and services, leaving the worker responsible for all the rest.[35] If, as is almost certain, ObamaCare significantly reduces the portion of medical care paid for out-of-pocket by shifting consumers to subsidized insurance purchased on governmental exchanges and expanding Medicaid, overall health care expenditures will continue to rise.

Another insidious side effect of the ACA is that it penalizes full-time work. As previously noted, the many millions of workers (and their families) not offered qualified employer-sponsored health insurance will be eligible for potentially large subsidies in purchasing individual insurance. Thus, as economist Casey Mulligan has noted, "Under the ACA it will not be extraordinary for people to be able to have more disposable income from a part-time position than from a full-time one."[36]

He calculates that for those considering whether to remain employed in order to access company-sponsored health insurance, the ACA will "raise marginal tax rates in 2015 by 10 percentage points of total compensation, on average, for about half of the nonelderly adult population and zero percentage points for the rest."[37] In other words, just like our welfare system, the ACA creates perverse incentives, the costs of which will be absorbed by the hapless taxpayers.[38]

Medicare cost containment

As previously discussed, much of our out-of-control health care spending is attributable to Medicare. The ACA attempts to rein this in by greatly expanding the program's use of "accountable care organizations" (ACOs). As health care expert Peter Suderman explains, "the basic idea . . . is that hospital systems or other networks of providers take responsibility for coordinating patient care. If those systems beat certain targets, while also hitting quality measures, they get to share some of the savings with Medicare."[39]

Like most social engineering projects, this one sounds good on paper; however, not only does it employ morally impermissible means, but it will also fail to achieve its ends. The first thing that must be understood about ACOs is that patients do not consciously agree to enroll in them, nor will they necessarily even know that they are "members." Rather, the entire arrangement is based on "passive enrollment," whereby Medicare patients are assigned to an ACO, for accounting purposes, if their primary care physician is part of a group that has registered (and qualified) as an ACO.

Importantly, Medicare beneficiaries get no share of any savings achieved by their ACO. Moreover, they are free to get outside care without authorization, and will pay no more for it than if provided by their group. Thus, as health care policy expert James Capretta has observed, "The result is that beneficiaries . . . have no incentive to behave any differently than they did before the ACO was initiated."[40]

On the other hand, hospitals, hospital or insurance-directed practice networks, and large physician-owned medical groups may be induced to organize and register as ACOs because they may benefit from the "shared savings payments" available to them under Medicare. And, even before passage, hospitals were aggressively purchasing physician practices, so that it is estimated that about half of all US doctors now work for a hospital or hospital-owned health system.[41] This will enable these institutions to satisfy the statutory requirement that an ACO manage the health care needs of a minimum of 5,000 Medicare beneficiaries for at least 3 years.

Unfortunately physician-employees are not as motivated, and therefore tend to work fewer hours and to be less productive, than physician-entrepreneurs, meaning, those who own and manage their own practices.[42] In all probability, ACOs run by hospital or hospital-owned systems will struggle to achieve greater efficiency.

While ObamaCare offers ACOs a share of any cost savings, organizing and registering as one comes at the heavy cost of being subject to an additional layer of complicated and potentially changing federal laws and regulations. Thus out of a universe of approximately 50 million Medicare beneficiaries, only about 4 million are now treated by ACOs.[43]

Even if many more medical providers register as ACOs and (passive) enrollment thereby dramatically increases, it will not be possible for bureaucrats to dictate rules and procedures for delivering quality health care, while simultaneously taming Medicare's cost spiral. While administrators can certainly track per-patient expenditures, it will be impossible to assess the value of such care without carefully controlled studies of similar medical populations extending over decades. Thus, there is a real and present danger that providers will game the system, earning profits not justified by better health outcomes. Moreover, there is also a reasonable concern that large ACOs will gain cartel-like pricing power in their geographic areas.

At some point, in order to avoid crushing tax increases and concomitant harm to the economy, limits will be placed on Medicare spending. The ACA contemplates doing this by means of bureaucratic fiat in the form of the Independent Payment Advisory Board.[44] However, if this technique were effective, the old USSR would still be going strong and China would never have embraced even modest property rights. Far better to allocate scarce health care resources via the price mechanism in a free market, in which patients would decide through their voluntary purchase decisions what care is worth having, and what can be forgone.

In summary, the ACA does not offer a strategy for controlling health care spending, within Medicare or outside of it. Even the Obama administration's own medical cost "bean counters" estimate that over the 2014–22 time horizon this legislation will add $621 billion to the tab over the pre-law baseline, and that health care spending will continue to grow faster than our GDP. Not coincidentally, the same report estimates that out-of-pocket spending will *fall* from 11.4 percent in 2012 to 9.1 percent by 2022.[45]

Free market medicine

The state has no moral authority for the ACA's massive nonconsensual taxation and redistribution, nor for coercively requiring competent adults to purchase insurance, employers to offer it, and insurance companies to sell only policies blessed by the authorities. The economic impact of these mandates is to move our health care system even further in the direction of prepaid, third-party reimbursement for almost all medical expenses. As a result, fewer dollars will be spent by individuals motivated to carefully weigh the costs and benefits of the service against alternative uses of scarce resources, and to hunt for the best deal from providers. In other words, we are moving away from introducing meaningful competition and cost control into the system.

Competitive capitalism would restore individual rights to our health care system and, as an added bonus, would likely improve the system from a utilitarian perspective. First, all laws against the unauthorized practice of medicine should be repealed. Medical professionals should not need licenses, and patients should not need prescriptions to obtain pharmaceuticals (see Chapter 5). However, fraud would remain illegal, so neither clinicians nor pharmaceutical firms could, with impunity, materially misrepresent their qualifications or their products.

Moreover, nothing in this proposal would prevent existing medical schools from seeking accreditation on a voluntary basis, or physicians from truthfully advertising that they graduated from an accredited institution. Additionally, medical professionals would be free to seek certification of their competence from independent organizations, as physicians must do now before they can hold themselves out as being "board certified" in a particular specialty.[46] The key difference is that consumers would decide for themselves whether they wish to pay extra for treatment by a licensed clinician.

All tax advantages for employer-based insurance should end, which would result in a dramatic increase in policies purchased directly by individuals and families. Similarly, all regulations, including coverage mandates, on the sale of insurance should be eliminated. If there were a single (national) market for individual policies, we would witness keen competition for this business, just as there is now for auto and homeowner's insurance. The problem of "portability," the loss of medical insurance when changing jobs, would thereby largely be solved, since a change of employment would have no impact on coverage.

We can anticipate that most consumers would elect to insure only against catastrophic illness. This in turn would require Americans to purchase much more of their health care on an out-of-pocket basis. The virtues of this arrangement are already on display in areas of medicine where federal intervention is relatively limited, and consumers pay for services themselves, as in the case of Lasik eye and cosmetic surgery. In both instances, prices have *fallen* over the last decade in inflation-adjusted terms, while patient satisfaction remains high.[47]

The issue of portability is closely related to a second problem under the status quo, namely, preexisting conditions. Many consumers now fear that if they develop a disease, and then lose their existing insurance for any reason, including a divorce or change of jobs, they will be stuck without coverage and face potential bankruptcy. However, in a free, competitive market, insurers can be expected to woo potential customers by offering "guaranteed renewable" policies. In other words, as health care economist John Cochrane explains, "once you sign up, you can keep the insurance for life, and your premiums do not rise if you get sicker."[48] Indeed, most individual policies already include this feature, as does virtually all term life insurance.

Naturally, insurers that offer guaranteed renewable policies lose money on healthy policyholders who subsequently are afflicted with expensive-to-treat conditions, but these losses are absorbed by the higher premiums paid by more typical customers. Consumers are willing to pay slightly more in exchange for the peace-of-mind that comes from ameliorating the risk of catastrophic illness, which is exactly how *insurance* is supposed to work.

It is true that in free markets many more people *who can afford insurance* will remain uninsured than under ObamaCare.[49] But it is not clear to me why this constitutes a material problem, and even less how it can justify the extensive violation of rights under the ACA. In the event that these persons face serious illness, they run the risk of receiving less than the optimal amount of care. However, under libertarian principles it is not unjust if people suffer as a result of their freely made choices.

It is also true that free market medicine would permit hospitals and insurers to shift costs from the uninsured to the insured, but there is even greater cost shifting under the ACA, in the form of its huge new taxes and subsidies. Furthermore, if we reduce or better yet eliminate the myriad of state coverage mandates, and allow insurance to be sold across state lines, the cost of catastrophic coverage would be substantially more affordable. In this case, there would be less cost shifting, as there would be fewer uninsured patients.

Under my proposal the truly needy would not be, as under the ACA, relegated to substandard care under Medicaid.[50] Rather, they would, as described in Chapter 7, receive medical services either as part of a holistic approach to the delivery of social services, or through financial support allowing them to purchase private care and insurance. Those receiving this assistance would shop for care and insurance like all other consumers, and would thereby place competitive pressure on providers hoping to capture this business.

For the reasons previously outlined, Medicare should also be dismantled. Hospitals and clinicians now waste endless hours and huge sums navigating their way through Medicare's and Medicaid's notoriously labyrinthine billing procedures.[51] Freed from these uniform, inflexible reimbursement rates, providers would have to compete for the patients now served by these programs, and would do so in the usual fashion, that is, on price and quality. In order not to violate the legitimate expectation interests of innocent people, those near retirement (say 55 or older) would be permitted to remain in Medicare on a means-tested basis, or they could elect to receive vouchers for private insurance. Younger workers would get back what they have contributed into the system, plus imputed interest, but no surplus of the sort enjoyed by earlier generations.

Obviously, this suggestion poses the challenge of transitional funding, since payroll withholdings will no longer be available for this purpose. Whatever the source or cost, it will save the government (and taxpayers) the enormous future burden of supporting this ever-more-expensive program. And, more importantly, restore each person's right to control his or her medical care. Because ending Medicare is politically impossible for the foreseeable future, the best practical reform would be to change its open-ended, third-party reimbursement structure to a defined benefit plan, in the form of vouchers.[52]

Due to the specialized nature of the psychological and physical wounds suffered by soldiers in combat, it would make sense even in a libertarian society for the state to assume responsibility for monitoring and treating these service-related conditions, as we do now through the Veterans Administration.[53] However, as in the case of the state's "backup" role in providing K-12 education when parents fail to do so, the government should supply this good through private channels, on a competitive basis. And, from a rights-based perspective, it is certainly irrational for the state to have any role in treating veterans' garden-variety ailments such as hypertension, diabetes, heart disease, and the like.

Free market medicine would enable consumers to purchase only the medical services they deem cost-effective, from providers eager to attract and retain their business. It thus aligns freedom with responsibility. This system would also avoid introducing perverse incentives into the economy that harm business owners and affect innocent persons' employment prospects and incomes. In light of the almost universally acknowledged major flaws in our existing system, which will only be exacerbated by the ACA, it is difficult to imagine how my prescription could make things materially worse from a utilitarian perspective, much less threaten the sort of moral catastrophe that would induce us to abandon libertarian principles.[54]

Given the existing political reality, adoption of the laissez faire alternative is highly unlikely in the foreseeable future. There may be room to make incremental improvements, such as laws promoting high-deductible plans linked to HSAs. However, the ACA represents an integrated, top-down approach to health care throughout, embracing the comprehensive, prepaid, third-party medical care model, and it is impossible to build a functional system on this base. When the utter failure of this strategy becomes obvious to the majority, the fateful question will then be posed: single payer or a much greater reliance on free markets.

CHAPTER TEN

Political issues for which there is no doctrinaire libertarian position

Natural rights philosophers rest their theories on a variety of ethical foundations. The best-known examples draw normative conclusions from observations regarding essential aspects of human nature. For Ayn Rand, it is our ability to reason, which obliges us to lead a life appropriate to our biological nature as a thinking, productive, independent, and self-interested being.[1] Murray Rothbard holds that our defining attribute, from the moral perspective, is self-ownership: "as a rational being with free will, it [ownership] extends over his own body, and it extends further over the material goods which he transforms with his labor."[2] And, for Nozick, it is what I have called our rational agency (see Chapter 1).

From these initial observations, each of these theorists independently arrive at certain fundamental libertarian positions: property rights are not categorically inferior to other sorts of rights; all rights, including those of property, are stringent; there is (at the minimum) a strong presumption against the coercion of innocent persons; claims of positive welfare rights should generally (if not always) be rejected. These core principles force us to condemn as morally impermissible most of the activities of the welfare/regulatory state.

However, there are also dominant views among "movement" libertarians and in the writings of prominent libertarian intellectuals regarding national security, abortion, and immigration. This chapter examines whether these judgments can be derived from our first principles, or just happen to be the views of a majority of committed libertarians based on a *different* set of normative judgments, or on controversial empirical assumptions. I conclude that the latter supposition is correct.[3]

Foreign policy

It is quite clear that the preferred national security strategy for most libertarian academics and public intellectuals is one of non-interventionism, understood in an operational sense as a rigid refusal to: (i) enter into military alliances with other nations, (ii) base troops and other military assets abroad, (iii) provide other nations (or rebel groups) with military assistance or foreign aid, and (iv) most critically, undertake military action other than in defense of the homeland or in response to other overt acts of war. This policy, or something very close to it, is expressed in the 2012 platform of the Libertarian Party ("LP"), has been consistently and forcefully defended by former Congressman Ron Paul, and is endorsed by leading libertarian think tanks, such as the Cato Institute.[4]

Recent events seem to vindicate this approach, as we have expended enormous human and financial resources in the Iraq and Afghanistan wars, with precious little to show for it. Moreover, it is certainly reasonable to question whether in this post-Cold War era, during which we have grown the national debt to over $17.4 trillion, our current defense budget and military posture are sustainable or in the best interests of the American people. Nevertheless, future events might make a more activist policy seem attractive, so the question remains: is the libertarian embrace of non-interventionism a matter of judgment, over which reasonable libertarians may differ, or is it integral to this ideology?

It does not appear possible to move in some straightforward logical progression from core libertarian precepts to a blanket condemnation of all "interventionist" tactics. One such argument, advanced by Murray Rothbard, relies on a very strict interpretation of just war theory. On this view, any harm inflicted on innocent persons, even in a purely defensive struggle, would violate the self-ownership principle and must be abjured: "War, then, even a defensive war, is only proper when the exercise of violence is rigorously limited to the individual criminals themselves. We may judge for ourselves how many wars or conflicts in history have met this criterion."[5] Given the inevitably of *some* collateral damage in modern warfare, this constraint would rule out all foreign interventions, and make even resistance to an unprovoked invasion all but impossible.

There are two major problems with this argument. First, as noticed by libertarian scholar George H. Smith, Rothbard assumes that rights are absolute, meaning they can never be overridden by other concerns, so that we must avoid killing a single innocent bystander even if this would prevent massive harm to a peaceful community under attack.[6] If consistently applied, this view produces absurd results. For example, it would be wrong for me to fleetingly trespass on another person's land, against the owner's wishes, in order to avoid a bear attack.

Additionally, Rothbard's version of just war theory is rejected by many philosophers, including Nozick and others with impeccable libertarian credentials, because they subscribe to some version of the doctrine of double effect ("DDE").[7] As described by philosopher Alison McIntyre, it holds "that sometimes it is permissible to bring about as a merely foreseen side effect a harmful event that it would be impermissible to bring about intentionally."[8]

In the context of warfare, this implies that a state fighting a defensive war may justly attack the military assets of the aggressor even if this results in the death of innocent bystanders, provided that such deaths are the foreseen but not intended effect of the strike, and provided further that the loss of innocent life is not disproportionate to the value of the military target. Accordingly, only those who reject *all* versions of the DDE will find Rothbard's absolutist position on just wars persuasive, and more importantly, libertarian principles do not compel us to agree with him.

Libertarian thinkers offer a second argument for non-interventionism, one that links the recognition of national sovereignty with constraints on the application of force. On this theory (often called "Westphalian" after the 1648 peace treaty of that name), national governments (even very repressive ones) are sovereign, and thus have, at least relative to all *other* states, the moral authority to decide all matters relating to their "own" populations.[9] Thus, interventions against even tyrannical states are ruled out, except in response to an actual (or imminently threatened) attack on one's own. This is at least superficially a *libertarian* stance because it purports to apply the NAP to international actors.[10]

But there are at least three serious weaknesses in this argument. First, minimal state libertarians accept the moral legitimacy of the state only on a highly conditional basis, specifically, its charter is limited to the supply of essential public goods and it does so in a manner that bears some reasonable resemblance to the rule of law. And, those most inclined to adopt non-interventionism, the anarcho-capitalists, generally echo Rothbard's view that "the State is an inherently illegitimate institution of organized aggression, of organized and regularized crime against the persons and properties of its subjects."[11]

Thus, the argument for non-interventionism based on the Westphalian view of sovereignty is subject to the telling objection that fundamentally unjust states are not, simply as a consequence of holding power, immune from the application of force (although this may generally be the prudent policy). As libertarian philosopher Aeon Skoble writes, "If rights are conceptually prior to the state, then state sovereignty must derive from a theory of legitimacy, which is based on protection of rights rather than a theory of moral equality of all states."[12]

Furthermore, assuming, *arguendo*, that even totalitarian states enjoy political authority, this would vindicate non-interventionism only to the extent of precluding so-called humanitarian interventions, meaning, military operations conducted for the purpose of liberating oppressed peoples.[13] The Westphalian doctrine provides no ethical rationale that would forbid, for example, other nations coming to the defense of a peaceful state that has been attacked. Or, for that matter, a law-abiding nation launching a preemptive military strike under the appropriate circumstances. Thus, even if we accept non-interventionism with respect to the internal affairs of despotic states, this still does not establish that direct self-defense (or the like) is the only just cause for war.[14]

Finally, and ironically, the Westphalian theory would sanction many of the foreign policy tools that are anathema to non-interventionists. If foreign governments are recognized as the sole "voice" of their populations, it would seem that they are also authorized, on their behalf, to enter into alliances, accept foreign aid, grant rights to military bases, and so forth.

Accordingly, neither Rothbard's interpretation of the just war doctrine nor the Westphalian argument show that non-interventionism follows from libertarian principles. Moreover, there are moral considerations congenial to libertarians that might guide us on a different course, namely, John Locke's state of nature analysis. He holds that the international sphere closely resembles this imaginary, anarchistic world, because there is no single power that can claim a monopoly on the legitimate use of force.

Rather, there are a large number of states, all acting in what they perceive to be their self-interest, with varying degrees of ruthlessness and willingness to resort to unprovoked violence. Locke held that in a state of nature any peaceful party may justly punish an aggressor, even though the aggressor has not specifically attacked them, because an unpunished aggressor represents a real, immediate danger to the entire community.[15] This conclusion seems intuitively compelling and unobjectionable.

An unconstrained aggressor imposes two serious costs on those who wish to abide by what Locke called the law of nature, that is, showing due regard for the equal rights of other persons. First, a party willing to take the life or property of one innocent victim is not likely to stop there. Accordingly, criminals cause fear in people not directly harmed by their aggression.

Second, violent outlaws impose significant material costs on society at large. Because of the threat they pose, peaceful persons will be required to expend time and resources in providing security for themselves and their loved ones. Individuals wishing to conduct mutually beneficial trade may be prevented from doing so because the goods or the payment will be stolen. Farmers may not plant crops because thieves will seize the harvest, and so on. An analogous dynamic exists in the realm of nations.

As a great trading power and source of investment capital, our citizens and businesses conduct important, mutually beneficial and consensual commercial transactions with their counterparts around the globe. Many millions of Americans also enjoy tourism. These activities and relationships are morally innocent, and conducted as a matter of right. Therefore, it would be unjust for the host government or a third party to arbitrarily interfere with them.

Hostile powers might do so by outright aggression against friendly states, such as Saddam Hussein's invasion of Kuwait in 1990, or by gaining a choke-hold over the air and sea lanes through which our trade must flow. One logical response to this danger is to protect our legitimate interests through alliances and the (admittedly costly) global projection of American military power. Libertarians might regard this policy as unwise, but this conclusion does not follow from our first principles.

Against this perspective, non-interventionist libertarians make a public choice/institutional design argument. Specifically, due to political pressures, informational constraints, bureaucratic bungling, and so forth, even the governments of "liberal" states are incapable of making rational decisions with respect to the costs and benefits of foreign interventions. Moreover, as Robert Higgs and other have argued, they may use the existence of armed conflicts to curtail the civil liberties of their citizens, then refuse to repeal these measures once the crisis is over.[16] The inevitable effect would be a ratcheting up of infringements over time. Arguably, therefore, libertarians in even relatively benign states should oppose the use of force in all but the most clear-cut cases.

But these are substantive empirical claims that need to be tested. Skeptics might cite a variety of important counter-examples. In the approximately 2 years prior to our entry into the Second World War, the United States pursued a foreign policy directly at odds with non-interventionism, assisting Great Britain and the Soviets in ways that not only violated international law, but crossed over into actual belligerency.[17] Yet, quite plausibly, this policy prevented a Nazi victory, which would have had catastrophic consequences for freedom generally.

A comparable claim of success can be made for our activist foreign policy during the Cold War, which sought to "contain" and deter the Soviet Union through a massive military buildup and by establishing and maintaining NATO and other formal and informal alliances, including foreign military bases.[18] Much smaller-scale, putative counter-examples to non-interventionism would include the first Gulf War in 1990–1 and the 1999 NATO-led humanitarian intervention in Kosovo.

Higgs's thesis regarding the inexorable erosion of civil liberties as a result of warfare is also debatable. While it is true that even democratic governments expand their powers during armed conflicts, it is far less certain that this tide does not recede in peacetime. For example, Lincoln is excoriated by many libertarians for, among other things, suspending the writ of habeas corpus during the Civil War, but this suspension was revoked by President Johnson on December 1, 1865, and this legal right is available today to all US citizens.

Similarly, First World War witnessed passage of the Sedition Act of 1918 which criminalized speech critical of the government or the armed forces, expressions of disloyalty, dissenting views regarding the necessity for war, and so forth. Although upheld by the Supreme Court then, this law is blatantly unconstitutional under more modern Supreme Court jurisprudence, and in any case was repealed in 1920. By the same token, surveillance and intelligence gathering methods that were accepted almost without dissent in the wake of the 9/11 terrorist attack are now the subject of a vigorous and healthy public debate.[19]

Of course, libertarians may reasonably conclude on the basis of their historical analysis and empirical assessment of the international environment that non-interventionism is the best foreign policy. But this opinion is just that, and cannot be derived from the moral foundations of natural rights. Thus, I think we are left with libertarian scholar Randy Barnett's commonsense conclusion that "Devising a military defense strategy is a matter of judgment and prudence about which reasonable libertarians may differ greatly."[20]

Abortion rights

Most committed libertarians hold strong (if not extreme) pro-choice views, as reflected in section 1.4 (Abortion) of the LP's 2012 platform: "we believe that government should be kept out of the matter, leaving the question to each person for their conscientious consideration." On its face, this would permit legal abortion up to the actual moment of birth. And, it is also true that Rand and Rothbard have expressed opinions consistent with the LP's platform.

However, this does not mean that this position flows naturally from one or more of the basic principles that undergird libertarianism. A rights-based approach to this issue must focus on identifying the strength of the respective moral claims of prospective parents (particularly the mother) on the one hand and the fetus on the other. Central to this analysis will be the question of when, if ever, the fetus acquires "moral status," meaning, in the words of philosophers Agnieska Jaworska and Julie Tannenbaum, that "its interests morally matter to some degree for the entity's own sake, such that it can be wronged."[21]

Recognizing that an entity has moral status does not imply that its interests are as important as those of a mature, fully functioning person. For example, it is certainly plausible to think that animals have some rights, but not the full panoply owed persons. However, if we were to conclude on the basis of our reasoning that a fetus at some stage of its development enjoys full moral status ("FMS"), or nearly FMS, then an abortion at this stage would surely require powerful justification.

Central to this debate is the significance we attach to the undeniable fact that the fetus is *potentially* a person, and will become one in the normal course of events. Some philosophers argue that it is only wrong to harm persons, and that since the fetus is *only* a potential person, it lacks moral status, and therefore abortion is morally permissible.[22] At some point in its development (perhaps at around 26 weeks), the fetus gains consciousness and the ability to experience pain (and presumably pleasure). However, even a late-term fetus lacks most indicia of personhood, including reasoning ability, self-motivation, communication skills, autonomy, and so forth.

But, this argument faces a daunting objection. There is (quite appropriately) in our society a strong moral consensus that a typical, healthy newborn human enjoys FMS, such that its unexcused killing would constitute a grievous wrong, indeed murder. Under our laws, it is just as much the crime of murder to kill (without excuse) a 9-day-old baby as a 39 or 99-year-old adult. Equally horrific would be the deliberate withholding of food and other basic necessities from a newborn by those obliged to supply them, like parents and guardians. So, while a late-term fetus is missing certain important attributes of personhood, this is equally true of the newborn.[23]

Other philosophers believe that potentiality cuts the other way, especially when coupled with notions of individual identity. The relevance of this last concept is captured by the following influential argument, made by the philosopher Don Marquis.[24] Assume "Joe" is a normal, healthy 21-year-old. It is wrong to murder Joe, not just now, but at any point in Joe's life. It is wrong to murder Joe because doing so deprives him of the value of his future life.

According to Marquis, Joe came into existence when those embryonic cells that became Joe-the-adult were organized in such a way that he and only he could develop from them. As a purely biological fact, this individualization occurs perhaps 3 weeks after fertilization. Therefore, the abortion of Joe after this development deprives him of the value of his future life (I would add, "as a rational agent"), and is tantamount to murder. Clearly, this verdict runs counter to the strong, widely held intuition that an organism *so unlike* a "standard" adult human (or even a newborn) should be entitled to FMS.[25]

Quite obviously, this is a thorny issue, with no easy answers. Based on considerations of the sort enumerated earlier, most thoughtful people hold that *at some point* in its development (perhaps at the point of consciousness), the fetus enjoys or nearly enjoys FMS and that good cause must then exist to justify an abortion. Of course, that the majority of people hold something like this view does not make it right, but I don't believe that libertarian theory offers us any good reason to reject it, either.

Ayn Rand offers one rights-based argument in favor of strong (perhaps absolute) abortion rights. She holds that: "An embryo *has no rights*. Rights do not pertain to a *potential*, only to an *actual* being. A child cannot acquire any rights until it is born. The living take precedence over the not-yet-living (or the unborn)" (emphasis in original).[26] Thus, Rand's argument relies on the distinction between actual (independently living) rights holders and mere potential beings (fetuses) who have none.[27]

However, this argument clearly fails because she simply assumes what needs to be established. What is it, exactly, that transforms a just-about-to-be-born fetus, utterly without rights, into a full rights bearing being moments later, as it exists the birth canal? This question is urgent because arguably what the late-term fetus and the newborn *share*, in addition to consciousness, is of overriding moral significance, specifically, the value of their future lives. Rand does not say, and there is no obvious answer within the confines of her ethical theory, either.

For Rand, libertarian rights derive from Man's nature as a "rational" being (understood in her particular way).[28] But a just-born baby is no more rational in this way than the about-to-be-born fetus. But, since Rand holds that the newborn, an "actual" being, *does* have rights, she owes us an argument for the momentous distinction she asserts.

At another point, she invokes the hardship that an unwanted birth inflicts on the parents, especially the mother.[29] But this claim relies on the dubious empirical assumption that carrying the fetus to term and then giving it up for adoption causes serious harm. Worse, given her own understanding of rights, this stance plainly begs the question against those who hold that the late-term fetus does enjoy FMS.

In all other contexts Rand assigns absolute stringency to rights, so that, for example, under no circumstances can the state redistribute resources from the super-rich to innocent people in desperate need. If the fetus does have rights, then for Rand any hardship imposed on others should be irrelevant. Rand shows no evidence of even appreciating the dilemma posed by her conflicting positions.

Additionally, many libertarians may be influenced by Rothbard's views on abortion, which purport to follow from the self-ownership principle: "Abortion should be looked upon, not as 'murder' of a living person, but as the expulsion of an unwanted invader from the mother's body. Any laws restricting or prohibiting abortion are therefore invasions of the rights of mothers" (footnote omitted).[30] In other words, we *own* our bodies and are thus entitled to do with them as we wish, including disposing as we like of any unwanted beings found therein.[31]

But this can hardly count as a dispositive argument for absolute abortion rights.[32] First, there are well-known problems with grounding libertarian rights in the self-ownership thesis. Not only does Rothbard fail to provide a convincing argument for it, but there are troubling gaps in this theory.[33] For example, how did we come to "own" ourselves, and what level of stringency applies to this property right? Also, why does self-ownership confer FMS on human beings but not earthworms or chickens, since in purely biological and physiological terms there seems to be no difference in interspecies self-ownership?

Moreover, unless Rothbard wishes to take the position that infanticide is morally permissible, he must explain, in terms of self-ownership, the different moral status of the infant and the fetus. His effort is entirely unpersuasive. For him, the newborn has only certain, very limited rights, because "the parents—or rather the mother, who is the only *certain* and visible parent—as the creators of the baby become its owners. A newborn baby cannot be an existent self-owner *in any sense*" (last phrase, my emphasis).

He then elaborates, seemingly unaware that he now contradicts his earlier claim: "even from birth, the parental ownership is not absolute but of a 'trustee' or guardianship kind. In short, every baby as soon as it is born and is therefore no longer contained within his mother's body possesses the right of self-ownership by virtue of being a separate entity and a potential adult." But, why does being a separate entity confer self-ownership, and aren't fetuses also potential adults?[34]

From this intellectual hash, Rothbard draws the odious conclusion that, "The parent therefore may not murder or mutilate his child, and the law properly outlaws a parent from doing so. But the parent should have the legal right *not* to feed the child, i.e., to allow it to die" (emphasis in original).[35] Many will no doubt join me in regarding this claim as reducing his entire position to absurdity. However, even apart from this, Rothbard never explains why a change in location of several inches (and the severing of the umbilical cord) transforms a fetus from a nonself-owner without moral status into a (partial) self-owner, which confers the right not to be murdered or mutilated.[36]

There is a second fatal objection. As Rothbard himself recognizes, an agent's otherwise justified use of force in defense of his property is rendered immoral if it is disproportionate to the right being vindicated. To use his example, a merchant may be justified in grabbing hold of a shoplifter to prevent him from absconding with his bubble gum, but he is not justified in shooting the shoplifter in the back as he flees.[37]

Rothbard offers no argument for the view that a late-term fetus lacks self-ownership and thus moral status. Accordingly, even assuming that we own ourselves in the way he claims, this fact only establishes that the prospective mother has the right to *evict* the unwanted fetus, not to kill it. If the fetus *has* meaningful moral status at the time of the desired "eviction," it should—on Rothbard's own logic—be delivered safely if possible, or gestation should be allowed to proceed to the point when it can be.

To sum up, there is no "official" libertarian stance on abortion rights. While it is possible to formulate pro-choice arguments that invoke basic libertarian principles, they fall flat. They fail because they do not resolve in any convincing way the moral status of the fetus, the central issue in this debate.

Immigration

Most libertarian theorists support something very close to "open borders."[38] Section 3.4 (Free Trade and Migration) of the 2012 LP platform is typical. It provides that "Economic freedom demands the unrestricted movement of human as well as financial capital across national borders." While I believe that fundamental libertarian principles demand a *more* liberal immigration policy, they do not imply quite so radical a departure from the status quo. As in the case of defense policy, different factual premises will produce divergent policy recommendations.

I will use prominent libertarian philosopher Michael Huemer's excellent essay "Is There a Right to Immigrate?"[39] as my starting point, since his cogent arguments for open borders are explicitly rights-based (although not premised on a specifically libertarian interpretation of rights). He begins with the observation that our laws exclude "ordinary, noncriminal migrants who wish to leave their country of origin for morally innocent reasons," and therefore have three characteristics that mark them as prima facie rights violations.[40] Specifically, these laws are coercive, restrictive, and harmful to would-be immigrants. They require the agents of the state to *prevent* those in need from alleviating their deprivation by relocating to more hospitable ground.[41]

Thus, those who favor the regulation of immigration cannot rely on the traditional philosophical distinction made between culpably injuring others and the mere failure to intervene to prevent the occurrence of harm (caused by a third party). In light of the considerations just cited, one need not, says Huemer, accept any particular theory of justice to find this restriction troubling, and accordingly, the burden of argument shifts to its defenders.

Huemer is making what is essentially a property-rights argument. The owner of a business is entitled to hire as she sees fit, including foreign nationals; owners of apartment units are entitled to rent them out as they choose; and so forth. By the same token, migrants are entitled to travel and reside here in response to these opportunities. Huemer wisely makes no claim for immigrant voting rights or any entitlement to public assistance, since this would open up an additional set of arguments against open borders.[42]

But, as we have seen, property rights are not absolute. Libertarians acknowledge that they do not license property owners to generate harmful externalities in the operation of their businesses. Might unregulated immigration produce an analogous sort of harm (what free market economist Bryan Caplan terms "political externalities"[43]) that could be regulated under traditional libertarian principles? Huemer acknowledges that it is a mainstream philosophical view that citizens of a particular state have a legitimate interest in preserving the distinctive culture of their community, but does not think that this concern can justify coercive immigration restrictions.[44]

Unfortunately, his argument on this point misses the mark. Huemer uses as an example the possibility that many Buddhists might move into your neighborhood and thereby change its character from mostly Christian to predominately Buddhist. He rightly says that since "the Buddhists do not coercively interfere with your practice of your own religion, nor . . . do anything else to violate your rights," you are not justified in using force to try to exclude them from your community.[45]

However, under libertarian principles we *do* have the right to live under the rule of law. Thus, we should consider the contrary supposition, that is, what if the population inflows under open borders interfere not only with your freedom of religion, but also with your freedoms of speech and association? If such a fear is not fanciful, but realistic, then the regulation of immigration would be permitted under libertarian principles.[46] Otherwise, we would find ourselves in the paradoxical position of arguing that our commitment to natural rights requires us to surrender them. Note that this position does not commit me to the "utilitarianism of rights" idea that I rejected when discussing compulsory personal savings accounts as an alternative to Social Security (see Chapter 4), because the question here is whether an unconditional right to immigrate *exists*, not the stringency of a recognized right.

Accordingly, Huemer's argument leaves open the reply by libertarian opponents of open borders that US citizens and legal residents have a legitimate interest in the political culture that they have collectively shaped.[47] On this account, they have the moral right to defend the value of this asset by regulating the decisions of individual employers and landowners that might, in the aggregate, materially degrade it.

I daresay that the greatest potential danger in this regard would not be the Buddhist takeover imagined by Huemer, but migration to the United States of even a small portion of the world's 1.6 billion Muslims.[48] Generally, this population suffers a much more impoverished standard of living than exists in the developed world, and its members would therefore be more willing to relocate here than most. Huemer and many other libertarians do not view this possibility as posing any special problem. I sincerely wish I shared their confidence.

Based on recent, scientific polling done by the Pew Research Center (consisting of 38,000 face-to-face interviews in 39 countries), it is apparent that substantial minorities, if not outright majorities, within international Muslim publics have values inconsistent with the rule of law.[49] For example, large majorities, ranging from 84 percent to 64 percent, in four of the six regions surveyed (generally those with the largest Muslim populations) believe that *sharia* (Islamic law) should be the official law of the land. In 5 of the 21 nations surveyed (including Egypt and Indonesia), a *majority* of those holding this view also believe that *sharia* should be applied to non-Muslims, and in 13 of the countries, at least one-third did.

In half of the 20 countries where representative data was obtained, a majority of those endorsing *sharia* as the law of the land favored stoning adulterers. Among proponents of Islamic law, 76 percent in South Asia (Pakistan, Bangladesh, and Afghanistan) and 56 percent in Middle East/North Africa (including Egypt and Iraq) favored *executing* those who leave Islam. In the other three regions, the comparable figures ranged between 13 percent and 27 percent.

Equally discomforting from the perspective of maintaining liberal values here, strong majorities in three of the five regions for which data was obtained believe that religious leaders should have at least some influence over political matters, with substantial minorities in the other two. Similarly, attitudes about women's rights are generally premodern, if not prehistoric.[50]

In another recent Pew Research survey covering 11 Muslim nations (including the large populations in Turkey, Egypt, Indonesia, Nigeria, and Pakistan), 13 percent of respondents indicated that they had a favorable opinion of both Al Qaeda and the Taliban, and an additional 23 percent either responded that they didn't know or refused to answer.[51] These groups routinely use violence to kill nonbelievers and to impose their seventh-century Islam on unwilling others, so to approve of them is to reject toleration and pluralism. And, perhaps most significantly, in those nations where dictatorial rulers have been overthrown, fundamentalist Muslims have waged an unrelenting campaign of murder and intimidation against Christians (such as the Copts)[52] and other Islamic movements, such as the Sufis and Ahmadiyya, that embrace more modern, liberal values.[53]

Recall, Huemer limits his claim of a right to immigrate to those who wish to do so for "morally innocent reasons." The problem is that even immigrants with the most illiberal values may have unobjectionable motives, such as economic opportunity. Yet they will still bring their intolerance with them, just as they bring other elements of their culture. And, if these beliefs express themselves in violence against those with different opinions, lifestyles, religions, and so on, then it hardly matters whether they have been granted the franchise or receive public assistance.

Would open borders, especially in the long-run, result in the degradation of what we have left of the rule of law *here*? I don't claim to have a definitive answer, but such fears are not unreasonable. For one thing, we may already be closer to the tipping point than we like to think. In 1988, Salmon Rushdie's *The Satanic Verses* was published, which caused widespread outrage and deadly mob violence in the Muslim world, and provoked Ayatollah Khomeini's fatwa ordering the death of all those responsible for the book's publication. Almost all nations with majority or substantial Muslim populations banned the book's importation.

In the United States, there were hundreds of threats to bookstores and several actual fire bombings. As a consequence, approximately one-third of our bookstores refused to sell it and many others kept it out of sight, like convenience stores used to do with pornographic magazines.[54]

Another well-known example of self-censorship in the United States caused by the fear of Muslim violence is provided by the Yale University Press. On September 30, 2005, the Danish newspaper *Jyllands-Posten* published 12 editorial cartoons of the Prophet Muhammad. As in the case of *The Satanic Verses*, this event sparked riots in many Muslim nations and at least 200 deaths.[55]

In late 2009, Yale published *The Cartoons That Shook the World*, by Brandeis professor Jytte Klausen, which explores the larger meaning of this episode.

Quite naturally, Klausen's manuscript included reproductions of the 12 cartoons that set these events in motion. But over the author's objection, Yale pulled these cartoons from the book at the last minute, because as stated by John Donatich, its Director, "there existed an appreciable chance of violence occurring if either the cartoons or other depictions of the Prophet Muhammad were printed in a book about the cartoons published by Yale University Press."[56]

These two episodes demonstrate that free speech already has been chilled here by the fear of Muslim extremism, but they are only the tip of the iceberg.[57] Every case of this sort represents a disgraceful breakdown in the rule of law. Central to libertarianism is the principle that *no* idea is off limits, and that those offended by the words of others must respond, if they wish to, with speech of their own, not actual or threatened physical aggression.

Second, although Muslims in the United States have values much more closely aligned with the mainstream than say their Pakistani co-religionists, even here there have been several deliberate murders of Jews by first and second-generation Muslim immigrants, and numerous attacks on Jewish houses of worship.[58] Moreover, since the 9/11 mega-terrorism, more than 250 American Muslim extremists have been arrested on terror-related charges involving Jewish targets or motivated at least in part by anti-Semitism.[59]

Thankfully, most of these plots are thwarted early in their gestation, and they are derided by many as the work of amateurs and cranks. That is, until innocent people actually get killed, as in the 2013 Boston Marathon bombings. The essential point is that it requires only a handful of violent fanatics to intimidate the exercise of important rights. How many film makers in Holland are now brave enough to make documentaries critical of Islam in the face of Theo van Gogh's murder on the streets of Amsterdam in 2004?

Accordingly, under plausible empirical assumptions, the view that we should limit immigration from certain populations is consistent with basic libertarian principles.[60] Nevertheless, it seems clear that our current immigration policy does run counter to these values. For the reasons adduced by Huemer, there is absolutely no reason why foreign students who earn degrees from our colleges or graduate schools should not be entitled to remain and seek employment here.

Additionally, we should emulate the European Union's policy of open borders within their polity. Since January 1, 2014, the European Union permits all citizens within its 28 states to move freely and seek employment anywhere in this bloc (the rules regarding welfare eligibility for immigrants are yet to be finalized).[61] We should likewise permit citizens of all nations that broadly share our values to work here. This access need not include voting rights or unconditional rights to public assistance. Freedom of contract demands this much, and we have nothing to fear, and much to gain, from being "overrun" by such workers.

CHAPTER ELEVEN

What is to be done?

One of Hayek's great political insights is that the rule of law is not found in statute books and constitutions but in deeply ingrained social traditions and attitudes that are *evidenced* in such writings. Accordingly, our politics will move in a more libertarian direction only if voters change their convictions regarding the content and stringency of rights, and consequently their views regarding the scope of permissible state action. One obvious way to attempt this is by means of the democratic process, through which ideas can be disseminated, debated, and then implemented.

There is a tendency in books written by libertarians to accentuate the positive when it comes to the prospect of political change. For example, David Boaz in his popular 1997 book, *Libertarianism: A Primer*, speaks of "the coming libertarian age."[1] I am less sanguine, for it seems to me that the last decade or so has been, at best, a mixed bag for libertarianism in America.

On the one hand, there has been notable, if incremental progress, in some areas, including educational choice, expansion of right-to-work laws, reform of eminent domain, and the glimmerings of a cease fire in our eternal war on drugs. Marriage equality has dramatically expanded, and certain aspects of political speech have recently been held by the Supreme Court in *Citizens United* to be protected by the First Amendment.

On the other hand, our national debt and unfunded entitlement program liabilities have exploded, with comparable pension-related deficits at the state and local levels. In this, we have used the coercive power of the state to finance current consumption, while sticking future generations with the bill. Also, total government spending (federal, state, and local) as a percentage of GDP has reached levels not seen since the Second World War.

Our politicians bailed out the domestic automobile industry and the Federal Reserve rescued several major financial institutions. Regulators continue to unroll and apply new spools of red tape, including the incredibly complex and onerous reregulation of the financial industry. Certain of our more "progressive" states and major cities seem to be competing to determine who can set the highest minimum wage. Meanwhile, the Federal Reserve is aggressively *managing* our economy, rather than simply conducting monetary policy in a way that facilitates organic growth.

As marriage equality has become law in an ever greater number of states, the authorities have become emboldened to use antidiscrimination laws to punish those who do not, as a matter of conscience, wish to endorse, even symbolically, same sex marriage. Last, but certainly not least, the federal government has assumed an even larger and more intrusive role in managing our health care, one-sixth of the US economy.

For those wishing to engage their fellow citizens in an effort to limit the reach of the state, this chapter offers a variety of argumentative strategies. For those who simply wish to live in a more rights-friendly environment, I make certain suggestions.

Arguing for libertarianism

Many people reject libertarianism because they seriously misunderstand natural rights theory or hold naive empirical assumptions. The most common errors are rebutted below. I do not claim that my arguments will suddenly convert modern liberals into libertarians, but they should at least be sufficient to prompt those with an open mind to think more deeply about these issues. I think no more can reasonably be expected, as it is notoriously difficult to persuade people to change their convictions, especially with respect to those that have, as political ones surely do, an emotional or psychological component.

First, libertarianism is often seen as merely an expedient ideological excuse for the wealthy to hold onto their (often undeserved) advantages at the expense of the poor. But, this ignores the historical record. Natural rights libertarianism has its roots firmly planted in the classical liberalism of such men as Locke, Hume, Smith, Montesquieu, Voltaire, and von Humboldt, and in popular movements such as "The Levelers."

These intellectuals and groups invoked the doctrine of natural rights in defense of the rule of law, including the right of ordinary people not to be harmed by the unearned economic privileges granted by monarchs to their political allies. These predatory import restrictions and domestic monopolies drove up the price of basic goods needed by the masses.[2]

Moreover, the mid-nineteenth century to early twentieth century American and European figures who are now recognized as forbearers of contemporary libertarianism—such as Josiah Warren, Benjamin Tucker, Lysander Spooner, Gustave de Molinari, and Herbert Spencer—generally saw the state as a formidable obstacle to the aspirations of the working classes and the poor. Until today, there are many prominent libertarians drawn to this doctrine at least in part because of its anticipated advantages for the less fortunate members of our society.[3] Accordingly, by insisting that the role of the state in our lives be limited to those functions that cannot be supplied adequately by voluntary means, natural rights libertarians do not seek to promote the interests of any class or group. Rather, all we ask from the state is the rule of law, and we hold that whatever distribution of holdings emerges from this arrangement is just (subject to the rectification of past wrongs).

Closely related to this first objection is the perception that libertarians are indifferent to the plight of the needy, and would let them suffer and die rather than resort to coercive taxation. As explained earlier, libertarianism is compatible with moral pluralism, including the recognition that rights may have to yield in the face of sufficiently powerful consequentialist considerations. Moreover, the foundational logic of Lockean appropriation requires that non-appropriators not be harmed by the institution of private property, either at the time of initial acquisition or subsequently. Clearly, there is nothing inherent in libertarian theory that enshrines callousness toward the truly helpless.

However, as a matter of actual social policy, I think libertarians need not apologize for being highly skeptical of the efficacy of coercive governmental "charity." Our "war on poverty" has a dismal track record, and no carefully controlled, grand scientific experiment has yet been conducted that proves that the interventionist state is better at alleviating poverty than free markets.[4] Nevertheless, libertarians would support coercively supplied aid to those unable to provide for themselves, if there were reasonable assurance that it would have the desired effect (see Chapter 7).

Another reason that many people find libertarianism implausible is that they suffer from the illusion that our country's astonishing industrial and economic progress over the course of its history is somehow an artifact of big government. So, without the state to guide and direct our activities, we would all still be living in log cabins, traveling on horseback, and dying young. This belief can be quickly dispelled by reference to the government's own economic statistics.

For example, in the four decades between 1870 and 1910 our per capita GDP grew from $223 to $608 (both figures expressed in constant 1929 dollars), an impressive gain of 270 percent in real terms.[5] This figure rose to $857 in 1929, an increase of almost 400 percent in real terms over a 60-year period, all before the start of the New Deal.[6] This is a significantly higher growth rate than experienced in recent decades. Even life expectancy in the United States (at birth, both genders, all races) went from 49.2 years in 1900 to 59.2 years in 1930.[7]

This impressive improvement in our standard of living between (roughly) the end of the Civil War and the start of the New Deal should not surprise us, since it is largely the private sector that is responsible for technological advances, and for devising new business models to exploit them. In the period between 1870 and 1930, there were enormous improvements in transportation, electrification, communication, and metallurgy, which were pioneered and commercialized by entrepreneurs such as Edison, Carnegie, Morgan, Ford, and Frick.

Naturally, as our population worried less about meeting its basic needs, the trade-offs we made between wages and other important goods (e.g., workplace safety, the environment, and children's education), began to change. This happened not as a consequence of governmental fiat, but almost entirely as a result of market forces. For example, as workers live longer and better, they become, in general, less willing to accept the risk of a job-related death. Accordingly, employers must either reduce this exposure or raise wages to compensate for it. This puts financial pressure on owners to make their factories and mines safer, and as a result the incidence of industrial accidents declines.[8]

If pre-New Deal America still seems a little like the Dark Ages to us, it is only because additional transformative inventions and innovations were yet to come, not because government bureaucrats rode to our rescue. Since almost all of us have lived all our adult lives under the welfare state, we have a hard time imagining life without it. The idea that interventionist government is the key to social progress is a failure of the imagination, not of laissez faire.

Additionally, many people are hostile to the concept of natural rights because they have difficulty accepting the idea that rights exist independently of the political process. As Hayek ruefully observes, "since the theoreticians of democracy have for over a hundred years taught the majorities that whatever they desire is just, we must not be surprised if the majorities no longer even ask whether what they decide is just."[9] So, since Medicare, for example, was enacted by our duly elected representatives, opponents should just accept its moral legitimacy.

Although frequently encountered, this is an astonishingly weak stance. It implies that in the absence of government, what Locke called a state of nature, there would be no moral rules governing our conduct toward other human beings. Now, there are certainly academic philosophers who will defend this view, but most ordinary people, who believe in an objective morality, would be rightly shocked by this conclusion.

On the same logic, those who assert that only political rights are real must hold that any apparent injustice inflicted on individuals or minority groups, no matter how egregious, does not count as such, provided that it was committed by democratically elected politicians. Both the Fugitive Slave Act of 1850 and the internment of Japanese-American citizens during the Second World War certainly had this sort of faux legitimacy.[10]

In contrast, those who hold the natural rights view are at liberty to denounce injustice wherever they find it. For example, attorney Salmon P. Chase, who would eventually become the Chief Justice of the Supreme Court, condemned the Fugitive Slave Act in just these terms: "the law of the Creator, which invests every human being with an inalienable title to freedom, cannot be repealed by any inferior law, which asserts that man is property."[11]

It should also be said that many opponents of libertarianism appear to have adopted certain philosophical doctrines without thinking them through very carefully. One common idea is that we should redistribute wealth because the rich don't "need it" as much, which relies on a crude utilitarianism, namely, the notion of marginal utility. But the idea that things should be allocated on the basis of need or utility is subject to devastating counterexamples.

For instance, the philosopher Judith Jarvis Thomson poses a case she calls "Transplant," which involves a skilled surgeon who realizes that she can save five lives if she kills one of her patients and harvests his organs.[12] If she is sure she can get away with it, isn't she obligated to do this in order to promote the greater good? Clearly, the answer is "no," because people have *rights* against being treated in such a horrific way.

There is another, equally devastating objection to utilitarianism. That is, since actions are adjudged right or wrong on the basis of the utility they produce, the doctrine commands us to value everyone's happiness (or whatever measure of utility is on offer) equally. In other words, the welfare of complete strangers should count as much as our own, and that of our spouse, children, and close friends. But, as libertarian philosopher Matt Zwolinski notes, this claim "is not only implausible. It is an almost entirely unargued-for assumption. And it is one that we should reject."[13] Those who rely on this moral theory should be prepared to answer these and other objections.

There is also the allure of what I call the egalitarian fetish, which views equality in holdings as some sort of transcendent value that should be enforced at almost any cost. One hears this mantra virtually every day as pundits point out the great disparities in resources owned by the "1 percent" and everyone else, or the supposed trend showing the income of the upper quintile pulling away from the lower quintile, and so on.

But this notion explodes upon first contact with philosophical scrutiny. Imagine two societies. In one, everyone has *exactly* the same level of wealth; unfortunately, all members are equally impoverished and miserable, barely sustaining life. In a second society, there is great inequality. A few possess the sort of superriches held by Bill Gates and Warren Buffett, while a much larger number, say 20 percent, are "mere" multimillionaires; everyone else just makes ends meet, with no hardship, but few luxuries.

No sane person would think that the former state of affairs is superior to the latter. More than this, despite the fact that the first society is *perfect* from the strict egalitarian perspective, I can see *nothing* good about it. This judgment strongly suggests that equality has no intrinsic value, meaning, there is no reason to promote it for its own sake.[14] At best, equality might have *instrumental* value in achieving some other (purported) good. For example, given the assumption of diminishing marginal utility, a utilitarian might claim that an egalitarian distribution of wealth would, all other things being equal, maximize utility and therefore be morally superior to an inegalitarian pattern. However, as previously noted, libertarians reject utilitarianism as a moral theory.

Accordingly, inequality has no independent moral significance. Before condemning it, we must ask whether it exists because social and political institutions are rigged to arbitrarily favor some over others, or because it simply reflects the familiar "bell curve" distribution of talent, character, and luck. The former is reprehensible, the latter is morally innocent, even if not cosmically just.

Finally, when libertarians decry governmental "coercion," critics often reply that there is nothing invidious about this since every property scheme, including a libertarian one, will involve the use of force to protect whatever rights it upholds. This observation is correct, but entirely besides the point. When libertarians condemn coercion they don't do so because it involves the threat of force, since this would be argument by tautology. Rather, their verdict is based on the view that the state is coercing *wrongly*.

Even the most die-hard libertarians should not object when a state, even a badly flawed one, enforces laws against the murder, robbery, and assault of innocent persons. However, for the reasons outlined in Chapter 1, natural rights libertarians uniformly protest when the state coerces people who are *not* committing violence or fraud against others (except as required to supply essential public goods). Naturally, egalitarians endorse a conflicting ethical framework that implies a more active role for the state, but it does not help their cause to simply claim that "coercion is coercion."

Living free (is the best revenge)

Libertarians correctly hold that our current laws and institutions are promiscuously rights violating. One response is to attempt change through the political process. But this strategy is quite probably futile: each of us has only a single vote out of the millions cast in any federal election. So, the likelihood that our ballot, and those whom we might influence, will decide even a single contest is extremely remote.

Moreover, to even have a chance of moving public opinion in a libertarian direction, an individual would have to commit gigantic sums to political advertising and education. So, unless you are extraordinarily wealthy, and willing to invest heavily in politics, your impact will be trivial at best. Therefore, libertarians who desire to escape the state's interference might rationally decide not to devote their energy to the art of persuasion, but rather to take concrete actions that will maximize their own freedom.

Recall Hayek's dictum that the drive to accumulate wealth is merely "the desire for general opportunity." The more resources we have available to us, the greater our ability to enforce the legal rights we have, thereby enhancing our prospects of achieving those things that are important to us. In this regard, the careful study of economics and the principles of investing are surely important. If, as I contend, there is a strong empirical connection between secure property rights and economic growth, then those who believe that we are regressing relative to other nations may wish to invest some of their savings abroad or in nondollar denominated assets.

Additionally, and probably more importantly, we can vote with our feet. One of the great advantages of federalism, at least as envisioned by the founding fathers, is that it permits, even encourages, the evolution of distinctly different political and social institutions in the various states. If federalism were allowed to operate as intended, not only would states function as what Justice Brandeis termed "laboratories of democracy," but there would also be a great diversity of political environments in which citizens might elect to live.

Sadly, as a result of the Supreme Court's jurisprudence upholding key elements of the New Deal, most legislative power is now concentrated in the hands of the federal government. Today, the massive federal regulatory apparatus, entitlement programs, payroll and income taxes, and so forth apply uniformly throughout the nation. Unless preempted by federal law, the various states are permitted to pile their tax schemes and regulations *on top of* the federal ones; however, some display much greater reticence about this than others. In addition, they differ markedly in their commitment to educational choice, labor laws, and other important matters.

Thus, those wishing to live as freely as possible should be sensitive to these potential advantages. Naturally, these disparities will have more or less appeal to people as a result of their individual circumstances. For example, a budding entrepreneur may wish to locate in a state with a friendly regulatory climate. On the other hand, a person who has already made their fortune may be influenced by tax policy, while a working class family with young children may wish to move to a state that encourages charter schools or even provides vouchers. Depending on one's specific interests, there may even be differences at the county level that should be explored.

Finally, it is also worth considering international options. For the six decades following the Second World War, the United States was rightly regarded as one of the countries most committed to free market principles, rivaled only by Hong Kong and Singapore. However, in its most recent 2011 international ranking of economic freedom, the Fraser Institute (a respected libertarian-leaning Canadian think tank) placed the United States seventeenth. This is behind not only Hong Kong and Singapore, but also New Zealand, Australia, Switzerland, the United Arab Emirates, Estonia, Finland, Canada, the United Kingdom, Chile, and Denmark, among others.[15] Our fall from the top echelon began, according to Fraser, between 2000 and 2005, (when, based on their analysis, we fell from second to eighth), and accelerated between 2005 and their most recent 2011 report.

It must be noted at once that this survey considers only economic freedom, and thus ignores other important rights, such as free expression, association, and so on, where the United States might shine, at least relatively. And, reasonable libertarians can differ with regard to the accuracy of these rankings, which will certainly fluctuate over time. But, the point here is simply to caution that we should not naively assume that the United States is the epitome of freedom, now or in the future.

This understanding is important, because living, working, or starting a business abroad is not just a theoretical possibility. Many developed countries have special visa programs for skilled workers, and in addition will grant visas to those receiving a job offer from a local employer.[16] Additionally, at least some first world countries have programs that allow foreign students to work full time after graduation from one of their colleges or universities.[17] And, others have special visa opportunities for those able to commit to certain levels of investment in the host country.[18] All of these programs may be pathways to foreign citizenship.

This step would not necessarily result in the loss of US citizenship, since most developed countries recognize dual citizenship. Of equal importance, the United States does as well, unless foreign citizenship is obtained voluntarily, and "with the intention to give up US citizenship."[19] Those Americans wishing to no longer be subject to our tax code may renounce their citizenship, an increasingly popular step, despite the presence of a burdensome "exit" tax.[20]

I have confidence that something approximating the libertarian conception of freedom will *eventually* triumph in our politics because the alternatives unduly restrict and hamper the exercise of our most fundamental attribute, our rational agency. Because of this, they will produce manifestly inferior economic outcomes over time. However, I fear it will be a very long and rocky road from here to there, and things may get substantially worse before they get better. Inasmuch as we each have only a single life to live, I cannot blame those who in the meantime seek greener pastures elsewhere.

NOTES

Introduction

1 See David Kirby and David Boaz, "The Libertarian Vote in the Age of Obama," *Policy Analysis*, No. 658, Cato Institute, January 21, 2010, http://www.cato.org/publications/policy-analysis/libertarian-vote-age-obama. A 2006 Zogby survey commissioned by the Cato Institute, and discussed in the essay referenced immediately above, found that 44 percent of respondents identified themselves as "fiscally conservative/socially liberal, also known as libertarian." A more recent survey, using a different methodology, found that 7 percent of Americans are consistent libertarians, while 15 percent lean libertarian. See Public Religion Research Institute, "2013 American Values Survey: In Search of Libertarians in America," October 29, 2013, http://publicreligion.org/research/2013/10/2013-american-values-survey/.

2 A very useful summary of Locke's political philosophy is found in Alex Tuckness, "Locke's Political Philosophy," *The Stanford Encyclopedia of Philosophy* (Winter 2012 Edition), Edward N. Zalta, ed., http://plato.stanford.edu/archives/win2012/entries/locke-political/.

3 For all references to Locke in this chapter, see John Locke, in Peter Laslett, ed., *Two Treatises of Government* (Cambridge: Cambridge University Press, 1988), Second Treatise, chapters V, VI, and IX, sections 26–37, 57, and 123.

4 Locke did not employ the term "private property," but used "several property" in its stead. As Randy Barnett, a leading libertarian scholar, has explained, he did so because his preferred expression "makes it clearer that jurisdiction to use resources is dispersed among the 'several'—meaning 'diverse, many, numerous, distinct, particular, or separate'—persons and associations that comprise a society, rather than being reposed in a monolithic centralized institution." Randy E. Barnett, "Coping With Partiality: Justice,

the Rule of Law, and the Role of Lawyers," *Roger Williams U. L. Rev.* 3 (Fall 1997), http://randybarnett.com/coping.htm. I thank Tom Palmer for calling this point to my attention. However, given the prevalence of "private property" in the contemporary political lexicon, I have elected to employ the more familiar term.

5 On the distinction between the positive and negative conceptions of rights, see John Hospers, "What Libertarianism Is," in Tibor Machan and Douglass Rasmussen, eds, *Liberty for the Twenty-First Century: Contemporary Libertarian Thought* (Lantham, MD: Rowman & Littlefield, 1995), 11–2; and Jan Narveson, *The Libertarian Idea* (Philadelphia, PA: Temple University Press, 1988), 57–61.

6 This conclusion is sound, I believe, as a matter of moral theory. I am leaving aside here a range of *practical* problems that might arise as a consequence of granting the state even this limited power. These include the possibility that well-intentioned assistance to the destitute might harm them or their offspring in the long run, and problems of institutional design. By the latter, I mean that given the nature of politics it might prove impossible to limit the state's social welfare efforts to assisting deserving persons in dire need. Once the door is opened even this far, massive entitlement programs, single-payer health care, and other rights-violating programs may inevitably follow, changing the entire character of society for the worse.

7 Philip Petit, "Non-Consequentialism and Political Philosophy," in David Schmidtz, ed., *Robert Nozick* (Cambridge: Cambridge University Press, 2002), 83.

8 For a much more comprehensive defense of Nozick's core philosophical principles, see Mark D. Friedman, *Nozick's Libertarian Project: An Elaboration and Defense* (London: Continuum International, 2011).

9 The following chapter summarizes the much more extensive argument for libertarian rights set forth in *Nozick's Libertarian Project*. In doing so, I occasionally quote or paraphrase passages from my earlier book, without specific attribution.

10 For a summary of utilitarianism, see Julia Driver, "The History of Utilitarianism," *Stanford Encyclopedia Philosophy* (Summer 2009 Edition), section 2, http://plato.stanford.edu/archives/sum2009/entries/utilitarianism-history/.

11 Walter Sinnott-Armstrong, "Consequentialism," *Stanford Encyclopedia Philosophy* (Winter 2011 Edition), section 1, http://plato.stanford.edu/archives/win2011/entries/consequentialism/.

12. See Larry Alexander and Michael Moore, s.v. "Deontological Ethics," *Stanford Encyclopedia Philosophy* (Winter 2012 Edition), http://plato.stanford.edu/archives/win2012/entries/ethics-deontological/.
13. There is empirical support for this hypothesis. See James Gwartney et al., *Economic Freedom in the World: 2013 Annual Report*, Fraser Institute, September 8, 2013, chapter 1, http://www.freetheworld.com/datasets_Efw.html.
14. In this regard, see David S. Landes, *The Wealth and Poverty of Nations: Why Some Are So Rich and Some So Poor* (New York: W.W. Norton, 1999), 217–8 (arguing that the Industrial Revolution happened first in Great Britain because to a much greater extent than other nations it upheld private property rights, the ability of parties to enforce contracts, and the rule of law).
15. Adam Smith, *The Wealth of Nations* (New York: Penguin Books, 1986), book 1, chapter II, 118–9.
16. See Friedrich A. Hayek, *The Constitution of Liberty* (Chicago: University of Chicago Press, 1960), 148–56, 206–10.
17. Milton Friedman, *Capitalism and Freedom* (Chicago: Chicago University Press, 1982), 4.

Chapter 1

1. In addition to Locke and ancient sources, we should note the important influence of Baron de Montesquieu, David Hume, and Thomas Paine, among others. See Carolyn Scearce, "A Revolutionary Reading List: The Intellectual Tradition That Influenced the U.S. Founding Fathers," ProQuest, April 2010, http://www.csa.com/discoveryguides/revolution/review2.php.
2. Mark Murphy, "The Natural Law Tradition in Ethics," in Edward N. Zalta, ed., *The Stanford Encyclopedia of Philosophy* (Winter 2011 Edition), section 1.2, http://plato.stanford.edu/archives/win2011/entries/natural-law-ethics/.
3. Ayn Rand, "Man's Rights," in Ayn Rand, with additional articles by Nathan Brandon, *The Virtue of Selfishness* (New York: Signet Books, 1970), 95.
4. Ayn Rand, "The Nature of Government," in *Virtue of Selfishness*, 108.
5. To the best of my knowledge, Rand never literally speaks of "natural rights," but instead uses the cognate locution, "the source

of rights is man's nature." Rand, "Man's Rights," in ibid., 94. Nevertheless, she clearly adopts the concept of *negative* rights outlined earlier. See ibid., 96–7.

6 See Mark D. Friedman, *Nozick's Libertarian Project: An Elaboration and Defense* (London: Continuum Books, 2011), 11–5. Nozick expressly rejects Objectivist ethics in "On the Randian Argument," in Jeffrey Paul ed., *Reading Nozick: Essays on "Anarchy, State and Utopia"* (Oxford: Basil Blackwell, 1982), 206–31.

7 Just before this passage, Nozick suggests that:

> In conjunction, don't they [rationality, free will, and moral agency] add up to something whose significance is clear: a being able to formulate long-term plans for its life, able to consider and decide on the basis of abstract principles or considerations it formulates to itself and hence not merely the plaything of immediate stimuli . . . and so on. (*ASU*, 49)

However, he then notes that a being might potentially possess the three key traits he identifies, yet still in some way be impeded "from operating in terms of an overall conception of its life, and what it is to add up to." Ibid. The need to foreclose this possibility gives rise to the language quoted in the text.

8 Immanuel Kant, *Groundwork of the Metaphysic of Morals* [1785], H. J. Paton, translator (New York: Harper & Row, 1964), 96.

9 A much more detailed reconstruction and defense of Nozick's argument is presented in Friedman, *Nozick's Libertarian Project*, 20–9.

10 I thank Danny Frederick for bringing home to me the need to address this point.

11 According to Locke, "God and his Reason commanded [Mankind] to subdue the Earth, i.e. improve it for the benefit of Life, and therein lay out something upon it that was his own, his labour." Nozick echoes this idea in defending his principle of justice in acquisition: "Perhaps the idea . . . is that laboring on something improves it and makes it more valuable; and anyone is entitled to own a thing whose value he has created" (*ASU*, 175). An individual or community that uses land for hunting, or that occupies it without transforming it, is morally entitled to retain *possession* indefinitely. However, if the user vacates the land, it is subject to being homesteaded by others on a first-come, first-served basis.

12 Our political authorities did not expressly justify the "war on poverty" programs in terms of rectification. Nevertheless, it was

understood that African-Americans were disproportionately impoverished, unemployed, and undereducated as a result of slavery and its aftermath. Thus, it was clearly expected that they would be the primary beneficiaries, as a group, from these programs. Certainly this was the understanding of President Johnson when he articulated his vision of the Great Society and the agenda intended to bring it about. See President Lyndon Johnson, Commencement Address at Howard University: "To Fulfill These Rights," June 4, 1965, achieved at http://www.lbjlib.utexas.edu/johnson/archives.hom/speeches.hom/650604.asp. With respect to the negative effect of our welfare state on African-Americans see, for example, Charles Murray, *Losing Ground: American Social Policy 1950–1980* (New York: Basic Books, 1984), especially 56–68, 219–20, 227–33 and Brad Plumer, "These Ten Charts Show the Black–White Economic Gap Hasn't Budged in 50 Years," Wonkblog, *WashingtonPost*.com, August 28, 2013, http://www.washingtonpost.com/blogs/wonkblog/wp/2013/08/28/these-seven-charts-show-the-black-white-economic-gap-hasnt-budged-in-50-years/.

Our effort to redress the great wrongs done to Native Americans takes the form of transfer payments, health and educational services, and other benefits offered through the Bureau of Indian Affairs (and other agencies). For the destructive effect of these welfare programs on Native Americans, see Calvin Helin, *Dances With Dependency Trap: Out of Poverty Through Self-Reliance* (Woodland Hills, CA: Cubbie Blue Publishing, 2008); Andrei Znamenski, "Native American Reservations: 'Socialist Archipelago,'" *Mises Daily*, April 26, 2013, http://mises.org/daily/6416/Native-American-Reservations-Socialist-Archipelago; and Chris Edwards, "Indian Lands, Indian Subsidies, and the Bureau of Indian Affairs," in *Downsizing the Federal Government* (Washington, DC: Cato Institute, February 2012).

13 For a powerful argument along these lines, see Tyler Cowen, "How Far Back Should We Go? Why Restitution Should be Small," in Jon Elster, ed., *Retribution and Restitution in the Transition to Democracy Since 1945* (Cambridge: Cambridge University Press, 2006), 17–32.

14 See Michael Sandel, "Interview, Michael Sandel on Justice," by Nigel Warburton, *Prospect Magazine*.co.uk, January 21, 2011, http://www.prospectmagazine.co.uk/magazine/interview-michael-sandel-on-justice-bbc4-justice-citizens-guide/#.UpTYBt7Tk5s.

15 See, for example, Friedrich A. Hayek, *Constitution of Liberty* (Chicago: University of Chicago Press, 1960), 94–8.

16 Ibid., 99.

17. For a summary and discussion of this view, see Daniel Shapiro, *Is the Welfare State Justified?* (Cambridge: Cambridge University Press, 2007), 18–22.
18. See Shapiro, *Welfare State*, 205–8 (arguing that elements of free choice and brute luck reciprocally influence each other, so there is no way to identify that portion of a person's holdings that is attributable to the latter).
19. One of the plain meanings of "deserve" is "to have a rightful claim, and thus be entitled to," so libertarians could fairly say, on the basis of the argument just presented, that under laissez faire the successful deserve their property. However, because desert is also commonly understood to mean "according to moral merit or virtue," I have elected to avoid this usage, in favor of "entitled."
20. Perhaps the best known and most thoroughly developed of these critiques is Peter Railton, "Locke, Stock and Peril: Natural Property Rights, Pollution, and Risk," in Mary Gibson, ed., *To Breathe Freely* (Tolowa, NJ: Rowman & Littlefield, 1985), 89–123.
21. For a useful introduction to this procedure, see Raymond Kopp et al., "Cost-Benefit Analysis and Regulatory Reform: An Assessment of the Science and the Art," Discussion Paper 97-19, Resources for the Future, 1997, http://www.rff.org/documents/rff-dp-97-19.pdf.
22. See James W. Child, "Can Libertarianism Sustain a Fraud Standard?" *Ethics* 104 (July 1994), 722–38, especially 733–4. Child does not interpret Nozick as urged earlier, but instead makes the error of regarding him as an advocate of the self-ownership thesis. See Chapter 10, under "Abortion rights." Accordingly, Child does not consider the justification for the punishment of fraud suggested in the text.
23. See, for example, David Boaz, *Libertarianism: A Primer* (New York: The Free Press, 1997), 75.
24. Isaiah Berlin, "Two Concepts of Liberty," collected in *Four Essays on Liberty* (Oxford: Oxford University Press, 1969), 137.
25. For a more detailed description of Nozick's justification of the minimal state and a summary of the flaws identified by critics, see Friedman, *Nozick's Libertarian Project*, 76–83.
26. It is possible that other citizens may elect to pick up the slack left by those who decide to free ride on the supply of security services by the minimal state. However, as one commentator has written, "Contributors must pay more to obtain any given level of protection precisely because others gain without contributing . . . Free riding

[on essential public goods] is clearly a form of theft, and libertarian theory itself admits the legitimacy of using government force to stop thefts, even where they are occurring through stealth rather than force." James Rolph Edwards, "Taxation, Forced Labor, and Theft: Comment," *Independent Review* VI(2) (Fall 2001), 255, http://www.independent.org/publications/tir/article.asp?a=162.

27 According to standard economic theory, a public good is one that satisfies two technical criteria: it is neither "excludable" (people cannot be prevented from benefiting from it) nor "rival" (one individual's consumption of the good does not diminish any other person's enjoyment of it). See Greg N. Mankiw, *Principles of Economics*, 3rd edn (New York: Dryden Press, 1998), 225–31. National defense is a classic example because as Mankiw explains, "Once the country is defended from foreign aggressors, it is impossible to prevent any single person from enjoying the benefit . . . [and] when one person enjoys the benefit of national defense, he does not reduce the benefit to anyone else." Ibid., 228. In other words, without universal taxation citizens are able to free ride because they can refuse to pay yet still receive the benefit, potentially resulting in an undersupply of this essential good.

The administration of justice is not a public good because free riders can largely be excluded from receiving its benefits, but the state's monopoly of force is justified in a society at least roughly governed by the rule of law because the independent enforcement of law and order represents too grave a threat to other members of the community. See Friedman, *Nozick's Libertarian Project*, 96–101. See also Eric Mack, "Nozickian Arguments for the More-Than-Minimal State," in Ralf M. Bader and John Meadowcroft, eds, *The Cambridge Companion to Nozick's "Anarchy, State, and Utopia"* (Cambridge: Cambridge University Press, 2011), 89–115 (making a libertarian argument for the provision of coercively funded "protective services" by the state, based on the public good/free rider problem).

28 John Locke, in Peter Laslett, ed., *Two Treatises of Government* (Cambridge: Cambridge University Press, 1988), Second Treatise, chapter V, section 28.

29 A much fuller discussion of this idea may be found at Friedman, *Nozick's Libertarian Project*, 137–41.

30 John Kekes, *The Illusions of Egalitarianism* (Ithaca, NY: Cornell University Press, 2003), 113–4.

31 See Joel Feinberg, "Voluntary Euthanasia and the Inalienable Right to Life," in Sterling McMurrin, ed., Vol. 1, *The Tanner*

Lectures on Human Value (Salt Lake City, UT: University of Utah Press, 1980), 233.

32 I note in this regard our society's general unwillingness to enact "required rescue" laws. Only two states (Vermont and Rhode Island) impose on their residents any duty to actively assist an injured or endangered person, and even in these states this requirement applies only to non-risky rescues. See David A. Hyman, "Rescue Without Law: An Empirical Perspective on the Duty to Rescue," *Tex. L. Rev.*, 84 (2006), 683–4. See also Eugene Volokh, "Duty to Rescue/Report Statutes," The Voklokh Conspiracy.com, November 3, 2009, http://volokh.com/2009/11/03/duty-to-rescuereport-statutes/. Several other states impose on bystanders a duty to report serious crimes they witness, but this is obviously a much less onerous requirement than a mandate to actually provide help.

The general absence of such mandatory rescue laws, and the fact that the two existing statutes excuse performance if there is even a minimal risk to potential rescuers or bystanders, reflects our society's general reluctance to impose positive duties of beneficence on its citizenry. This stance seems to be premised on the important distinction that many philosophers draw between an agent's culpability in causing harm to an innocent person and merely allowing foreseeable harm, caused by someone else, to occur. I believe that the ethical considerations that underlie this distinction also support the claim that persons are entitled to a great deal of moral discretion in deciding how and to what extent they should assist those in financial distress. Accordingly, the acknowledgment that the autonomy of well-off persons may be overridden when minor sacrifices by them are required to prevent a moral catastrophe, such as innocent persons starving in the streets, does not imply that it must also give way in order to lift people out of what are merely unpleasant living conditions.

33 Whether positive welfare rights extend to foreigners is a complicated issue that cannot be fully addressed here. I believe that several considerations converge to suggest that it is more difficult to justify coercive taxation to save foreigners, relative to innocent members of our own community. I admit that I have no conclusive argument here, but I would note: (i) our intuitive feeling that we have more stringent obligations to our fellow citizens than to the world at large (as demonstrated by our pattern of charitable giving); (ii) that to make a meaningful dent in global poverty, if possible at all, would require very substantial financial contributions from all middle class and more affluent Americans, which goes well beyond what can reasonably be *demanded* of people; and (iii) that it is plausible that

our fellow citizens contribute to our welfare in a way that foreigners do not; that is, by (to a greater extent) embracing values such as mutual respect and tolerance that produce political stability and something resembling the rule of law, which make affluent societies like ours possible.

Chapter 2

1. For a relatively recent and influential example of this perspective, defended by two prominent left-leaning philosophers, see Liam Murphy and Thomas Nagel, *The Myth of Ownership: Taxes and Justice* (London: Oxford University Press, 2004). Very briefly, Murphy and Nagel assert that since the apparatus of the liberal/democratic state establishes the background conditions that enable talented people to acquire great wealth, there is no injustice in the state imposing heavy (redistributive) taxation as the "price" of this good. For a concise but devastating rebuttal to this line of argument, see Jason Brennan's blog post on *Bleeding Heart Libertarians*.com, June 7, 2012, http://bleedingheartlibertarians.com/2012/06/if-you-want-to-keep-dating-me-youd-better-let-me-fuck-you/. As Brennan (a libertarian academic philosopher) notes, Murphy and Nagel's argument would apply equally to civil, associative, and other noneconomic rights; but they reject out of hand any state interference with these liberties. So, they do not actually provide an *argument* for applying different degrees of stringency to economic liberty on the one hand and other rights on the other, but simply presuppose that this disparity is just.

2. Tibor Machan, *Individuals and Their Rights* (La Salle, IL: Open Court, 1989), 140.

3. Professor Barnett defines "economic liberty" as "the right to acquire, use and possess private property and the right to enter into private contracts of one's choosing." Randy E. Barnett, "Does the Constitution Protect Economic Liberty," *Harv. J.L. & Pub Pol'y* 35 (2012), 5, http://scholarship.law.georgetown.edu/facpub/821/.

4. Ayn Rand wrote that "The right to life is the source of all rights—and the right to property is their only implementation. Without property rights, no other rights are possible." Rand, "Man's Rights," in Ayn Rand, with additional articles by Nathan Brandon, *The Virtue of Selfishness* (New York: Signet Books, 1970), 94.

Murray Rothbard, an important libertarian economist/philosopher and one of the leading exponents of anarcho-capitalism, went so far as to claim that all rights are property rights. This claim is based, very briefly, on the idea that we own ourselves and our labor, and therefore all the fruits thereof. Moreover, he thought it was incoherent to think of rights existing apart from property ownership, since a person cannot exercise rights without owning or having permission to use the property that enables such rights; for instance, one cannot exercise one's right of free speech without controlling some means of expression. See Rothbard, *For a New Liberty: The Libertarian Manifesto*, revised edn (New York: Macmillan, 1978), 39–44, accessible online at The Ludwig von Mises Institute's website, http://mises.org/rothbard/newlibertywhole.asp.

See also Eric Mack, "The Natural Right of Property," *Social Philosophy and Policy* 27, no. 1 (January 2010), 54 ("individuals have a basic moral claim . . . not to be precluded from engaging in the acquisition and discretionary disposal of extrapersonal objects").

5 Friedrich A. Hayek, *The Road to Serfdom*, anniversary edn (Chicago: University of Chicago Press, 1994), 98.
6 Leon Trotsky, *The Revolution Betrayed: What is the Soviet Union and Where is It Going?* (Garden City, NY: Doubleday, Doran & Co., 1937), 283.
7 Richard Pipes, *Property and Freedom* (New York: Alfred A. Knopf, 1999), 281.
8 See Mark D. Friedman, *Nozick's Libertarian Project: An Elaboration and Defense* (London: Continuum Publishing, 2011), chapter 5, for a more in-depth exploration of this subject.
9 See the discussion and sources cited ibid., 100–1.
10 Of course, this will involve difficult problems of proof, but burdens of this sort are inherent in the law of torts generally where, for example, juries are routinely called upon to award damages for pain and suffering or loss of reputation.
11 See Institute for Justice, "Five Years After *Kelo*: The Sweeping Backlash Against One of the Supreme Court's Most-Despised Decision" (2010), http://www.ij.org/five-years-after-kelo-the-sweeping-backlash-against-one-of-the-supreme-courts-most-despised-decisions.
12 See James R. Hagerty, "A Neighborhood's Comeback: Part of Pittsburgh Finally Recovers from 1950s Planners; Google Sets Up Office," *Wall Street Journal* (July 18, 2012), A3; and Jason Dearen

(Associated Press), "Troubled Half-Century of Urban Renewal in SF," *USA Today*, November 9, 2008, http://www.usatoday.com/news/nation/2008-11-09-2450995649_x.htm.

13 See "Statement of Mr. Hilary O. Shelton, Director NAACP Washington Bureau, before the House Energy and Commerce Committee, Subcommittee on Commerce, Trade and Consumer Protection," October 19, 2005, http://action.naacp.org/page/-/washington%20bureau/testimonies/Kelo.FINAL.pdf.

14 Editorial, *New York Times*, "The Limits of Property Rights," June 24, 2005, http://www.nytimes.com/2005/06/24/opinion/24fri1.html?_r=1.

15 Hayek, *Law, Legislation and Liberty: Vol. 1, Rules and Order* (London: Routledge, 1973), 36. The language quoted in the text originates with the eighteenth-century Scottish philosopher, Adam Ferguson.

16 Richard Epstein, "Physical and Regulatory Takings: One Distinction Too Many," 64 *Stan. L. Rev. Online* 99 (March 1, 2012), http://www.stanfordlawreview.org/online/physical-regulatory-takings; and see "Chapter 34. Property Rights and the Constitution," in *Cato Handbook for Policymakers*, 7th edn (2007), prepared by Roger Pilon, http://www.cato.org/pubs/handbook/hb111/hb111-34.pdf.

17 See Robert C. Ellickson, "Alternatives to Zoning: Covenants, Nuisance Rules and Fines as Land Use Controls," *U. Chi. L. Rev.* 40, no. 4 (Summer 1973), 691–2, http://digitalcommons.law.yale.edu/fss_papers/471/.

18 Houston does not have what might be called "classical" zoning, that is, laws that specify particular land uses, such as industrial, commercial, high-density housing, single family, and so on. However, this city does have ordinances governing such matters as minimum lot size, setbacks, minimum parking spaces, street width, and so on that would often be specified by zoning laws. See Michael Lewyn, "How Overregulation Creates Sprawl (Even in a City Without Zoning)," *Wayne L. Rev.* 50, no. 1171 (Winter 2005), http://papers.ssrn.com/sol3/papers.cfm?abstract_id=837244. Lewyn argues that these "quasi-zoning" laws are primarily responsible for the Houston's notorious suburban sprawl.

19 A "restrictive covenant" is "a clause in a deed or lease to real property that limits what the owner of the land or lease can do with the property. Restrictive covenants allow surrounding property owners, who have similar covenants in their deeds, to enforce the terms of the covenants in a court of law. They are intended to

enhance property values by controlling development." *The Free Dictionary*.com, Legal Dictionary, s.v. "Restrictive Covenant," http://legal-dictionary.thefreedictionary.com/Restrictive+Covenant.

20 Bernard Siegan, "Non-Zoning is the Best Zoning," *Cal. W. L. Rev.* 31 (1994), 132.

21 See, for example, William A. Fischel, *The Economics of Zoning Laws: A Property Rights Approach to American Land Use* (Baltimore, MD: Johns Hopkins University Press, 1985); Siegan, "Non-Zoning is the Best Zoning," 137–8; George W. Liebmann, "Modernization of Zoning: A Means to Reform," *Regulation* no. 2 (1996), 71–7; Ellickson, "Alternatives to Zoning," 691–710; and Jonathan Rothwell, "Housing Costs, Zoning, and Access to High-Scoring Schools," Brookings Institute, April 19, 2012, 16–9, http:www.brookings.edu/research/papers/2012/04/19-school-inequality-rothwell.

22 Bradley C. Karkkainen, "Zoning: A Reply to the Critics," *J. Land Use & Envtl. L.* 10, no. 1 (Fall 1994), 3, http://www.law.fsu.edu/journals/landuse/vol101/karkkain.html.

23 Siegan, "Best Zoning," 135–6 and references cited there.

24 Ibid., 128.

25 See Ben O'Neill, "How Zoning Rules Would Work in a Free Society," Mises Daily (blog), June 17, 2009, http:mises.org/daily/3506.

26 See Ellickson, "Alternatives to Zoning," 711–9.

27 *Restatement (Second) of Torts*, vol. 4, section 821D (American Law Institute, 1979).

28 See Ellickson, "Alternatives to Zoning," 719–22.

29 See ibid.

30 For this paragraph, I am relying substantially on Liebman, "Modernization of Zoning," 74–7.

Chapter 3

1 Thomas Nagel, "Personal Rights and Public Space," *Philosophy and Public Affairs* 24, no. 2 (Spring 1995), 98. Nagel is figuratively prepared to fight to the death in defense of the rights of free expression and association, but will not lift a finger to defend economic liberty. See Chapter 2, Note 1.

2 See Eric Barendt, *Freedom of Speech*, 2nd edn (Oxford: Oxford University Press, 2007), 7–13.

3 Critics of utilitarianism (and consequentialism generally) argue that rigid rules derived from these doctrines will "collapse" into the act versions of the theory. For example, utilitarians may hold that the justification for free speech should not apply to particular expressive *acts* but solely to the question of whether we should have a general *rule* in favor of free speech. Hate speech would then be protected under this general rule, even if isolated examples produce negative utility. But, critics have pointed out that there is no apparent reason to abide by a rigid rule if we can "improve" it by admitting certain exceptions, like one for hate speech. See Brad Hooker, s.v. "Rule Consequentialism," in Edward N. Zalta, ed., *The Stanford Encyclopedia of Philosophy* (Spring 2011 Edition), section 8, http://plato.stanford.edu/archives/spr2011/entries/consequentialism-rule/. Hooker proposes a version of rule consequentialism that he contends escapes the collapse problem, but his proposal has its own distinct set of conceptual difficulties that still leaves rule consequentialism in a delicate, if not untenable, position. See, for example, Philip Stratton-Lake, "Can Hooker's Rule-Consequentialist Principle Justify Ross's Prima Facie Duties?" in *Mind* 106 (October 1997), 751–8; and Richard Arneson, "Sophisticated Rule Consequentialism: Some Simple Objections," *Philosophical Issues* 15, no. 1 (2005), 235–51.

4 Letter from US Senators John D. Rockefeller IV and Senator Olympia J. Snowe to Rex W. Tillerson, October 27, 2006, available at Archive. org, http://archive.is/MDC0D.

5 See Michael Barone, "The Tyranny of Good Intentions at U.S. Colleges," Creators.com (2012), http://www.creators.com/conservative/michael-barone/the-tyranny-of-good-intentions-at-u-s-colleges.html. See also the cases involving the selective enforcement of college speech codes described at the Students for Academic Freedom website, http://www.studentsforacademicfreedom.org/.

6 See Samantha Harris, Foundation for Individual Rights in Education.org., "Speech Code of the Month: Oakland University," April 3, 2012, http://thefire.org/article/14356.html.

7 Almost all "private" colleges and universities are subsidized by taxpayers in various ways, including a variety of tax breaks and exemptions, grants, research funding, and most importantly of all, by the financial assistance provided to a substantial portion of their student bodies. See John V. Lombardi, "Public and Private; What's the Difference?" InsideHigherEducation.com, March 6, 2006, http://www.insidehighered.com/views/2006/03/06/lombardi. The federal and state governments that supply this aid could condition it on these institutions honoring the free speech rights of their

students, faculty, and staff. The fact that this is not done speaks volumes about how little our elected representatives care about the First Amendment.

8. For this paragraph, see David Keating and Edward Crane, "Meet the Parents of the Super PACs," (opinion column) *Wall Street Journal*, February 11–2, 2012, A13; Bradley A. Smith, "The War on Political Free Speech," (opinion column) *Wall Street Journal*, January 23, 2012; and Robert A. Levy, "Campaign Finance Reform: A Libertarian Primer," Cato Institute: Commentary, January 29, 2010, http://www.cato.org/pub_display.php?pub_id=11176.

9. See "Stephen Ohlemacher (Associated Press), "IRS Apologizes for Targeting Conservative Groups," May 10, 2013, http://bigstory.ap.org/article/irs-apologizes-targeting-conservative-groups.

10. See Alan M. Dershowitz, "Shouting 'Fire!'" *Atlantic Monthly*, January 1989, http:www.theatlantic.com/issues/89jan/dershowitz.html.

11. These statutes also banned discrimination in voting, and mandated equal access to state and municipal facilities. As explained in the text, since these aspects of the law apply to *state* action, libertarians fully support them.

12. See David E. Bernstein, "Context Matters: A Better Libertarian Approach to Antidiscrimination Law," Cato Institute: Cato Unbound blog, June 16, 2010, http://www.cato-unbound.org/2010/06/16/david-bernstein/context-matters-a-better-libertarian-approach-to-antidiscrimination-law/.

13. It is sometimes argued that bigotry on the part of commercial establishments should be distinguished from bigotry in personal relationships because the former "hold themselves out" as serving the public at large, and thus are guilty of misrepresentation if they discriminate. But, businesses rarely affirmatively state that they will do business with *everyone*, and simply make no representations on this subject. In any case, interested parties may easily determine a particular business's policy in this regard by a phone call or through social media.

14. See Sherry F. Colb, "The New Mexico Supreme Court Applies Anti-Discrimination Law to Wedding Photographer Refusing to Photograph Same-Sex Commitment Ceremonies," Justia.com, September 4, 2013, http://verdict.justia.com/2013/09/04/new-mexico-supreme-court-anti-discrimination-law-to-wedding-photographer.

15. See Ashby Jones, "Judge Rules Colorado Bakery Discriminated Against Gay Couple," *WallStreetJournal*.com, December 6, 2013,

http://online.wsj.com/news/articles/SB10001424052702303722104579242750485975452; and Ros Krasney (Reuters), "Lesbian Brides Win Settlement From Vermont Inn," Yahoo! News, August 23, 2012, http://news.yahoo.com/lesbian-brides-win-settlement-vermont-inn-201458939.html.

16 With respect to torts committed by corporations against noncustomers, it would be manifestly unjust for passive investors to be personally liable, potentially for their entire net worth, as a result of such malfeasance. Here again, the state is not doing shareholders any special favors by granting them limited liability (i.e., only to the extent of their investment) for wrongs committed by corporate employees.

17 See Milton Friedman, *Capitalism and Freedom* (Chicago: Chicago University Press, 1982), 109–10.

Chapter 4

1 Gerald Dworkin, s.v. "Paternalism," in, Edward N. Zalta, ed., *The Stanford Encyclopedia of Philosophy* (Summer 2010 Edition), preface, http://plato.stanford.edu/archives/sum2010/entries/paternalism/.

2 Alexis de Tocqueville, *Democracy in America*, volume II [1840], Henry Reeve translation (1899), section 4, chapter 6, posted by the University of Virginia, http://xroads.virginia.edu/~Hyper/DETOC/toc_indx.html. F. A. Hayek has echoed this theme, asserting that citizens develop a distinct "moral sense" under capitalism that atrophies in more collectivist polities. See Hayek, *The Road to Serfdom* [1944] (Chicago: University of Chicago Press, 1994), 231–2.

3 See Centers for Medicare and Medicaid Services, "National Health Expenditures 2012 Highlights," http://www.cms.gov/Research-Statistics-Data-and-Systems/Statistics-Trends-and-Reports/NationalHealthExpendData/downloads/highlights.pdf.

4 Milton Friedman, *Capitalism and Freedom* (Chicago: University of Chicago Press, 1982), 188.

5 Hayek, *The Constitution of Liberty* (Chicago: University of Chicago Press, 1960), 286.

6 See Social Security Administration.gov, "Primary Insurance Amount: PIA definition," http://www.ssa.gov/OACT/COLA/piaformula.html.

7   Social Security also redistributes from single to married participants (due to survivors' benefits) and from two-earner couples to one-earner couples. See T. Teresa King and H. Wayne Cecil, "The History of Major Changes to the Social Security System," *CPA Journal* (May 2006), http://www.nysscpa.org/cpajournal/2006/506/infocus/p.15htm.

8   See C. Eugene Steuerle and Stephanie Rennane, "Social Security and Medicare Taxes Over a Lifetime," June 20, 2010, http://www.urban.org/UploadedPDF/social-security-medicare-benefits-over-lifetime.pdf. Amazingly, the first worker to retire under Social Security (in 1940), one Ida May Fuller, contributed $24.75 in withholdings, lived to 100, and received $22,888.92 in benefits. See Social Security Administration.gov, Agency History, "Research Note #3, Details of Ida May Fuller's Payroll Tax Contributions," https://www.socialsecurity.gov/history/idepayroll.html. More recent retirees have not done this well, of course, but even the typical worker retiring in 1980 received more than twice the benefits (in real terms) than the taxes they paid. See Steuerle, "Social Security and Medicare Taxes."

9   See Jagadeesh Gokhale, "Democrats' Social Security Policy Dilemma," (opinion column) *Washington Times*, April 7, 2011, http://www.washingtontimes.com/news/2011/apr/7/democrats-social-security-policy-dilemma/.

10 According to the Social Security Administration's own figures, the ratio of workers to retirees has progressed as follows: 41.9:1 in 1945; 4:1 in 1965; 3.4:1 in 1990; 2.9:1 in 2010. See Social Security Administration.gov, History, FAQ, "Ratio of Covered Workers to Beneficiaries," http://www.ssa.gov/history/ratios.html. According to the agency's projections, the ratio will fall to 2.1:1 by 2040. See Gayle L. Reznik et al., "Coping With the Demographic Challenge: Fewer Children and Living Longer," *Social Security Bulletin* 66, no. 4 (Winter 2005/2006), Social Security Administration, Office of Policy, http://www.ssa.gov/policy/docs/ssb/v66n4/v66n4p37.html.

11 According to the Board of Trustees of Social Security and Medicare, to keep the social security system solvent for the next 75 years, we will have to either raise the payroll tax by 20 percent or decrease benefits by 25 percent. See *The 2012 Annual Report of the Board of Trustees of the Federal Old-Age and Survivors Insurance and Federal Disability Insurance Funds*, 20, transmitted to Congress on, April 23, 2012, http://www.ssa.gov/oact/tr/2012/tr2012.pdf.

12 Hayek, *Constitution of Liberty*, 296.

13 The Cato Institute has proposed a detailed long-term plan along these lines for ending Social Security and transitioning entirely to a

system of private accounts. See Michael D. Tanner, "The 6.2 Percent Solution: A Plan for Reforming Social Security," *Social Security Choice Paper* No. 32, February 17, 2004, http://www.cato.org/publications/social-security-choice-paper/62-percent-solution-plan-reforming-social-security.

14. For a discussion of the Chilean system, see Daniel Shapiro, *Is the Welfare State Justified?* (Cambridge: Cambridge University Press, 2007), 164–7. Shapiro argues that if it were reformed to eliminate some of its costly and ineffective regulations, the Chilean system would be markedly superior to defined benefit PAYGO plans, including our social security system. See also, Editorial, "Yes, Chile's Private Pension Model Works, Big Time," *Investor's Business Daily*, September 26, 2013, http://news.investors.com/ibd-editorials/092613-672776-score-another-one-for-the-chilean-model-of-private-pensions.htm.

15. According to one recent study by the US Centers for Disease Control, motorcycle helmet laws saved 1,500 lives and more than $3 billion in health care expenses, lost wages, and other costs in 2010. See David Beasley (Reuters), "Motorcycle Helmet Use Saved $3 Billion in 2010: CDC," Yahoo! News, June 14, 2012, http://news.yahoo.com/motocycle-helmet-saved-3-billion-2010-ced-003226754.html. This study is unable to determine precisely how much of this benefit is due to these laws, and how much would have occurred in any case as a result of voluntary decisions by riders and passengers. Nevertheless, it is clear that a substantial portion is attributable to the mandates.

16. I thank Mark Pennington for this suggestion.

17. Jane Gravelle, "Do Smokers Have Rights? The Science and Politics of Tobacco," Cato Policy Report, XVI, no. 6 (November/December 1994), https://www.cato.org/pubs/policy report/smoke-pr.html.

18. See the studies cited by Sijbren Cnossen, in "Tobacco Taxation in the European Union," *FinanzArchiv/Public Finance Analysis* 62, no. 2 (June 2006), 305–22, http://www.jstor.org/discover/10.2307/40913115?uid=3739960&uid=2&uid=4&uid=3739256&sid=21103346124567; ungated version available at Social Science Research Network, http://papers.ssrn.com/sol3/papers.cfm?abstract_id=905502, see 8–10.

19. See American Lung Association, "State Cigarette Excise Tax Rates," http://www.stateoftobaccocontrol.org/state-grades/methodology/state-cigarette-excise-tax.html. Some localities impose additional taxes.

20 See Thomas A. Lambert, "The Case Against Smoking Bans," *Regulation* (Winter 2006–7), 38–40, http://www.cato.org/pubs/regulation/regv29n4/v29n4-4.pdf.

21 See, for example, "Chapter 33: The War on Drugs," *Cato Handbook for Policymakers*, 7th edn (Washington, DC: Cato Institute, 2009), prepared by David Boaz and Timothy Lynch, 337–44; John McWhorter, "How the War on Drugs Is Destroying Black America," *Cato's Letter* 9, no. 1 (Winter 2011), http://www.cato.org/sites/cato.org/files/pubs/pdf/catosletterv9n1.pdf; and Jeffrey A. Miron and Katherine Waldock, "The Budgetary Impact of Ending Drug Prohibition," White Paper, Cato Institute, September 27, 2010, http://www.cato.org/publications/white-paper/budgetary-impact-ending-drug-prohibition.

22 See Jeffry A. Miron, "Anti-Sex School for Johns?" Cato Institute, Cato at Liberty blog, August 31, 2009, http://www.cato.org/blog/anti-sex-school-johns.

23 Richard H. Thaler and Cass Sunstein, *Nudge: Improving Decisions About Health, Wealth, and Happiness* (New Haven, CT: Yale University Press, 2008).

24 Will Wilkerson, "Why Opting Out Is No 'Third Way': The Perplexing Banality of 'Libertarian Paternalism,'" Reason.com, October 2008, http://reason.com/archives/2008/09/29/why-opting-out-is-no-third-way.

Chapter 5

1 See Wayne Crews, "Code of Federal Regulations Expanding, Faster Pace Under Obama," CompetitiveEnterpriseInstitute.org, March 17, 2014, http://cei.org/2014/03/17/new-data-code-of-federal-regulations-expanding-faster-pace-under-obama.

2 Charles Murray, *What It Means to be a Libertarian* (New York: Broadway Books, 1997), 62. See also Stephen Moore and Julian L. Simon, *It's Getting Better All the Time: 100 Greatest Trends of the Last 100 Years* (Washington, DC: Cato Institute, 2000), 174–5 (confirming Murray's claim). Murray applies the same analysis to the 55 mph speed limit imposed by the federal government in 1974, showing that it had no discernible impact on highway deaths. See Murray, *What It Means*, 52–4.

3 See Burton G. Malkiel, "Innovation, Competition and the FDA," *Forbes*, August 8, 2011, 16.

4   See Matthew Herper, "The Cost of Creating a New Drug Now $5 Billion, Pushing Big Pharma to Change," *Forbes*.com, August 11, 2013, http://www.forbes.com/sites/matthewherper/2013/08/11/how-the-staggering-cost-of-inventing-new-drugs-is-shaping-the-future-of-medicine/2/. This calculation is highly sensitive to methodology, and the results will vary greatly with one's assumptions about the allocation of overhead expenses and so on. See Note 5. Suffice it to say that the number used in the text is, if anything, conservative.

5   See Joseph A. DiMasi et al., "The Price of Innovation: New Estimates of Drug Development Costs," *Journal of Health Economics* 22 (2003), 151–85, http://moglen.law.columbia.edu/twiki/pub/LawNetSoc/BahradSokhansanjFirstPaper/22JHealthEcon151_drug_development_costs_2003.pdf; and Christopher P. Adams and Van V. Brantner, "Estimating the Cost of New Drug Development: Is It Really $802 Million?" *Health Affairs* 25, no. 2 (2006), 420–8, http://content.healthaffairs.org/content/25/2/420.long.

6   Charles Murray makes essentially the same argument presented in this and the following paragraph at Murray, *What It Means*, 69–70.

7   In fact, Consumer Reports.org, the best known of the private testing firms, already offers a free website that evaluates and advises on the safety, efficacy, and pricing of both prescription and OTC drugs (http://www.consumerreports.org/health/prescription-drugs/index.htm), as well as a more extensive subscription service, http://www.ConsumersReportsMedicalGuide.org.

8   See Doug Bandow, "End the FDA Drug Monopoly: Let Patients Choose Their Medicines," *Forbes*, June 11, 2012, http://www.cato.org/publications/commentary/end-fda-drug-monopoly-let-patients-choose-their-medicines.

9   It is not uncommon for a drug that fails to satisfy the FDA's efficacy requirement to show promise for one of more subgroups of patients, for example, those with a particular genetic makeup.

10 I note in this regard that the FDA recently refused to permit the sale of the drug Lemtrada as a treatment for multiple sclerosis, even though it has been approved in 30 other countries, including the entire European Union. Its proponents argue that Lemtrada offers clear clinical advantages relative to the alternatives in treating this terrible disease. Now, to get this drug, US patients will have to cross borders or find a physician willing to prescribe it for an off-label use (it is currently approved and in use for the treatment of leukemia). See Susan Jeffrey, "FDA Declines Approval of Alemtuzumab (Lemtrada) in MS," Medscape Medical News.com, December 30,

2013, http://www.medscape.com/viewarticle/818420; and Christopher DeMuth, Sr. and Cristopher Demuth, Jr., "The FDA Nixes a Pathbreaking Drug for MS," (opinion column) *Wall Street Journal*, January 17, 2014.

11   See Patrick A. Malone, "The Role of FDA Approval in Drug Cases," *Trial*, November 1998, http://www.patrickmalonelaw.com/files/role_of_fda_approval_in_drug_cases.pdf.

12   See Bandow, "FDA Drug Monopoly."

13   See FDA Review.org (Independent Institute), "Theory, Evidence and Examples of FDA Harm," http://www.fdareview.org/harm.shtml; and Thomas Philipson and Eric Sun, "Cost of Caution: The Impact on Patients of Delayed Drug Approvals," Manhattan Institute, Project FDA Report, no. 2 (June 2010), http://www.manhattan-institute.org/html/fda_02.htm.

In June, 2013, the FDA adopted a new "Fast Track" approval process for drugs deemed by the agency to fill an unmet need for the treatment of serious conditions. See US Food and Drug Administration, FDA.gov, "Fast Track, Breakthrough Therapy, Accelerated Approval and Priority Review," last updated June 26, 2013, http://www.fda.gov/forconsumers/byaudience/forpatientadvocates/speedingaccesstoimportantnewtherapies/ucm128291.htm. Only time will tell whether this new procedure is effective.

14   See, for example, Milton Friedman and Rose Friedman, *Free to Choose: A Personal Statement* (New York: Harcourt Brace Jovanovich, 1980), 207–8. The Friedmans' analysis of the various harms caused by FDA regulation is exemplary, and instructive in many respects. See ibid., 203–10.

15   See Lindsey Tanner (Associated Press), "New Drugs Have Side Effects," May 1, 2002 (citing research by Dr. Karen Lasser showing that between 1975 and 1999 more than 10 percent of FDA approved drugs had to be subsequently given a serious side effects warning or withdrawn from the market), http://www.pspinformation.com/medications/interactions/drug_sideeffects.shtml.

16   See, for example, Daniel Park, "Conflicts of Interest: Monitoring the FDA's Relationship with Pharmaceutical Companies," *Yale Journal of Medicine and Law*, November 1, 2005, http://www.yalemedlaw.com/2005/11/conflicts-of-interest-monitoring-the-fda%E2%80%99s-relationship-with-pharmaceutical-companies/.

17   This criticism has come from across the entire ideological spectrum. See, for example, Friedman, *Free to Choose*, chapter 7 and Gabriel

Kolko, "The New Deal Illusion," Counterpunch.org, August 29, 2012, http://www.counterpunch.org/2012/08/29/the-new-deal-illusion/.

18 See Michele Boldrin and S. Joshua Swamidass, "A New Bargain for Drug Approvals," (opinion column) *Wall Street Journal*, July 27, 2011, A15.

19 Fredric Bastiat, "What Is Seen and What Is Not Seen" [1848] in his *Selected Essays on Political Economy* (Irvington-on-Hudson, NY: The Foundation for Economic Education, Inc., 1995), http://www.econlib.org/library/Bastiat/basEss1.html.

20 See Adrian Moore, "Don't Be Fooled, Regulations Cost Jobs," August 9, 2012, RealClearMarkets.com (citing a study by the Small Business Administration), http://www.realclearmarkets.com/articles/2012/08/09/dont_be_fooled_regulations_cost_jobs_99812.html.

21 See Swedish Agency for Growth Policy Analysis, "The Economic Effects of the Regulatory Burden—A Theoretical and Empirical Analysis" (based on research done by The Ratio Institute, an independent Swedish think-tank), December 2010, http://ec.europa.eu/enterprise/policies/industrial-competitiveness/competitiveness-analysis/seminars/files/bbs_falkenhall_report_en.pdf.

22 See US Department of Labor, Wage and Hour Division, "Minimum Wage: Frequently Asked Questions," http://webapps.dol.gov/dolfaq/dolfaqBYsubtopic.asp?faqpage=1&subtopicid=8&topicid=1.

23 See National Conference of State Legislatures, "State Minimum Wages," http://www.ncsl.org/research/labor-and-employment/state-minimum-wage-chart.aspx. As of this writing, there is an accelerating push in our "blue" states to raise the minimum wage to even higher levels, with four states (Connecticut, Maryland, Hawaii, and Vermont) enacting a $10.10 minimum, to take effect in 2015 or later. See Paul Davidson, "More States, Cities, Raising Minimum Wage," *USA Today*, May 15, 2014, http://www.usatoday.com/story/money/business/2014/05/15/minimum-wage-increases/9129183/.

24 A clear majority of economists accept that raising the minimum wage will cost jobs, and that the higher the rate, the more jobs will be lost. See, for example, Mark Wilson, "The Negative Effects of Minimum Wage Laws," Cato Institute: *Policy Analysis*, June 21, 2012, 6–8, http://www.cato.org/pubs/pas/PA701.pdf; and Richard Cowan (Reuters), "U.S. Minimum Wage Hike Would Kill Jobs But Alleviate Poverty: CBO," February 18, 2014 (reporting that the Congressional Budget Office found that raising the minimum

wage to $10.10 in three annual steps would cost 500,000 jobs by 2016), http://news.yahoo.com/cbo-sees-job-losses-rising-incomes-minimum-wage-195151711-business.html.

25 See Mike Konczal, "Economists Agree: Raising the Minimum Wage Reduces Poverty," WashingtonPost.com, January 4, 2014, http://www.washingtonpost.com/blogs/wonkblog/wp/2014/01/04/economists-agree-raising-the-minimum-wage-reduces-poverty/. For the opposing view, see Wilson, "Minimum Wage Laws," 9–11 and Joseph J. Sabia, "Does Raising the Minimum Wage Reduce Poverty?" (opinion column), *U-T San Diego*, April 12, 2012, http://www.utsandiego.com/news/2012/Apr/12/does-raising-the-minimum-wage-reduce-poverty/?#article-copy.

26 Friedman, *Free to Choose*, 238.

27 See Dick M. Carpenter et al., "License to Work: A National Study of Burdens from Occupational Licensing," Institute for Justice, May 2012, https://www.ij.org/licensetowork.

28 See sections 8(a)(5) and 8(b)(3) of National Labor Relations Act of 1935, Public Law 74–198, codified at 29 U.S.C. sections 158(a)(5) and (b)(3).

29 See Peter Levine, "The Libertarian Critique of Labor Unions," *Philosophy & Public Policy Quarterly* 21, no. 4 (Fall 2001), 17–8. Agency shops are permitted and enforced in states that do not have "right to work" laws. Ibid., 18.

30 Oklahoma became a RTW state in 2001, Indiana did so in 2012, and Michigan in the following year, while none have gone the other way. So, the trend seems to be moving slowly in favor of workers' freedom of contract. See *The Morning Sun*, "Michigan News Round-up: State Evenly Divided on Right to Work law," April 1, 2013, http://www.themorningsun.com/article/20130401/NEWS03/130339911/michigan-news-roundup-state-evenly-divided-on-right-to-work-law.

31 See Richard Vedder, "Right-To-Work Laws: Liberty, Prosperity, and Quality of Life," *Cato Journal* 30, no. 1 (Winter 2010), 175, http://www.cato.org/sites/cato.org/files/serials/files/cato-journal/2010/1/cj30n1-9.pdf. According to Vedder, as of 2007, 6.7 percent of all workers (public and private sector) in RTW states were union members, versus 14.2 percent in the others. According to Census Bureau data, as of the end of 2012, the overall percentage of workers in unions (nationally) was 11.3 percent, down from 11.8 percent in 2011, with only 6.6 percent belonging to private sector unions. See Steven Greenhouse, "Share of the Work Force

in Union Falls to a 97-Year Low, 11.3%," *New York Times*, January 23, 2013, http://www.nytimes.com/2013/01/24/business/union-membership-drops-despite-job-growth.html?_r=0. I have not been able to find a comparative breakdown of private sector union membership in RTW and non-RTW states.

32 See Veder, "Right-To-Work-Laws," 175–8.

33 See F. A. Hayek, *The Constitution of Liberty* (Chicago: University of Chicago, 1960), 270 and Friedman, *Free to Choose*, 233.

34 See Sheldon Richman, "The Libertarian Case Against Right-to-Work Laws," *Reason*.com, December 16, 2012, http://reason.com/archives/2012/12/16/libertarian-case-against-right-to-work-l.

35 Once a union is legally recognized as the exclusive bargaining representative for workers at a particular business, employees have no opportunity to decertify the union until the labor agreement expires, and unions can nullify this possibility by renewing the agreement prior to maturity. Even removing the contractual requirement that workers pay dues as a condition of employment is subject to substantial legal and practical obstacles. See Russ Brown, "A Deep Secret That Labor Unions Don't Want Workers to Know," *Forbes*.com, August 16, 2012, http://www.forbes.com/sites/realspin/2012/08/16/a-deep-secret-that-labor-unions-dont-want-workers-to-know/.

36 See, for example, Alicia Mundy, "Teachers Unions Give Broadly," *Wall Street Journal*, July 13, 2012, A4 (from 2007 to 2011 the two major teachers unions spent more than $330 million on political contributions, lobbying, issue education, and other activities designed to promote their interests).

37 See, for example, Joan Gralla (Reuters), "U.S. Munis' $2 Trillion in Unfunded Pensions May Cause Some Public Workers to Lose Benefits," HuffPost Buiness.com, July 2, 2012, http://www.huffingtonpost.com/2012/07/02/pensions-us-munis-unfunded-lose-benefits_n_1644772.html; Andrew Biggs and Jason Richwine, "Overpaid Public Workers: The Evidence Mounts," *Wall Street Journal*, April 11, 2012, A13; Chris Edwards, "Public Sector Unions and the Rising Cost of Employee Compensation," *Cato Journal* 30, no. 1 (Winter 2010), 87–115, http://www.cato.org/sites/cato.org/files/serials/files/cato-journal/2010/1/cj30n1-5.pdf; and Allysia Finley, "California Prison Academy: Better Than a Harvard Degree," (opinion column) *Wall Street Journal*, April 30, 2011, http://online.wsj.com/news/articles/SB10001424052748704132204576285471510530398.

38 See Chris Edwards, "Public-Sector Unions," *Tax & Budget Bulletin*, no. 61 (March 2010), http://www.cato.org/sites/cato.org/files/pubs/pdf/tbb_61.pdf; and Bob Williams, "Why Government Employee Collective Bargaining Laws Must Be Reformed Now," State Budget Solutions.org, June 5, 2012, http://www.statebudgetsolutions.org/publications/detail/why-government-employee-collective-bargaining-laws-must-be-reformed-now.

39 By comparable reasoning, less stringent property rights should apply to holders of natural monopolies, such as certain utility services.

40 Franklin Roosevelt cited the unique and irreplaceable nature of governmental services in his famous August 1937 letter to Luther C. Steward, head of the National Federation of Federal Employees, cautioning him that "the process of collective bargaining, as usually understood, cannot be transplanted into the public service." See Franklin D. Roosevelt: "Letter on the Resolution of Federation of Federal Employees Against Strikes in Federal Service," August 16, 1937. Online by Gerhard Peters and John T. Woolley, *The American Presidency Project*. http://www.presidency.ucsb.edu/ws/?pid=15445.

41 See Joseph E. Slater, "The Assault on Public Sector Collective Bargaining: Real Harms and Imaginary Benefits," American Constitution Society, June 2011, http://www.acslaw.org/sites/default/files/Slater_Collective_Bargaining.pdf; and Chris Edwards, "Public-Sector Unions." I have not found a more recent exact total of states permitting public sector collective bargaining, so the figure in the text may be slightly in error.

42 See Richard N. Langlois, "Cost-Benefit Analysis, Environmentalism and Rights," *Cato Journal* 2, no. 1 (1982), 294–7. As Langlois puts it: "[I]f we *must* make a centralized decision about 'public' resources, then we should prefer something like utilitarianism to a criteria involving the decision-maker's perception of 'social values' or of the 'higher preferences' the citizen would like to see emphasized in public policy but which, alas, he is unable to incorporate into his own decisions." Ibid., 296, Note 45 (his emphasis).

43 See, for example, Nam D. Pham and Daniel J. Ikenson, "A Critical Review of the Benefits and Costs of EPA Regulations on the U.S. Economy," NDP Consulting, November 2012, http://www.nam.org/~/media/423A1826BF0747258F22BB9C68E31F8F.ashx; Kenneth P. Green, "Fostering Quality Science at EPA: Perspectives on Common Sense Reform," Statement before House Committee on Science, November 30, 2011, http://www.aei.org/print/fostering-

quality-science-at-epa-perspectives-on-common-sense-reform; and Anne E. Smith, "Prepared Statement of Anne E. Smith, Ph.D. before the House Committee on Science, Space and Technology," October 4, 2011, http://www.nera.com/nera-files/PUB_Smith_QualityAir_testimony_1011.pdf.

44 Nozick toys with this idea, but does not reach a final conclusion about whether the tort system could fairly balance the competing rights at issue (see *ASU*, 79–81), while Rothbard advocates just this approach. See Murray N. Rothbard, "Law, Property Rights, and Air Pollution," *Cato Journal* 2, no. 1 (Spring 1982), 55–99, http://library.mises.org/books/Murray%20N%20Rothbard/Law,%20Property%20Rights,%20and%20Air%20Pollution.pdf. A detailed, nuanced defense of the classical liberalism perspective on environmental protection is found in Mark Pennington's *Robust Political Economy: Classical Liberalism and the Future of Public Policy* (Cheltenham, UK: Edward Elgar, 2011), chapter 8.

45 Environmental Protection Agency, "Summary of the Toxic Substances Control Act," July 26, 2013, http://www2.epa.gov/laws-regulations/summary-toxic-substances-control-act.

46 See David Boaz, *Libertarianism: A Primer* (New York: The Free Press, 1997), 250.

47 Ibid.

48 See Steven P. Calandrillo, "Responsible Regulation: A Sensible Cost-Benefit, Risk Versus Risk, Approach to Federal Health and Safety Regulation," *B.U.L. Rev.* 81 (December 2001), 988–9.

49 See the discussion in the sources cited in Note 43.

50 See, for example, David Schoenbrod and Melissa White, "Statutory Arteriosclerosis," in *The Environmental Forum* 28, no. 5, American Enterprise Institute, September/October 2011, http://www.aei.org/article/energy-and-the-environment/contaminants/air/statutory-arteriosclerosis/; and *Cato Handbook for Policymakers*, 7th edn, 2009, chapter 44 ("Environmental Policy"), prepared by Jerry Taylor, 467–9, http://object.cato.org/sites/cato.org/files/serials/files/cato-handbook-policymakers/2009/9/hb111-44.pdf.

Chapter 6

1 A previous federal income tax had been in effect during the Civil War, but it lapsed in 1873. In 1894, Congress attempted to revive the tax, but it fell victim to a constitutional challenge based on

the objection that it represented an "unapportioned" direct tax in contravention of the requirements of article 1, section 9, clause 4. In 1909, Congress enacted a corporate income tax (in the guise of an "excise" tax), which the Court upheld, based on the idea that it was a special tax for the privilege of doing business. That same year Congress adopted the Sixteenth Amendment, which eliminated the "apportionment" requirement for taxes on all forms of income. In 1913, the amendment was ratified by the requisite number of states, and the Revenue Act of 1913 followed soon after. See John Steele Gordon, *An Empire of Wealth* (New York: Harper Collins, 2004), 272–7.

2 In tandem, the individual and corporate income taxes account for about 60 percent of all federal tax revenues. However, the percentage is approximately 85 percent if payroll taxes are excluded from this calculation. See Tax Policy Center (Urban Institute/Brookings Institution), "Tax Facts: Historical Amount of Revenue by Source," http://www.taxpolicycenter.org/taxfacts/displayafact.cfm?Docid=203.

3 As one economist and persistent Fed critic has accurately observed, "The power to create money is the power to tax, because inflation is merely a form of taxation. It is a regressive tax—it hurts lower income people more than the rich—it is a dishonest tax, and it strains the social fabric of nations. Nevertheless, throughout history it has been politicians' preferred form of taxation." Jerry L. Jordan, "Who Will Guard the Monetary Guardians?" Cato Institute, Cato Unbound blog, November 12, 2013, http://www.cato-unbound.org/2013/11/12/jerry-l-jordan/who-will-guard-monetary-guardians.

4 Here and elsewhere when I refer to the federal income tax, I am speaking of both the corporate and individual tax components, codified in Title 26 of the United States Code. A list of all federal tax breaks, and the lost revenue represented by each, can be found in Office of Management and Budget, "Fiscal Year 2014 Analytical Perspectives, Budget of the U.S. Government" (2013), Table 16-1 (Estimates of Total Income Tax Expenditures for Fiscal Years 2012–8), 243–7, http://www.whitehouse.gov/sites/default/files/omb/budget/fy2014/assets/spec.pdf.

5 Clearly, from a practical perspective, it makes no sense to tax a person whose income is so meager that he would qualify for public assistance, and then to provide him relief with this revenue. Therefore, the application of the tax should begin at an income level in excess of that required for the bare necessities.

6   See William McBride, "What is the Evidence on Taxes and Growth?" Tax Foundation, Special Report No. 207, December 12, 2012, http://taxfoundation.org/article/what-evidence-taxes-and-growth.

7   At the time of enactment, most of the federal government's receipts came from import duties, but the income tax soon came to dwarf these as a source of revenue.

8   See Burton Abrams, "Income Tax Turns 100," (opinion column) *Washington Times*, October 29, 2013, http://www.washingtontimes.com/news/2013/oct/29/abrams-income-tax-turns-100/?page=all; and Gordon, *An Empire of Wealth*, 277.

9   See Gordon, *An Empire of Wealth*, 277.

10 See the discussion in Chapter 1 under "The Legitimate Functions of the State," including Note 26 thereto, arguing that free riding on taxes paid by others to support the morally legitimate functions of the state is akin to theft under libertarian principles.

11 Domestic security probably does not qualify as a "public good" in the technical economic sense, but it is a public good in the sense that it cannot be provided in a just way without state involvement. See the analysis in Chapter 1, including Note 27.

12 See generally Eric Rakowski, "Can Wealth Taxes Be Justified?" 53 *Tax L. Rev.* (1999–2000), 300–9; Kip Hagopian, "The Inequality of the Progressive Income Tax," *Policy Review*, No. 166 (Hoover Institution, April 1, 2011), under "The Benefits Principle," http://www.hoover.org/publications/policy-review/article/72291; and Richard A. Epstein, *Simple Rules for a Complex World* (Cambridge, MA: Harvard University Press, 1995), 138–9. For a penetrating critique of the competing "sacrifice theory" of taxation, see Hagopian, "The Progressive Income Tax," under "Sacrifice Theory and the Marginal Utility of Money."

13 The issues raised in this paragraph are explored in much greater depth in Mark D. Friedman, *Nozick's Libertarian Project: An Elaboration and Defense* (London: Continuum International, 2011), 83–101.

14 Kip Hagopian, "The Progressive Income Tax," under "The Benefits Principle" (quoting Blum and Kalven, *The Uneasy Case for Progressive Taxation* [1953], 38).

15 James Rolph Edwards, "Taxation, Forced Labor, and Theft: Comment," *Independent Review* VI, no. 2 (Fall 2001), 255, http://www.independent.org/publications/tir/article.asp?a=162.

16 See Hagopian, "Progressive Income Tax," under "Critique of the Doctrine." For an extended argument *against* the moral

legitimacy of a proportionate wealth tax, see Rakowski, "Wealth Taxes," 300–9. Proceeding under the assumption that the benefit theory of taxation is correct, and assuming further that the distribution of resources in a society is just (so there is no mandate for redistributive taxation), he concludes that "The natural implication of the benefit principle against the backdrop of a just distribution of resources seems to be a head tax" (footnote omitted). Ibid., at 304.

17 For reasons of accountability and respect for the virtues of federalism, it will generally be preferable to collect taxes to fund non-classic goods at the state or local level. Nevertheless, the same reasoning that supports the justice of a proportional levy for classic public goods applies equally here.

18 If practical from an administrative standpoint, the benefit theory of taxation might best be vindicated in certain cases by the imposition of user fees as a partial substitute for proportional taxation. For example, with respect to civil litigation, while it is certainly true that society at large profits from having a reasonably convenient and fair means of peacefully resolving disputes, some parties—those who use the courts most frequently—clearly gain on a disproportionate basis. Therefore, it would not be unjust to impose a surcharge on them. This logic would equally apply to users of infrastructure, which should be funded, at least in part, by tolls or similar user fees. See Richard Rahn, "Flat Tax? Sales Tax? Value-Added Tax?" (opinion column) *Washington Times*, July 16, 2013, http://www.washingtontimes.com/news/2013/jul/16/flat-tax-sales-tax-value-added-tax/.

19 See Hagopian, "The Progressive Income Tax," under "A New Doctrine of Fairness."

20 There is an obvious practical reason to prefer the income tax: the greater administrative costs associated with a wealth tax. A very substantial portion of our holdings are illiquid and thus hard to value, including interests in non-publicly traded businesses, antiques and collectibles, certain types of real estate, art, jewelry, and so on. It would be very expensive and time consuming to audit the value of such assets, which would fluctuate on a year-by-year basis. In contrast, income generally leaves a paper trail, and raises no problems of valuation. So, if both levies equally satisfy the criteria identified in the text, the income tax should be selected.

21 Allister Heath, "A Wealth Tax Would be Ethically Wrong and Economically Destructive," (opinion column) *The Telegraph*, February 19, 2012, http://www.telegraph.co.uk/finance/

comment/9880714/A-wealth-tax-would-be-ethically-wrong-and-economically-destructive.html.

22 Our laws make a half-hearted gesture toward addressing the double taxation problem by taxing dividend income at a lower rate (20%) than the highest individual marginal tax rate, but since the corporate tax rate should be zero, this hardly corrects this injustice.

23 The tax code is rife with loopholes that enable the well-off, with careful tax planning, to avoid paying their fair share. All of these should end. By the same token, due to the size of the standard deduction and the availability of other deductions, such as for mortgage interest, 43 percent of households pay *no* federal income tax, which is also unfair. See Alison Linn, "Now It's the 43 Percent: Fewer Paying No Income Tax," CNBC.com, September 9, 2013, http://www.cnbc.com/id/101015065.

The common "liberal" response to the just cited 43 percent statistic is to point out that these individuals are subject to payroll taxes. But this is irrelevant, because payroll taxes are involuntary contributions to our entitlement programs in which everyone is compelled to participate, and which in theory everyone is supposed to benefit. In fact, the largest component of the payroll tax, Social Security, is steeply progressive (see Chapter 4), so low-income workers are certainly not paying more than their fair share. Furthermore, although payroll taxes are in fact routinely comingled with general federal revenues, the government has pledged to repay these loans when the entitlement program liabilities come due. Accordingly, non-payers of the federal income tax simply free ride on the backs of those whose income taxes pay for military defense, federal law enforcement, federal courts, poverty relief, and so on.

Kerk Phillips, an associate professor of economics at Brigham Young University, has calculated that a 20 percent tax rate applied to *all* income (with no deductions, exemptions, etc.), combined with a $10,000 refundable tax credit for all filers (e.g., a negative income tax for the poor) would be revenue neutral. See Kerk Phillips, "A Flat Tax is Not Incapable of Funding the Government and the Poor," (opinion column) *Deseret News*, February 19, 2013, http://www.deseretnews.com/article/865573462/A-flat-tax-system.html. This proposal seems to be a reasonable starting point in the search for a tax system that could pass libertarian muster.

24 The awesome political power wielded by homeowners, the housing industry, and the advocacy groups that push "affordable housing" explains not only these tax breaks, but the continued existence of Freddie Mac and Fannie Mae, the GSEs that played a crucial role

in the recent financial crisis and the ensuing major recession. See, for example, Gretchen Morgenson and Joshua Rosner, *Reckless Endangerment: How Outsized Ambition, Greed and Corruption Led to Economic Armageddon* (New York: Times Books, 2011).

25. There are many philosophers who accept the justice of unfettered gifting, while objecting to the institution of inheritance. For example, Hillel Steiner acknowledges that the former is "an unimpeachable incident of natural property rights," while attempting to distinguish it in a principled way from the latter. Hillel Steiner, *An Essay on Rights* (Oxford: Blackwell, 1994), 253. His argument fails; see Friedman, *Nozick's Libertarian Project*, 50–1.

26. Much (if not most) of the value of the resources handed down by inheritance have already been taxed at least once, so the "death tax" would run afoul of the principle prohibiting double taxation. However, it is possible that great wealth in the form of unrealized capital gains, that is, stock issued to the founders of very successful corporations, could escape taxation for generations. Thus, the argument in the text exonerates even those transfers at death that don't run afoul of the double taxation principle.

27. See David Miller, "Tiny Little Hope for Tax Reform," HuffPost Business, April 4, 2012, http://www.huffingtonpost.com/david-miller/obama-romney-tax-reform_b_1415041.html.

28. For a very useful summary of the history and operation of the national banking system, see Bruce Champ, "The National Banking System: A Brief History," Federal Reserve Bank of Cleveland Working Paper No. 07-23R (originally published 2007, revised May 2011), http://www.clevelandfed.org/research/research_publication.cfm?id=35&y=2007&DCS.nav=Local.

29. See George Selgin, "Milton Friedman and the Case Against Currency Competition," *Cato Journal* 28, no. 2 (Spring/Summer 2008), 292–4, http://citeseerx.ist.psu.edu/viewdoc/download?doi=10.1.1.170.4468&rep=rep1&type=pdf; and Kurt Schuler, "Note Issue by Banks: A Step Toward Free Banking in the United States?" *Cato Journal* 20, no. 3 (Winter 2001), 456–7, http://object.cato.org/sites/cato.org/files/serials/files/cato-journal/2001/1/cj20n3-8.pdf.

30. Champ, "National Banking System," 9. Since demand for funds was greater in the large cities, banks there could pay higher interest on deposits than smaller-city national banks, in effect outbidding other institutions for this capital.

31. Roger T. Johnson, "Historical Beginnings . . . The Federal Reserve" (Federal Reserve Bank of Boston, 2010), 14.

32 See ibid., 14–5; and Gerald P. O'Driscoll, Jr., "The Fed at 100," Cato Institute, Cato Unbound blog, November 4, 2013, http://www.cato-unbound.org/issues/november-2013/federal-reserve-100.

33 See Johnson, "Historical Beginnings," 16–32.

34 The 12 Federal Regional Banks are "owned" by their shareholders, which consist of the thousands of federally chartered member banks who must by law purchase a specified number of shares, and state-chartered institutions, that have this option. Shareholders receive statutory dividends, and elect the majority of the Regional Banks' board of directors, but there is no market for their shares, and the operations of the Banks are strictly controlled by statute. So, they are essentially instrumentalities of the larger system. See Wikipedia.com, s.v. "Federal Reserve System," under "Federal Reserve Banks," http://en.wikipedia.org/wiki/Federal_Reserve_banks.

35 See Schuler, "Note Issue by Banks," 457.

36 See Dror Goldberg, "Legal Tender," Bar-Ilan University, Working Paper 2009-4 (April 2009), http://ideas.repec.org/p/biu/wpaper/2009-4.html.

37 See Milton Friedman and Rose Friedman, *Free to Choose: A Personal Statement* (New York: Harcourt Brace Jovanovich, 1980), 86–7.

38 Ibid., 76.

39 See Craig K. Elwell, "Brief History of the Gold Standard in the United States," Congressional Research Service, June 23, 2011, 13, http://www.fas.org/sgp/crs/misc/R41887.pdf.

40 See Steven Horwitz, "An Introduction to U.S. Monetary Policy," Mercatus Center, April 2, 2013, 19–20, http://mercatus.org/sites/default/files/Horwitz_MonetaryPolicy_v1.pdf; and Anna J. Schwartz and Walter F. Todd, "Why a Dual Mandate is Wrong for Monetary Policy," *International Finance* 11, no. 2 (2008), 179, http://www.aei.org/files/2009/01/28/Todd%20-%20Schwartz%20-%20Why%20a%20Dual%20Mandate%20Is%20Wrong%20for%20Monetary%20Policy.pdf.

41 Horwitz, "U.S. Monetary Policy," 20–1.

42 See Clive Crook, "The Fed Needs a New, Simpler Mandate," Bloomberg.com, April 12, 2012, http://www.bloomberg.com/news/2012-04-10/the-fed-needs-a-new-simpler-mandate.html; and Mike Moffatt, "Why the Fed Should Abandon Its Dual Mandate," (opinion column) *Globe and Mail*, July 18, 2012, http://www.theglobeandmail.com/report-on-business/economy/economy-lab/why-the-fed-should-abandon-its-dual-mandate/article4425062/.

43 Marc Labonte, "Changing the Federal Reserve's Mandate: An Economic Analysis," Congressional Research Service, August 12, 2013, https://www.fas.org/sgp/crs/misc/R41656.pdf.

44 See Schwartz, "Dual Mandate," 171–2.

45 See Annalyn Kurtz, "This Could be the Largest Fed Stimulus Ever," CNN Money, October 28, 2013, http://money.cnn.com/2013/10/28/news/economy/federal-reserve-qe-stimulus/.

46 See Jeffrey Rogers Hummel, "Ben Bernanke versus Milton Friedman," *Independent Review* 15, no. 4 (Spring 2011), 509, http://www.independent.org/pdf/tir/tir_15_04_1_hummel.pdf.

47 See Jon Hilsinrath et al., "Fed's Yellen Sets Course for Steady Bond-Buy Cuts," *Wall Street Journal*, February 12, 2014, A4.

48 In June 2013, the Fed strongly suggested that it would soon begin reducing the volume of its security purchases (i.e., "tapering") as the economy apparently was on the mend. Three months later, without further ado, it changed its mind. See "Shares at Record High as Federal Reserve Refrains from Tapering," BBC News/Business, September 18, 2013, http://www.bbc.co.uk/news/business-24152993.

49 Richard Fisher, "We Are Sailing Deeper Into Uncharted Waters," RealClearPolitics.com, September 22, 2012, http://www.realclearpolitics.com/articles/2012/09/22/we_are_sailing_deeper_into_uncharted_waters_115536.html.

50 Hummel, "Ben Bernanke," 510.

51 See Lawrence H. White, "The Federal Reserve and the Rule of Law," Testimony Before the Subcommittee on Monetary Policy and Trade, House Committee on Financial Services, September 12, 2013, Cato.org, http://www.cato.org/publications/testimony/federal-reserve-rule-law.

52 Federal Reserve.gov., Transcript of Chairman Bernanke's Press Conference, September 13, 2012, 10–1, http://www.federalreserve.gov/mediacenter/files/FOMCpresconf20120913.pdf.

53 See Anthony Randazzo, "How Quantitative Easing Helps the Rich and Soaks the Rest of Us," Reason.com, September 13, 2012, http://reason.com/archives/2012/09/13/occupy-the-fed.

54 See Tracy Alloway, "Banks Reap Profits on Mortgages After QE3," *Financial Times*, October 1, 2012, http://www.ft.com/cms/s/0/3406bba8-08bb-11e2-9176-00144feabdc0.html#axzz2tLMoG7sI.

55 See Andre F. Perold, "Negative Real Interest Rates: The Conundrum for Investment and Spending Policies," *Enterprising Investor*, July 3,

2012, http://blogs.cfainstitute.org/investor/2012/07/03/negative-real-interest-rates-the-conundrum-for-investment-and-spending-policies/; and US Department of the Treasury, Resource Center, "Interest Rate Statistics, Daily Treasury Real Yield Curve Rates," http://www.treasury.gov/resource-center/data-chart-center/interest-rates/Pages/TextView.aspx?data=realyield.

56 Bill Gross, "*Barron's* 2011 Roundtable, Part 1," *Baron's*, January 24, 2011, 38. See also Martin Feldstein, *Wall Street Journal*, January 3, 2013, A13 (criticizing recent Fed policy). It is perhaps worth remembering in this context the "stagflation" of 1970s and early 1980s, during which inflation raged, peaking at 14.8 percent (year-over-year) in 1980. In these years, investors in long-term fixed rate bonds saw their savings ravaged by this hidden tax.

57 Federal Reserve.gov, Transcript of Chairman Press Conference, federalreserve.gov, November 3, 2011, 20, http://www.federalreserve.gov/mediacenter/files/FOMCpresconf20111102.pdf.

58 See Reuters, "Fed Missed Warning Signs in 2007 as Crisis Gained," January 18, 2013, http://www.reuters.com/article/2013/01/18/us-usa-fed-idUSBRE90H13Q20130118.

59 See ibid. It is fair to say that as a general matter the Fed's record of forecasting key economic variables, even in the short-term, is pretty dismal. For example, as noted by economist Diana Furchtgott-Roth, "In 2010 the median Fed forecast for 2011 growth was 3.3 percent. The reality was 1.8 percent growth in 2011." Diana Furchtgott-Roth, "If Possible, Fed Forecasts are Worse Than Its Policies," RealClearMarkets.com, December 24, 2013, http://www.realclearmarkets.com/articles/2013/12/24/if_possible_fed_forecasts_are_worse_than_its_policies_100814.html.

60 Alan Greenspan, "Alan Greenspan, Former Chairman of the Federal Reserve Tells *CBS Sunday Morning With Charles Osgood* He Missed Signals That Led to the 2008 Economic Collapse," CBS News, Press Release, October 18, 2013, http://www.cbspressexpress.com/cbs-news/releases/view?id=37044.

61 See Robert J. Schiller, "Is Economics a Science?" *Project Syndicate*, November 6, 2013, http://www.project-syndicate.org/commentary/robert-j-shilleron-whether-he-is-a-scientist.

62 It was the Fed's disastrous mismanagement of monetary policy that caused the Great Depression or at least significantly deepened and lengthened it. The analysis done by Milton Friedman and Anna Swartz in their *Monetary History of the United States, 1867–1960* (Princeton, NJ: Princeton University Press, 1963) makes this

conclusion virtually inescapable. In 2002, during the celebration of Friedman's ninetieth birthday, Bernanke (then merely a member of the Fed's board of governors) acknowledged this fact, even if in a jocular fashion: "I would like to say to Milton and Anna: Regarding the Great Depression. You're right, we did it. We're very sorry. But thanks to you, we won't do it again." See Federal Reserve. gov, "Remarks at the Conference to Honor Milton Friedman," November 8, 2002, http://www.federalreserve.gov/boarddocs/speeches/2002/20021108/default.htm.

63 Horwitz, "U.S. Monetary Policy," 29.
64 Ibid.
65 Labonte, "Federal Reserve's Mandate," 16.
66 Choice no. 2, eliminating the dual mandate, could also include an inflexible rule for maintaining price stability, for example, something like the "Taylor Rule." Such a policy would then, like choices nos. 1 and 4, attempt to bring the Fed into compliance with the rule of law by forcing it to adhere to a fixed, preannounced rule. For an elaboration of the Taylor Rule, see EconModel.com, "Taylor Rule," http://www.econmodel.com/classic/terms/taylor_rule.htm.
67 Donald Wells and L. S. Scruggs, "The Free Banking Alternative," *The Freeman*, February 1, 1985, http://www.fee.org/the_freeman/detail/the-free-banking-alternative#axzz2tLXAVOfU.
68 Lawrence H. White, s.v. "Competing Money Supplies," *The Concise Encyclopedia of Economics*, Library of Economics and Liberty, 2008, http://www.econlib.org/library/Enc/CompetingMoneySupplies.html. See also Horwitz, "U.S. Monetary Policy," 31–2.
69 F. A. Hayek, *Denationalization of Money* (London: Institute of Economic Affairs, 1976), available at http://www.iea.org.uk/publications/research/denationalisation-of-money. Because of what Hayek regarded as irreversible political forces, he did not propose a return to a commodity-backed currency. Instead, he suggested the repeal of all laws that favor government-issued currency, thus permitting private banks the unregulated issuance of competing notes, which he anticipated would be backed by various fiat currencies (dollars, marks, etc.). Private parties would be free to choose between them for all purposes. See ibid., 46–54.
70 See, for example, Ignacio Briones and Hugh Rockoff, "Do Economists Reach a Conclusion About Free-Banking Episodes?" *Economics Journal Watch* 2, no. 2 (August 2005), 279–324, http://econjwatch.org/articles/do-economists-reach-a-conclusion-on-free-banking-episodes.

71 See Gerald P. Dwyer, Jr., "Wildcat Banking, Bank Panics, and Free Banking in the United States," Federal Reserve Bank of Atlanta, *Economic Review* (December 1996), 1–20; and The Federal Reserve Bank of Minneapolis, "A History of Central Banking in the United States," under "'Free' Banks: 1837–1863," http://www.minneapolisfed.org/community_education/student/centralbankhistory/bank.cfm?#free. According to Dwyer, "Free banking in the United States was not the disaster portrayed by some, but it was also not problem free . . . With the exception of episodic events that generated atypical losses, free banking's performance improved over time." Dwyer, "Free Banking," 16.

72 See Champ, "National Banking System," 10.

73 A list of ten of the most frequently heard criticisms of free banking are compiled and discussed in chapter 10 of Selgin's *The Theory of Free Banking: Money Supply Under Competitive Note Issue* (Washington, DC: Cato Institute, 1988), http://oll.libertyfund.org/?option=com_staticxt&staticfile=show.php%3Ftitle=2307&chapter=218729&layout=html&Itemid=27.

74 See, for example, Scott Sumner, "In Defense of a Flexible Monetary Policy," Cato Institute, Cato Unbound, November 8, 2013, http://www.cato-unbound.org/2013/11/08/scott-sumner/defense-flexible-monetary-policy; and Milton Friedman and Anna J. Schwartz, "Has Government Any Role in Money?" *Journal of Monetary Economics* 17 (1986), 37–62, collected in Anna J. Schwartz, ed., *Money in Historical Perspective* (Chicago: University of Chicago Press, 1987), 311–3, http://www.nber.org/chapter/c7507.

Chapter 7

1 See Tad DeHaven, "Corporate Welfare in the Federal Budget," Cato Institute, *Policy Analysis*, No. 703, July 25, 2012, http://www.cato.org/publications/policy-analysis/corporate-welfare-federal-budget.

2 See Notes 13 and 14.

3 The Cato Institute's tally of corporate welfare excludes that more than $16 billion spent by the NIH each year on basic research because "[t]here is a theoretical argument for the government doing some 'basic' scientific research." DeHaven, "Corporate Welfare," 9. While there is a good argument that such research is a public good, and thus might be underfunded in the absence of government intervention, it does not follow that taxation to

support it is morally legitimate. This activity does not establish the preconditions for the exercise of rational agency, and its absence would hardly qualify as a moral catastrophe, so coercive funding is impermissible.

4   See Allison Linn, "Now It's the 43 Percent: Fewer Paying No Income Tax," CNBC.com, September 9, 2013, http://www.cnbc.com/id/101015065.

5   For a helpful discussion of this political dynamic, see Mark Pennington, *Robust Political Economy: Classical Liberalism and the Future of Public Policy* (Cheltenham, UK: Edward Elgar, 2011), 65–9.

6   John O. Ledyard, "Market Failure," in John Eatwell et al., eds, *The World of Economics* (New York: W.W. Norton, 1991), 407.

7   Ibid.

8   On the economic harm of crony capitalism, see, for example, David R. Henderson, "The Economics and History of Cronyism," *Mercatus Research*, July 27, 2012, http://mercatus.org/sites/default/files/Henderson_cronyism_1.1%20final.pdf; and DeHaven, "Corporate Welfare," 6–12. On the dangers inherent in governmental efforts to correct market failure, see Pennington, *Robust Political Economy*, 19–40.

9   There are, of course, other serious deficiencies in the process, including lack of sufficient competition among contractors, an overly bureaucratic approach, and the quest for "perfect" weapon systems. For a brief overview, see Arthur Herman, "What if Apple Designed an iFighter?" (opinion column) *Wall Street Journal*, July 24, 2012, A15.

10 See Wikipedia.org, s.v. "2005 Base Realignment and Closure Commission," http://en.wikipedia.org/wiki/2005_Base_Realignment_and_Closure_Commission.

11 Both cases are discussed in Major Zachary J. Buettner, "Defense Acquisition Reform: Doing the Same Thing All Over Again," School of Advanced Military Studies, US Army Command and General Staff College, April 19, 2010, 40–5, http://www.dtic.mil/cgi-bin/GetTRDoc?AD=ADA522660. An even more recent example is the effort of certain powerful federal legislators to reverse the Air Force's decision to phase-out its venerable A-10 "Warthog." See W. J. Hennigan, "Cold War-era 'Warthog' Plane Targeted for Retirement Amid Budget Cuts," *LosAngelesTimes*.com, November 20, 2013, http://www.latimes.com/business/la-fi-endangered-warthog-a10-20131120,0,355220.story#ixzz2ru6HywCI

12 This was proposed by Stephen Slivinski in his "The Corporate Welfare State: How the Federal Government Subsidizes U.S. Businesses," *Policy Analysis*, 592, Cato Institute, May 14, 2007, 10–1, http://object.cato.org/sites/cato.org/files/pubs/pdf/pa592.pdf.

13 See Robert Rector, "Examining the Means-tested Welfare State: 79 Programs and $927 Billion in Annual Spending," Testimony before Committee on the Budget, US House of Representatives, April 17, 2012, http://budget.house.gov/uploadedfiles/rectortestimony04172012.pdf.

14 See Michael Tanner, "The American Welfare State: How We Spend Nearly $1 Trillion a Year Fighting Poverty—and Fail," *Policy Analysis*, No. 694 (Washington, DC: Cato Institute, April 11, 2013), 1, 11–6, http://www.cato.org/publications/policy-analysis/american-welfare-state-how-we-spend-nearly-$1-trillion-year-fighting-poverty-fail. Both Rector and Tanner acknowledge that some of this spending goes to individuals and families that have incomes above the official poverty line. See ibid., 2 and Rector, "The Means-tested Welfare State," 5–6. But, as Tanner correctly notes, this doesn't exonerate such spending; rather, it shows that we are using impermissible means to redistribute resources to those not in need even under the government's liberal standard. See Tanner, "American Welfare State," 2.

15 The benchmark used by the federal government to determine whether an individual or family is living in "poverty" is found at United States Census Bureau, Census.gov, "People and Households/Poverty Data," http://www.census.gov/hhes/www/poverty/data/threshld/. Rector's $33,000 per family calculation assumes that the $462 billion in means-tested spending on families with children is equally divided among the one-third of households that earn the lowest income. This demographic covers about 14 million families. See Rector, "The Means-tested Welfare State," 6.

16 According to Rector's figures, even accounting for inflation and population growth, "the U.S. now spends 50 percent more on means-tested cash, food and housing than it did when Bill Clinton entered office on a promise to 'end welfare as we know it.'" Rector, "The Means-tested Welfare State," 2.

17 Daniel Shapiro, *Is the Welfare State Justified?* (Cambridge: Cambridge University Press, 2007), 277.

18 President Lyndon Baines Johnson, Transcript, "Annual Message to the Congress on the State of the Union, January 8, 1964," LBJ Presidential Library.org, http://www.lbjlib.utexas.edu/johnson/archives.hom/speeches.hom/640108.asp. See also Thomas Sowell,

The Vision of the Anointed: Self-Congratulation as a Basis for Social Policy (New York: Basic Books, 1995), 9–10 (stated purpose of the "war on poverty" was a reduction in dependency).

19 See Robert Rector, "How the War on Poverty Was Lost," (opinion column) *Wall Street Journal*, January 8, 2014, A15.

20 See US Census Bureau, Carmen DeNavas-Walt et al., Current Population Reports, "Income, Poverty and Health Insurance Coverage in the United States: 2012," issued September 2013, 13, http://www.census.gov/hhes/www/poverty/data/incpovhlth/2012/index.html.

21 The government's method of measuring poverty is (characteristically) deeply flawed, as it based solely on income, and thus ignores people's ability to maintain a "normal" standard of living by drawing down their savings. Using a more realistic, consumption-based standard, economists have estimated that the poverty rate was only 5 percent in 2010. See Robert Samuelson, "How We Won—and Lost—the War on Poverty," RealClearPolitics.com, January 12, 2014 (quoting a study done by Bruce Meyer of the University of Chicago and James Sullivan of the University of Notre Dame), http://www.washingtonpost.com/opinions/robert-j-samuelson-how-we-won-and-lost-the-war-on-poverty/2014/01/12/9bf4696e-7a24-11e3-b1c5-739e63e9c9a7_story.html. Samuelson notes that according to this report, "Among the official poor, half have computers, 43 percent have central air conditioning and 36 percent have dishwashers," which suggests that measures of poverty based solely on income may not be appropriate.

22 See US Census Bureau, Carmen DeNavas-Walt et al., "Income and Poverty," 13.

23 See the data cited in the text of Chapter 11, under "Arguing for Libertarianism." Prior to the New Deal and, for all practical purposes, until the start of the "war on poverty," assistance to the destitute was primarily supplied by nongovernmental sources. The needy were served by religious institutions, fraternal organizations, mutual aid societies, trade unions, and private charities. Because of the availability of such assistance, there is no evidence of widespread deadly starvation in America even during the Great Depression. See William H. Young and Nancy K. Young, *The 1930s (American Popular Culture Through History)* (Westport, CT: Greenwood Publishing, 2002), 8; David T. Beito, *From Mutual Aid to the Welfare State: Fraternal Societies and Social Services, 1890–1967* (Chapel Hill, NC: University of North Carolina Press, 1999); and Yaron Brook and Don Watkins, "America Before the Entitlement

State," *Forbes*, January 16, 2012, 28. Sadly, here as in many other instances, the government's decision to provide a particular social good tends to crowd out the private supply of the same good.

24 Charles Murray, *What It Means to Be a Libertarian* (New York: Broadway Books, 1997), 51. He is citing here his earlier research in *Losing Ground: American Social Policy 1950–1980* (New York: Basic Books, 1984). The government's own data appear to support the claim that not only was poverty diminishing before the "war on poverty" began, but that this trend was even more pronounced for blacks and other minorities. In 1939, white year-round full-time male workers had a median wage or salary of $1,419, compared to $639 for nonwhites, a more than two-to-one gap. By 1957, this deficit had shrunk, as these figures were $4,950 and $3,137, respectively. A similar pattern is shown for female wages over these two decades. See US Department of Commerce, Bureau of the Census, *Historical Statistics of the United States, Colonial Times to 1957* (1960), Table Series G 147-168 ("Median Money Wage or Salary Income of All Workers With Wage or Salary Income, and of Year-Round Full-Time Workers, by Sex, Color, and Major Occupational Group: 1939–1957"), 168.

25 Department of Health and Human Services, "Fiscal Year 2013, Budget in Brief," http://www.hhs.gov/budget/. The state matching figure is from FY 2011, see Rector, "The Means-tested Welfare State," 15.

26 See Department of Health and Human Services, Centers for Medicare and Medicaid Services, "Report to Congress: 2012 Actuarial Report on the Financial Outlook for Medicaid," released March 1, 2013, iv, http://medicaid.gov/Medicaid-CHIP-Program-Information/By-Topics/Financing-and-Reimbursement/Downloads/medicaid-actuarial-report-2012.pdf.

27 See Avik Roy, "Four Reasons Why the Oregon Medicaid Results Are Even Worse Than They Look," *Forbes*.com, May 11, 2013, http://www.forbes.com/sites/theapothecary/2013/05/11/four-reasons-why-the-oregon-medicaid-results-are-even-worse-than-they-look/; Scott Gottlieb, "Medicaid is Worse Than No Coverage at All," (opinion column) *Wall Street Journal*, March 10, 2011, A17; and Nina Owcharenko, "Saving Medicaid: A Path to Comprehensive Medicaid Reform," Statement before Committee on Finance, U.S. Senate, July 7, 2011, http://www.heritage.org/research/testimony/2011/07/saving-medicaid-a-path-to-comprehensive-medicaid-reform.

There are several reasons for Medicaid's inferior performance. These include the federal mandate that each state provide the same package of benefits to all recipients, preventing the states from prioritizing care or offering different coverage to subgroups of beneficiaries. A closely related problem is that due to the comprehensive coverage mandate, program funding is spread thin, and the reimbursement rate for certain services is so low that many providers simply refuse to serve Medicaid patients. Finally, because medical care is usually offered with little in the way of co-pays or deductibles, and because free transportation to appointments is offered, there is overutilization of marginal services, reducing the availability of high-priority care.

28 See US Department of Health and Human Services, Administration for Children and Families, FY 2011 TANF Financial Data, "Chart A.1, Federal TANF and State MOE Expenditures Summary by ACF-196 Spending Category, FY 2011," http://www.acf.hhs.gov/sites/default/files/ofa/2011_tanf_data_with_states.pdf.

29 Except as otherwise indicated, the figures in this paragraph are from Rector, "Means-Tested Welfare State," 15-8 (Appendix).

30 See Centers for Medicare and Medicaid, Medicaid.gov, Affordable Care Act, "Eligibility" (undated, last accessed March 3, 2014), http://www.medicaid.gov/AffordableCareAct/Provisions/Eligibility.html; and Chris Edwards, "Food Subsidies," Cato Institute, July 2009, http://www.downsizinggovernment.org/agriculture/food-subsidies.

31 Nicholas Eberstadt, "Poor Statistics," (opinion column) *Forbes*, March 2, 2009.

32 See D. Michael Tanner and Tad DeHaven, "TANF and Federal Welfare," Cato Institute, September 2010, http://www.downsizinggovernment.org/hhs/welfare-spending; and Edwards, "Food Subsidies."

33 See Chris Edwards and Tad DeHaven, "Fraud and Abuse in Federal Programs," Cato Institute, August 2009, http://www.downsizinggovernment.org/fraud-and-abuse. The authors cite the Government Accounting Office's April 22, 2009 report titled "Improper Payments: Progress Made but Challenges Remain in Estimating and Reducing Improper Payments," which found $72 billion in improper payments made in 2008 under the federal programs it examined. For obvious reasons, it is impossible in most cases to distinguish outright fraud from payments made to ineligible recipients, and the GAO does not attempt to do so. The GAO found the following amounts of improper payments in our welfare programs: $33 billion (about 10.5 percent of total program spending) for Medicaid; $1.7 billion for food stamps;

$4.6 billion for SSI; $1.7 billion for TANF; $1.4 billion for school lunch benefits; $800 million for the Children's Health Insurance Program (constituting about 15 percent of benefits paid); $1 billion in rental housing subsidies for low-income tenants; and $12 billion in improper EITC payments (constituting almost one-third of all benefits). Edwards notes that some experts believe that the GAO report substantially understates the extent of Medicare and Medicaid fraud.

34 Tanner, "American Welfare State," 10.
35 See Douglas J. Besharov, Testimony, Subcommittee on Human Resources, Committee on Ways and Means, US House of Representatives, "Use of Technology to Improve the Administration of SSI's Financial Eligibility Requirements," July 25, 2012, 12–3, http://waysandmeans.house.gov/uploadedfiles/doug_besharov_testimony_hr072512.pdf; Tanner, "TANF and Federal Welfare," 5 (and sources cited there); and C. Eugene Steuerle, "The Widespread Prevalence of Marriage Penalties," Testimony Before the Subcommittee on the District of Columbia Committee on Appropriations, United States Senate, May 3, 2006, 5–6, 10–1, http://www.urban.org/uploadedpdf/900952_Steuerle_050306.pdf.
36 See John Karl Scholz et al., "Trends in Income Support," September 2, 2008, 19 ("We conclude that the tax and transfer system has measurable effects on the behavior of low-income families, with the strongest effects on reducing work effort"), http://www.econ.wisc.edu/~scholz/Teaching_742/Transfers_Chapter_2008_V6.pdf.
37 See James Sherk, "Effects of Unemployment Benefits," Heritage Foundation blog, May 13, 2010, http://blog.heritage.org/2010/05/13/effects-of-unemployment-benefits/.
38 See Elizabeth Dwoskin, "Why Americans Won't Do Dirty Jobs," BloombergBusinessweek.com, November 11, 2011, http://www.businessweek.com/magazine/why-americans-wont-do-dirty-jobs-11092011.html; and Aaron Smith, "Tons of Trucking Jobs . . . That Nobody Wants," CNN Money.com, July 24, 2012, http://money.cnn.com/2012/07/24/news/economy/trucking-jobs/.
39 See Janice Shaw Crouse, "Poverty Rates by Living Arrangements: 2000, 2007 & 2012," Beverly LaHaye Institute, *Data Digest* XIII, no. 1 (December 2013), http://www.cwfa.org/wp-content/uploads/2013/12/DD_BLI_Pov-rates-by-marital-status-living-arrangements-Dec-2013.pdf. Tanner reaches essentially the same conclusion: "children growing up in single parent families are four times more likely to be poor than children growing up in two-parent families." Tanner, "American Welfare State," 10.

40   See Steuerle, "Prevalence of Marriage Penalties," 6–7; and Scholz, "Trends in Income Support," 19, http://www.econ.wisc.edu/~scholz/Teaching_742/Transfers_Chapter_2008_V6.pdf.

41   The social costs that welfare dependency imposes on subsequent generations were understood even at the time we began our ill-stared war on poverty. Most famously, they were highlighted by the future Senator Daniel Patrick Moynihan when he was an obscure assistant secretary with the Department of Labor in his 1965 whitepaper, "The Negro Family: The Case for National Action." Available, with background information, in Lee Rainwater and W. L. Yancy, eds, *The Moynihan Report and the Politics of Controversy* (Cambridge, MA: MIT Press, 1967). Moynihan's concerns have proven to be well founded. For example, Tanner cites a 1988 study published in the highly respected journal *Science* that shows that "nearly 20 percent of daughters from families that were 'highly dependent' on welfare became 'highly dependent' themselves, whereas only 3 percent of daughters from non-welfare households became 'highly dependent.'" Studies have also shown a strong correlation between single-parent families and criminal activity by their children. See D. Michael Tanner and Tad DeHaven, "TANF and Federal Welfare," under "Breaking up Families," "Relationship to Crime Levels," and studies cited there in notes 32, 38–41. See also Rector, "War on Poverty" ("Children raised by single parents are three times more likely to end up in jail and 50% more likely to be poor as adults").

42   See Robert Rector, "Obama's End Run on Welfare Reform, Part One: Understanding Workfare," The Heritage Foundation, *Backgrounder*, No. 2730, September 19, 2012, 3, http://www.heritage.org/research/reports/2012/09/obamas-end-run-on-welfare-reform-part-one-understanding-workfare.

43   See ibid., 1.

44   See ibid., 4.

45   See ibid., 2. As Rector suggests, states have avoided federal penalties for failing to meet the statutory mandate regarding recipients' participation in work activities by "serving those with substantial barriers [to employment] through new solely state-funded programs." Heather Hahn et al., "TANF Work Requirements and State Strategies to Fulfill Them," Urban Institute, March 2012), under "How Do the States Meet the Work Requirement?" http://www.urban.org/UploadedPDF/412563-TANF-Work-Requirements-and-State-Strategies-to-Fulfill-Them.pdf. The same tactic is often used to avoid cutting people off benefits at the end of their five years of eligibility. Ibid.

46 Rector, "End Run Welfare Reform," 3–4.
47 To receive food stamps, participation in work or work-related activities is only required of recipients without dependent children. Section 8 housing subsidies are not conditioned on employment or even efforts to seek employment.
48 Marlin Stutzman and Michael Needham, "The 'Farm' Bill is No Such Thing," (opinion column) *Wall Street Journal*, August 2, 2012, A13.
49 President William Clinton, "Remarks at July 31, 1996 News Conference Following the US Senate's Passage of the Personal Responsibility and Work Opportunity Reconciliation Act of 1996," quoted in Charles P. Cozic, ed., *Welfare Reform* (San Diego, CA: Greenhaven Press, 1997), 41.
50 See Shapiro, *Welfare State Justified?* 233–42; and James Rolph Edwards, "The Costs of Public Income Redistribution and Private Charity," *Journal of Libertarian Studies* 21, no. 2 (Summer 2007), 10–6, http://mises.org/journals/jls/21_2/21_2_1.pdf.
51 See Edwards, "Redistribution and Private Charity," 3–5.
52 See Tarren Bragdon, "Florida's Medicaid Reform Shows the Way to Improve Health, Increase Satisfaction, and Control Costs," Heritage Foundation, *Backgrounder* 2620, November 9, 2011, http://www.heritage.org/research/reports/2011/11/floridas-medicaid-reform-shows-the-way-to-improve-health-increase-satisfaction-and-control-costs.
53 See Lloyd Dunkelberger, "Feds Approve Florida's Plan to Move Patients Into Managed Care," *Tallahassee Herald-Tribune*, February 20, 2013, http://politics.heraldtribune.com/2013/02/20/feds-approve-floridas-plan-to-move-medicaid-patients-into-managed-care/.
54 See Bragdon, "Florida's Medical Reform," 19. For another detailed analysis that endorses a block grant solution to Medicaid's chronic underperformance, see Linda Gorman, "Medicaid Block Grants and Medicaid Performance," Independence Institute, March 2012, http://healthcare.i2i.org/files/2012/03/IP_2_2012.pdf.

Chapter 8

1 See Andrew Young and Walter Block, "Enterprising Education: Doing Away with the Public School System," *International Journal of Value-Based Management* 12, 202–3 (1999), http://mises.org/daily/2216. The authors are describing, not endorsing, this argument.

2. See John Stuart Mill, *On Liberty* [1859] (London: Longmans, Green & Co., 1913), 62, http://books.google.com/books?id=f14SAAAAIAAJ&printsec=frontcover&source=gbs_ge_summary_r&cad=0#v=onepage&q&f=false.

3. See Milton Friedman, *Capitalism and Freedom* (Chicago: University of Chicago Press, 1982), 91–3.

4. Funding for the public schools comes from state income taxes, local property taxes, the federal income tax, and other taxes, none of which are paid exclusively or even predominantly by parents with children in the public schools. So, in additional to coercive taxation generally, we also have unjustified redistributive taxation between different segments of the population.

5. See Michael Flaherty, "The Latest Crime Wave: Sending Your Child to a Better School," (opinion column) *Wall Street Journal*, October 1–2, 2011, A13. Mr. Flaherty's essay describes the case of an Ohio single mother convicted on two felony counts of grand theft for enrolling her two children in what she regarded as a better public school outside her district. Ohio Governor John Kasich commuted her felonies to misdemeanors.

6. See Robert Balfanz et al., "Building a Grad Nation: Progress and Challenge in Ending the High School Dropout Epidemic, Annual Update, February 2013," America'sPromiseAlliance.org, 16–7, http://www.americaspromise.org/~/media/Files/Our%20Work/Grad%20Nation/Building%20a%20Grad%20Nation/BuildingAGradNation2013Full.ashx.

7. See Organization for Economic Cooperation and Development (OECD), "PISA 2012 Results in Focus," 5, http://www.oecd.org/pisa/keyfindings/pisa-2012-results-overview.pdf.

8. Quoted in Tim Walker, "What Do the 2012 PISA Scores Tell Us About U.S. Schools?" neatoday.org, December 3, 2013, http://neatoday.org/2013/12/03/what-do-the-2012-pisa-scores-tell-us-about-u-s-schools/.

9. Jay Greene, "Myths of the Teachers Unions," FrontPageMagazine.com, January 9, 2007, http://archive.frontpagemag.com/readArticle.aspx?ARTID=708.

10. See Andrew J. Coulson, "The Impact of Federal Involvement in America's Classrooms," Testimony Before Committee on Education & the Workforce United States House of Representatives, February 10, 2011, http://www.cato.org/publications/congressional-testimony/impact-federal-involvement-americas-classrooms.

11 See OECD (2013), *Education at a Glance 2013, OECD Indicators*, chapter B1, table B1.1a, http://dx.doi.org/10.1787/888932849350.

12 See Tess Stovall and Deirdre Dolan, "Incomplete: How Middle-Class Schools Aren't Making the Grade," Third Way, September 2011, http://thirdway.org/subjects/143/publications/435. See also Jason Richwine, PhD, "The Myth of Racial Disparities in Public School Funding," The Heritage Foundation, *Backgrounder* No. 2548, April 20, 2011; and Adam Schaeffer, "They Spend WHAT? The Real Cost of Public Schools," *Policy Analysis*, No. 662 (Washington, DC: Cato Institute, March 10, 2010), http://www.cato.org/publications/policy-analysis/they-spend-what-real-cost-public-schools.

The last report studied per capita spending levels for the five largest metropolitan school districts, plus the District of Columbia. It analyzed the funding for each central city school district, both on an official basis and as determined by the author, then compared it to the lowest and highest spending nearby districts. This report reveals that these districts underreported actual expenditures by an average of 44 percent, and that even using the official numbers, spending in districts with lower income residents is not significantly less than either the city-wide level or the national average. In fact, using the publically reported numbers, in two of the metropolitan areas (Chicago and Houston), spending in the low income district was *higher* than in the nearby affluent district.

13 See The Center for Education Reform, "Charter School Laws Across the States, Ranking and Scorecard," January 16, 2012, http://www.edreform.com/2013/01/annual-charter-school-law-report-card-issued/. To put the charter movement in some perspective, according to the National Center for Educational Statistics, as of 2011 only about 1.8 million K-12 students of the total student population of some 49 million, or about 3.6 percent, were attending charters. See National Center for Education Statistics, "Charter School Enrollment" (updated January 2013), http://nces.ed.gov/programs/coe/indicator_cgb.asp. Because of their rapid growth, the percentage is no doubt somewhat higher today.

14 The best evidence may be a recent study that tracked New York City students who were and were not selected by lottery to receive a relatively modest school voucher. The voucher could be used at any private school, but its value was only $1,400 per year (in 1998), insufficient even to fully pay for schooling at local Catholic parochial schools. These students were followed from kindergarten to college, and the authors claim to have controlled for all demographic factors other than the presence or absence of the voucher. This study

found that African-American students who received a voucher were 24 percent more likely to go on to college than those who remained in the public system. See Matthew M. Chingos and Paul E. Peterson, (opinion column) "A Generation of School-Voucher Success," *Wall Street Journal*, August 23, 2012, A13.

15 See National Center for Education Statistics, "Private School Enrollment" (updated January 2014), https://nces.ed.gov/programs/coe/indicator_cgc.asp.

16 See Schaeffer, "They Spend What?" 22–3. Median private school per pupil spending in the six metro areas studied was $9,173, and *tuition* was even less ($7,728), because about 20 percent of the cost is covered by non-tuition sources. This is considerably below the "official" average public school per capita spending in low-income districts ($11,580), and if the author's adjusted public school spending levels are correct ($15,221), quite substantially lower. The author uses median instead of average spending/tuition levels for private schools because the very high fees charged by a relatively few elite institutions distort the overall average, and in any case these schools do not represent a realistic option for typical parents.

17 Thankfully, although still small, there is a growing list of jurisdictions implementing voucher programs. As of early 2014, nine states, one Colorado county, and the District of Columbia have taxpayer funded programs, although they are often limited in size or restricted to certain types of students (e.g., special need). Other states have programs utilizing privately funded scholarships or tax credits. See American Federation for Children, "School Choice 101, Existing Programs, Voucher Programs in the United States," http://www.federationforchildren.org/existing-programs.

18 Federal aid to undergraduates consisted of grants ($45 billion), loans ($68 billion), and work-study/tax benefits ($18 billion), while aid to graduate students totaled almost $39 billion (mostly in the form of loans). See College Board (2013), "Trends in Student Aid 2013," 12–3, http://trends.collegeboard.org/student-aid. The figures are based on preliminary data.

19 See Douglas Belkin, *Wall Street Journal*, January 21, 2014, A2 (citing a report prepared by Illinois State University).

20 See *Fiscal Times*, October 28, 2010, "High College Dropout Rate Threatens U.S. Growth," http://www.thefiscaltimes.com/Articles/2010/10/28/High-College-Dropout-Rate-Threatens-US-Growth.aspx.

21 See Michael G. Morris, "Wanted: Ten Million Skilled Workers," *Washington Examiner*, November 13, 2011, http://www.washingtontimes.com/news/2011/nov/9/wanted-10-million-skilled-workers/.
22 See Steve Forbes, *Forbes*, "Dinosaur U.," February 28, 2011, 13.
23 See *Cato Handbook for Policymakers*, 7th edn (2009), chapter 21 ("Higher Education Policy"), prepared by Neal McCluskey, 231, http://www.cato.org/pubs/handbook/hb111/hb111-21.pdf.
24 See Rohit Chopra, "Too Big to Fail: Student Debt Hits a Trillion," Consumer Finance Protection Bureau, March 21, 2012, http://www.consumerfinance.gov/blog/too-big-to-fail-student-debt-hits-a-trillion/.
25 See College Board, "Trends in Student Aid," 21.

Chapter 9

1 For a catalog and description of the destructive effects of the federal and state regulation of health care and the sale of health care insurance, see *Cato Handbook for Policymakers*, 7th edn (Washington, DC: Cato Institute, 2009), chapter 15 ("Healthcare Regulation") and chapter 16 ("Health Insurance Regulation)," both prepared by Michael F. Cannon, http://www.cato.org/cato-handbook-policymakers/cato-handbook-policymakers-7th-edition-2009.
2 See, for example, Jeffrey L. Berlant, *Profession and Monopoly: A Study of Medicine in the United States and Great Britain* (Berkeley, CA: University of California Press, 1975), 177–252.
3 For example, see Lisa Katz, "Scope of Practice of Health Professionals in the State of Michigan," Public Sector Consultants, 2001, http://www.msms.org/Portals/0/Documents/ScopePracBook.pdf. See also Christine Vestal, "Nurse Practitioners Slowly Gaining Autonomy," *Kaiser Health News*, July 19, 2013, http://www.kaiserhealthnews.org/stories/2013/july/19/stateline-nurse-practitioners-scope-of-practice.aspx.
4 See Carolyne Krupa, "Medical Licensure: State Lines Pose Daunting Barriers," American Medical News.com (American Medical Association), September 17, 2012, http://www.amednews.com/article/20120917/profession/309179950/2/.
5 See *Cato Handbook for Policymakers*, 7th edn (Washington, DC: Cato Institute, 2009), chapter 14 ("The Tax Treatment of

Healthcare"), prepared by Michael F. Cannon, http://www.cato.org/cato-handbook-policymakers/cato-handbook-policymakers-7th-edition-2009.

6   As required by the Patient Protection and Affordable Care Act of 2010, this will partially change starting in January 2018, when so-called Cadillac insurance plans—those valued in excess of $27,500 annually for a family of four—will become subject to a 40 percent excise tax. See *Heath Affairs*, "Excise Tax on 'Cadillac' Plans," September 12, 2013, http://www.healthaffairs.org/healthpolicybriefs/brief.php?brief_id=99.

7   See Christopher J. Conover, "Featured Discussion: Understanding American Health Care, A Conversation With Christopher J. Conover," by Paul Howard, American Enterprise Institute, March 29, 2013, http://www.aei.org/article/featured-discussion-understanding-american-health-care-a-conversation-with-christopher-j-conover/. For the source of the 11.4 percent figure, see Note 45. In this interview, Conover states that the percentage of out-of-pocket payments is "just over 10 percent," which differs from the more accurate 11.4 percent estimate, almost certainly because he is relying on earlier, 2008 data.

8   Ibid.

9   Holman W. Jenkins, Jr., "The Young Won't Buy ObamaCare," (opinion column) *Wall Street Journal*, June 19, 2013, A13.

10 See Dr. Milton R. Wolf, "After Obamacare," (opinion column) *Washington Times*, June 21, 2012, http://www.washingtontimes.com/news/2012/jun/21/after-obamacare-997809127/; and *Cato Handbook* (chapter 16), 171–9.

All of the individual states mandate treatment for certain medical conditions and the right to receive treatment from certain categories of providers (in addition to the "conventional" ones), and some have as many as 69 specific requirements. According to one study, providing these benefits can drive up the cost of a policy by more than 50 percent. See Victoria C. Bunce, "Health Insurance Mandates in the States, 2012," Council for Affordable Health Insurance, April 9, 2013, http://www.cahi.org/article.asp?id=1115. Clearly, the effect of these mandates is to shift the mode of payment for health care away from out-of-pocket and toward third-party reimbursement.

11 The degree of the illegitimate coercion present in Medicare is much worse than commonly understood. Remarkably, as a result of obscure Social Security regulations written in 1993 under the Clinton Administration, and upheld against constitutional challenge

by the D.C. Circuit Court of Appeals in 2012, an individual eligible for Medicare cannot opt out of the program (i.e., disclaiming all reimbursement for Medicare services) without also forfeiting their Social Security benefits. See *Hall v. Sebelius*, 667 F.3d 1293 (D.C. Cir. 2012); and "Forced Into Medicare," Editorial, *Wall Street Journal*, March 24, 2011, A15. In January 2013, the Supreme Court denied the petition for certiorari filed in this case. See Ilya Shapiro, "Supreme Court Snubs Citizens Whose Social Security Will Be Confiscated If They Refuse Government Health Care," Cato at Liberty blog, January 25, 2013, http://www.cato.org/blog/supreme-court-snubs-citizens-whose-social-security-will-be-confiscated-they-refuse-government.

12 See Kelli Kennedy (Associated Press), "Medicare Yanks Licenses, Gives Them Right Back," Yahoo.com, October 16, 2011, http://news.yahoo.com/ap-medicare-yanks-licenses-gives-them-back-144410498.html.

13 See Merrill Matthew, "Scamming Uncle Sam," *Forbes*, May 10, 2010, 20.

14 In 2012, Medicare spent $536 billion, representing 21 percent of all US health care expenditures. See The Henry J. Kaiser Family Foundation, "Medicare Spending and Financing Fact Sheet," November 14, 2012, http://kff.org/medicare/fact-sheet/medicare-spending-and-financing-fact-sheet/. Obviously, for clinicians that specialize in treating the elderly, this percentage will be much higher.

15 Payroll taxes pay only 38 percent of the program's costs. The balance comes from general revenues (40%), beneficiary premiums (13%), state payments, and other minor sources. See ibid., under "Estimated Sources of Medicare Revenue, 2012" (Figure 3), http://kff.org/medicare/fact-sheet/medicare-spending-and-financing-fact-sheet/.

16 See, for example, Guy Boulton, "Efforts to Boost Number of Primary Care Physicians Face Pay Gap Hurdle," *Journal Sentinel Online*, December 1, 2012, http://www.jsonline.com/business/efforts-to-boost-number-of-primary-care-physicians-face-pay-gap-hurdle-la7r23f-181711331.html; and Annie Lowrey et al., "Doctor Shortage Likely to Worsen With Health Law," *New York Times*, July 28, 2012, http://www.nytimes.com/2012/07/29/health/policy/too-few-doctors-in-many-us-communities.html?_r=0.

17 See American Medical Association, "AMA Online Survey of Physicians: The Impact of Medicare Physician Payment on Seniors Access To Care," May 2010, http://www.ama-assn.org/resources/doc/washington/medicare-survey-results-0510.pdf.

18 See Greg Bengel, "Doctors Refuse to Accept Medicare Patients," *Healthcare Technology Online*, August 9, 2013, http://www.healthcaretechnologyonline.com/doc/doctors-refuse-to-accept-medicare-patients-0001. According to this source, 9,539 physicians dropped out of Medicare (meaning, neither they nor their patients can receive reimbursement from this program) in 2012, versus 3,700 in 2009. Almost certainly, a disproportionate number of these doctors were primary care practitioners.

19 See John Cogan, "The Millionaire Retirees Next Door," (opinion column) *Wall Street Journal*, May 12, 2011, A15; and Holman W. Jenkins, "Let's Begin Obama's 'Conversation' on Entitlements," (opinion column) *Wall Street Journal*, February 26–7, 2011, A15.

20 See John Goodman and Laurence Kotikoff, "Medicare by the Scary Numbers," (opinion column) *Wall Street Journal*, June 24, 2013, A15, http://online.wsj.com/article/SB10001424127887323393804578555461959256572.html. As the authors explain, even this staggering figure greatly underestimates our real liability because (i) the Medicare trustees were legally required to operate under the assumption that a 25 percent pay cut for physician reimbursement for treating Medicare patients would go into effect, even though Congress has uniformly nullified such cuts over the course of 15 years (aka the "doc fix") and (ii) the trustees assume that the cost-containment procedures mandated by ObamaCare will be effective, or the alternative method specified by the law—draconian cuts in fees to providers—will be implemented.

Medicare is one of our three major federal entitlement programs, the others being Social Security and federal employee pension benefits. According to one credible estimate, unfunded obligations for these three programs total some $87 trillion, meaning that this is the amount we would have to set aside *today* to fund them; so, we are not talking about far-in-the-future obligations that must be discounted to their present value. These liabilities are on top of the borrowings already incurred to pay for past spending, registered in the form of our national debt, now approaching $17.5 trillion. See Chris Cox and Bill Archer, "Why $16 Trillion Only Hints at the True U.S. Debt," (opinion column) *Wall Street Journal*, November 28, 2012, http://online.wsj.com/article/SB10001424127887323353204578127374039087636.html.

Unless drastic cuts are made to our federal entitlement programs over the next decade or so, or taxes increased substantially (which will choke off economic growth), we will have to borrow staggering sums in order to make good on our promises, raising our national debt to an unsustainable and dangerous level. The result of such irresponsibility is on display now in Greece, Italy, Portugal, and other European countries, and closer to home, in Detroit and Stockton. See Gene Epstein, "What, Me Worry?" *Barron's*, September 30, 2013, 21–3.

21 See Diana Furchtgott-Roth, "Medicare is Unsustainable in Current Form," MarketWatch.com, December 6, 2012, http://www.marketwatch.com/story/medicare-is-unsustainable-in-current-form-2012-12-06.

22 Even President Obama has recognized the need to reform Medicare (although he has made no serious effort to do so): "But with an aging population and rising health care costs, we are spending too fast to sustain the program. And if we don't gradually reform the system while protecting beneficiaries, it won't be there when future retirees need it. We have to reform Medicare to strengthen it." President Barack Obama, "Address to a Joint Session of Congress, September 8, 2011," http//www.whitehouse.gov/the-press-office/2011/09/08/address-president-joint-session-congress.

Medicare should be the "poster child" for politicians' inability to estimate the costs and thus the (relative) benefits of their massive social engineering projects. In 1967, 1 year after the legislation establishing Medicare became effective, the House Ways and Means Committee estimated that in 1990 the yearly cost would be $12 billion; the actual cost that year was $110 billion. See Conn Carroll, "Health Care Reform Cost Estimates: What is the Track Record?" Heritage Foundation, August 4, 2009, http://blog.heritage.org/2009/08/04/health-care-reform-cost-estimates-what-is-the-track-record/.

23 See Robert Samuelson, "The Folly of Obamacare," (opinion column) *Washington Post*, June 17, 2012, http://www.washingtonpost.com/opinions/robert-samuelson-the-folly-of-obamacare/2012/06/17/gJQAf5o1jV_story.html.

24 See Jason Kane, "Health Costs: How the U.S. Compares With Other Countries," PBS Newshour, October 22, 2012, http://www.pbs.org/newshour/rundown/2012/10/health-costs-how-the-us-compares-with-other-countries.html.

25 See Ricardo Alonso-Zaldivar (Associated Press), "Report: U.S. Health Care System Wastes $750B a Year," September 6, 2012, http://news.yahoo.com/report-us-health-care-system-wastes-750b-140106406.html.

26 New levies include a 3.8 percent tax on the investment income of high-income taxpayers; an increase of 0.9 percent in the Medicare payroll tax for these same persons; annual fees on health insurance

providers and the makers and importers of branded drugs; a 2.3 percent excise tax on the *sales* (not income) of manufacturers and importers of medical devices; and increasing the threshold for triggering the medical expense deduction from 7.5 percent to 10 percent of adjusted gross income. See Tom Wilemon, "Paying for Obamacare: Some Feel Singled Out," *Tennessean*, August 16, 2013, http://www.usatoday.com/story/news/nation/2013/08/18/paying-for-obamacare-some-feel-singled-out/2667879/; and Glenn Kessler (The Fact Checker blog), "Does 'Obamacare' Have $1 Trillion in Tax Hikes Aimed at the Middle Class?" *Washington Post*, March 12, 2013, http://www.washingtonpost.com/blogs/fact-checker/post/does-obamacare-have-1-trillion-in-tax-hikes-aimed-at-the-middle-class/2013/03/11/1e685f4c-8a9b-11e2-8d72-dc76641cb8d4_blog.html.

27 See Michael F. Cannon, "ObamaCare: The Plot Thickens," *Harvard Health Policy Review* 14, no. 1 (Spring 2013), 36, http://finance.townhall.com/columnists/michaelfcannon/2013/08/11/harvard-health-policy-review-on-the-irss-illegal-obamacare-taxes-n1661441. As described in this essay, there is a substantial constitutional issue regarding the authority of the federal government to pay subsidies to individuals for the purchase of policies on the state-level insurance exchanges it established after most of the individual states declined to do so.

28 See Kaiser Family Foundation, Health Reform, "Subsidy Calculator, Premium Assistance for Coverage in Exchanges," http://kff.org/interactive/subsidy-calculator/; and Editorial, "The Obamacare Bomb," *Washington Times*, September 9, 2013, http://www.washingtontimes.com/news/2013/sep/9/the-scheme-is-about-to-blow-up-the-ince-8889143/.

29 See Scott Gottlieb, "Meet the ObamaCare Mandate Committee," (opinion column) *Wall Street Journal*, February 16, 2012; and Christopher J. Conover, "Health Reform Breaks Bad," *Weekly Standard* 19, no. 7, October 21, 2013, http://www.weeklystandard.com/articles/health-reform-breaks-bad_762272.html.

30 See Peter Grier, "Millions Losing Health Plans Under Obamacare. Did President Mislead?" *Christian Science Monitor*, October 29, 2013, http://news.yahoo.com/millions-losing-health-plans-under-obamacare-did-president-165108996.html.

31 See Conover, "Breaks Bad"; and Darius Tahir, "Narrow-Network Health Plans Expected to Proliferate Under Obamacare," NationalJournal.com, October 9, 2013, http://www.nationaljournal.com/innovations-in-health/narrow-network-health-plans-expected-to-proliferate-under-obamacare-20131009.

32. See Megan McArdle, "Is Obamacare in a Death Spiral?" BloombergNews.com, October 21, 2013, http://www.bloomberg.com/news/2013-10-21/is-obamacare-in-a-death-spiral-.html.

33. See Avik Roy, "Yet Another White House Obamacare Delay: Out-of-Pocket Caps Waived Until 2015," *Forbes*.com, August 13, 2013, http://www.forbes.com/sites/theapothecary/2013/08/13/yet-another-white-house-obamacare-delay-out-of-pocket-caps-waived-until-2015/.

34. See *Kaiser Health News*, "Budget Report: More Employers Than Previously Estimated Will Drop Health Coverage," February 6, 2013, http://www.kaiserhealthnews.org/daily-reports/2013/february/06/cbo-and-employer-insurance.aspx; US Senator Ron Johnson, "Obamacare's Costs are Soaring," (opinion column) *Wall Street Journal*, March 21, 2012, A11; and Chris Burritt, "Home Depot Sending 20,000 Part-Timers to Health Exchanges," BloombergNews.com, http://www.bloomberg.com/news/2013-09-19/home-depot-sending-20-000-part-timers-to-health-exchanges.html.

35. In 2012, one-third of workers at relatively larger employers (over 200 employees) had coverage that included deductibles of $1,000 or more, compared to 10 percent in 2006. See Timothy Martin and Christopher Weaver, "Burden Shifts on Insurance," *Wall Street Journal*, September 18, 2013, A1. See also Jay Hancock, "FAQ: How Employer-Sponsored Health Insurance is Changing," *Kaiser Health News*, September 17, 2013, http://www.kaiserhealthnews.org/stories/2013/september/17/employer-sponsored-health-insurance-trends.aspx; and Eric Morath, "Health-Care Inflation the Slowest in 50 Years," *Wall Street Journal*, September 18, 2013, A6. The latter story cites a Price Waterhouse survey showing that the percentage of employers offering only a high-deductible plan increased from 13 percent in 2012 to 17 percent in 2013. As reported, "These plans typically require patients to use health savings accounts to pay the first *several thousand dollars of costs*" (my emphasis).

36. Ira Stoll, "Unhappy Labor Day: Obamacare Edition," Reason.com, September 2, 2013 (quoting Casey B. Mulligan, a professor of economics at the University of Chicago), http://reason.com/blog/2013/09/02/ira-stoll-unhappy-labor-day-obamacare-ed.

37. Ibid. See also Daniel P. Kessler, "How Health Reform Punishes Work," (opinion column) *Wall Street Journal*, April 25, 2011, A15.

38. Professor Mulligan's claim that ObamaCare includes significant disincentives for work was recently confirmed by the Congressional Budget Office. See Louise Radnofsky and Damien Paletta, "Health

Law to Cut Into Labor Force," *Wall Street Journal*, February 5, 2014, A1 (citing a February 2014 CBO report to the effect that "the new health law is projected to reduce the total number of hours Americans work by the equivalent of 2.3 million full-time jobs in 2021").

39 Peter Suderman, "Obamacare Savings Program Shows Partial Success—But Will It Last?" Reason.com, July 19, 2013, http://reason.com/blog/2013/07/19/obamacare-savings-program-shows-partial.

40 James C. Capretta, "Reforming Medicare Integrated Care: An Alternative to the Obama Administration's Accountable Care Organizations," American Enterprise Institute, August 21, 2013, http://www.aei.org/outlook/health/healthcare-reform/ppaca/reforming-medicare-integrated-care-an-alternative-to-the-obama-administrations-accountable-care-organizations/.

41 See Scott Gottlieb, "The Doctor Won't See You Now. He's Clocked Out," (opinion column) *Wall Street Journal*, March 15, 2013. Gottlieb suggests that part of this trend may result from the ACA's expanding and strengthening the existing federal mandate requiring *all* medical offices to install and use a system of electronic health records for their patients. Small medical practices find this burdensome, and it provides an added incentive for these physicians to give up their independence and become hospital employees or to work for hospital-owned groups.

42 Ibid.

43 See Jenny Gold, "FAQ On ACOs: Accountable Care Organizations, Explained," *Kaiser Health News* (Henry J. Kaiser Foundation), August 23, 2013, http://www.kaiserhealthnews.org/stories/2011/january/13/aco-accountable-care-organization-faq.aspx.

44 The Independent Payment Advisory Board ("IPAB") is subject to virtually no Congressional oversight, and is empowered to make deep cuts in Medicare expenditures, while being barred from rationing care. But, of course, the only way to control costs by administrative means is to either cut reimbursement rates to providers or refuse to cover certain treatments altogether. For obvious reasons, both methods will limit the *availability* of care ("rationing" by another name), and will provoke the ire of patients and doctors. Howard Dean, a prominent Democratic politician and supporter of the ACA, writes that "rate-setting—the essential mechanism of the IPAB—has a 40-year track record of failure." Later in this piece, he notes that the primary effect of these sorts of controls is to "drive up administrative costs." Howard Dean, "The

Affordable Care Act's Rate-Setting Won't Work," (opinion column) *Wall Street Journal*, July 28, 2013, http://online.wsj.com/article/SB10001424127887324110404578628542498014414.html. See also David B. Rivkin and Elizabeth Foley, "An ObamaCare Board Answerable to No One," (opinion column) *Wall Street Journal*, June 20, 2013, A21, http://online.wsj.com/news/articles/SB10001424127887324634304578539823614996636.

45 See Centers for Medicare and Medicaid Services, "National Health Expenditure Projections, 2012–2022," September 18, 2012, http://www.cms.gov/Research-Statistics-Data-and-Systems/Statistics-Trends-and-Reports/NationalHealthExpendData/NationalHealthAccountsProjected.html. It would be imprudent to place too much stock in long-range economic forecasts by government officials, and central planning is an unpromising technique for controlling costs. Accordingly, if our past experience with Medicare is any guide (see Note 22), it is likely that expenditures will far exceed the official prediction.

46 Currently the American Board of Medical Specialties, a private, nonprofit institution, certifies such competence in 24 different practice areas. See the American Board of Medical Specialties website, http://www.abms.org/.

47 See Matt Palumbo, "How the Free Market Can Cure Health Care," *American Thinker*, December 17, 2011, http://www.americanthinker.com/2011/12/how_the_free_market_can_cure_health_care.html#! And, see generally Christopher J. Conover, "Featured Discussion"; and Andrew Foy, MD, "The Medical Marketplace, Free and Unfree," *Mises Daily*, June 17, 2011, http://mises.daily.org/daily/5359/The-Medical-Marketplace-Free-and-Unfree.

48 John H. Cochrane, "What to do About Pre-existing Conditions," (opinion column) *Wall Street Journal*, August 14, 2009, http://online.wsj.com/article/SB10001424052970203609204574316172512242220.html.

49 A substantial minority of those now uninsured could afford coverage, but decline to purchase it. Our estimate of the size of this population depends on the assumptions we make about what is "affordable." According to Census Bureau data for 2011, 31 percent of Americans without health insurance live in households with incomes in excess of $50,000, including 15 percent with incomes in excess of $75,000. See Mark J. Perry, "31% of Americans Without Health Insurance Live in Households Making $50k or More, and 38% are Between 18–34 Years Old," American Enterprise Institute blog, October 5, 2012, http://www.aei-ideas.org/2012/10/31-of-

americans-without-health-insurance-live-in-households-making-50k-or-more-and-38-are-between-18–34-years-old/.

President Obama, and those who support the ACA, typically speak as if being uninsured is equivalent to not receiving medical care, but this is plainly false. The uninsured do get care: according to one study, the uninsured received a total of $116 billion worth in 2008 (the most recent data I could find). See Robert Samuelson, "Naive, Hypocritical and Dishonest," Real Clear Politics, June 15, 2009, http://www.realclearpolitics.com/articles/2009/06/15/wrong-way_health_reform_96997.htm (citing a study by Families USA). This study reports that the uninsured pay for about 30 percent of their care out-of-pocket, about an equal percentage is uncompensated, and the rest is paid for by the government or charities. Ibid. It is not clear that the uninsured would have materially better health care outcomes if they were covered, once we control for such confounding sociological factors as education, obesity, smoking, and so on. See ibid; and Daniel P. Kessler, (opinion column) "ObamaCare's Broken Promises," *Wall Street Journal*, February 1, 2013, A13.

50 The ACA dramatically expands eligibility for access to the badly flawed Medicaid program (see Chapter 7), especially for low-income, single adults. It encourages states to cooperate by providing that the federal government will cover all of the incremental cost for the first 3 years, gradually decreasing to 90 percent by 2020. Fearful that this 90 percent commitment will be unsustainable, about half of the states have refused to expand their programs or are considering alternatives to the conventional program. See The Advisory Board Company, "Beyond the Pledges: Where the States Stand on Medicaid," September 17, 2013, http://www.advisory.com/Daily-Briefing/Resources/Primers/MedicaidMap.

51 See Peter J. Cunningham and Ann S. O'Malley, "Do Reimbursement Delays Discourage Medicaid Participation By Physicians?" *Health Affairs* 28, no. 1 (2009), w17–w28, http://content.healthaffairs.org/content/28/1/w17.full.html.

52 In 2011, Representative Paul Ryan proposed to end Medicare as we know it by, beginning in 2022, eliminating traditional fee-for-service reimbursement and replacing it, for *new beneficiaries only*, with a voucher worth $8,000 for private insurance. During the 2012 presidential campaign, he added various sweeteners to make it more politically palatable. See Chris Good, "Paul Ryan's 2011 Medicare Plan: A Primer," ABC News.com, August 11, 2012, http://abcnews.go.com/blogs/politics/2012/08/paul-ryans-2011-medicare-plan-a-primer/.

53 As of this writing, the VA is embroiled in a nasty scandal arising from the revelation that high-level officials appear to have directed staff to cover up the rationing of care. See "VA to Send More Vets to Private Care," Associated Press, May 24, 2014, http://www.modernhealthcare.com/article/20140524/INFO/305249941. In my judgment, this is a harbinger of scandals to come under the ACA as we move ever farther away from free market medicine.

54 See John H. Cochrane, "What to Do When ObamaCare Unravels," *WallStreetJournal*.com, December 25, 2013 (arguing for deregulation of health care, and a transition to individual, catastrophic healthcare insurance), http://online.wsj.com/news/articles/SB10001424052702304866904579265932490593594.

Chapter 10

1 See Ayn Rand, "Objectivist Ethics," in *The Virtue of Selfishness* (New York: Signet Books, 1970), 16–20.

2 Murray Rothbard, *The Ethics of Liberty*, with a new introduction by Hans-Herman Hoppe (New York: New York University Press, 1998), 34, http://mises.org/rothbard/ethics/ethics.asp.

3 I have previously discussed each of these topics in some depth on my blog, NaturalRightsLibertarian.com, and accordingly this chapter may include scattered quotes or paraphrased passages from these posts.

4 Section 3.3 (International Affairs) of the Libertarian Party's 2012 platform (http://www.lp.org/platform) provides:

> American foreign policy should seek an America at peace with the world. Our foreign policy should emphasize defense against attack from abroad and enhance the likelihood of peace by avoiding foreign entanglements. We would end the current U.S. government policy of foreign intervention, including military and economic aid.

See also *Cato Handbook for Policymakers*, 7th edn (2009), chapter 19 (The Defense Budget), prepared by Benjamin Friedman, http://www.cato.org/pubs/handbook/hb111/hb111-19.pdf.

5 Rothbard, *The Ethics of Liberty*, 190.

6 See George H. Smith, "Thinking About War," *Liberty*, May 2008, part III, posted on Ozarkia.net, http://www.ozarkia.net/bill/anarchism/library/ThinkingAboutWar.html. Rothbard's argument also implies that an internal revolt against an absolute despot would

also be immoral if it would foreseeably lead to the death of even a few innocent non-combatants.

7. Nozick says nothing about the DDE in *ASU*, but endorses a version of it in his 1977 essay "War, Terrorism, Reprisals—Drawing Some Moral Lines," collected in Robert Nozick, *Socratic Puzzles* (Cambridge: Harvard University Press, 1997), 300–4. See also Eric Mack, "Rights, Just War, and National Defense," in Tibor Machan and Douglas B. Rasmussen, eds, *Liberty for the Twenty-First Century: Contemporary Libertarian Thought* (Latham, MD: Rowman & Littlefield, 1995), 105–7, 111; and Fernando R. Teson, "Targeted Killing in War and Peace: A Philosophical Analysis," in Claire Finkelstein et al., eds, *Targeted Killing: Morality and Law in an Asymmetrical World* (Oxford: Oxford University Press, 2012), chapter 16.

8. Alison McIntyre, s.v. "The Doctrine of Double Effect," in Edward N. Zalta, ed., *The Stanford Encyclopedia of Philosophy* (Fall 2011 Edition), introduction, http://plato.stanford.edu/archives/fall2011/entries/double-effect/.

9. For an example, see Chandran Kukathas, "The Mirage of Global Justice," *Social Philosophy and Policy* 28, no. 1 (2006), 1–28.

10. See Roger Donway, "The War Over Libertarian Foreign Policy," TheAtlasSociety.org, January 26, 2011, http://www.atlassociety.org/tni/war-over-libertarian-foreign-policy.

11. Rothbard, *Ethics of Liberty*, 187.

12. Aeon Skoble, "War and Liberty," *Reason Papers* 28 (Spring 2006), 45; and see also Randy Barnett, "Antiwar Libertarians and the Reification of the State," July 20, 2007, TheVolokhConspiracy.com, http://www.volokh.com/posts/1184891247.shtml.

13. There is a distinctly libertarian argument against humanitarian interventions. It draws on the fact that regardless of the moral merit of defending the innocent against murder by their own state, such intervention can only take place through impermissible means; that is, coercive taxes. Although we operate with a volunteer military, taxation for purposes of national defense is compulsory, and it may be asserted that such coercion is only morally justified because it supplies an essential public good that benefits all taxpayers. Levies to defend far-off strangers cannot be defended on this basis.

Powerful though it may be, I don't believe this argument excludes *all* humanitarian interventions because, as we have observed in other contexts, side constraints are not absolute. They may be relaxed in order to avoid what Nozick terms "catastrophic moral horror," and there are certainly cases where the potential costs of a humanitarian intervention are so low compared to the benefits, that action can be justified on this basis.

14 In traditional just war theory, in order for a war to be just, not only must there be a just cause, but the political leaders initiating it must also have the right intentions; it must be conducted under proper authority and with a public declaration; it must be the last resort; there must be a reasonable probability of success; and there must be proportionality between the overall expected benefits and harms. See Brian Orend, s.v. "War," *Stanford Encyclopedia Philosophy* (Fall 2008 Edition), section 2.1, http://plato.stanford.edu/archives/fall2008/entries/war/.

The major competitors to just war theory are realism and pacifism. Realism holds that ethical considerations simply have no place in war which, so to speak, takes place in a realm that is beyond good and evil. At the other extreme, pacifism holds that war can never be morally justified. Ibid. For reasons that are not entirely clear to me, very few, if any, natural rights libertarians subscribe to either of these competing theories.

15 See John Locke, *Two Treatises of Government*, edited and with an introduction by Peter Laslett (Cambridge: Cambridge University Press), Second Treatise, Chap. III, sections 16–9. Roger Donway suggests this argument when, in reference to the strategic options open to a relatively just nation surrounded by lawless aggressors, he writes: "The first order of business is for civilized people to defend themselves, certainly. But not wanting to live forever in an armed camp, their long-range goal would be to use persuasion and force to bring their neighbors into a condition of peace and freedom." Donway, "Libertarian Foreign Policy." See also Smith, "Thinking About War," part III.

16 See Robert Higgs, *Crisis and Leviathan* (Oxford: Oxford University Press, 1987) and Robert Higgs, "Are Questions of War and Peace Merely One Issue Among Many for Libertarians?" *Independent Review* (Fall 2011), http://www.independent.org/publications/tir/article.asp?a=856.

17 Alexander DeConde, *A History of American Foreign Policy*, 2nd edn (New York: Charles Scribner's Sons, 1971), 585–602.

18 Interestingly, the need for America to develop and maintain a credible nuclear deterrent against the USSR in the early 1970s was the subject of a heated debate between Rothbard and John Hospers, a distinguished academic philosopher and Libertarian Party candidate for president in 1972. As one might guess, Hospers argued that the Soviets were a real danger, and that military

deterrence was morally justified, while Rothbard disagreed. See John Hospers, "Hospers Replies" and Murray Rothbard, "The Editor Rebuts," *The Libertarian Forum*, February 1973, 2–5, https://mises.org/journals/lf/1973/1973_02.pdf.

19 For an instructive intra-libertarian debate on this subject, see Roger Pilon and Richard Epstein, "NSA Surveillance in Perspective," (opinion column) *Chicago Tribune*, June 12, 2013, http://articles.chicagotribune.com/2013-06-12/opinion/ct-perspec-0612-nsa-20130612_1_nsa-national-security-agency-privacy (defending the NSA's collection of metadata) and Julian Sanchez, "A Reply to Epstein and Pilon on the NSA's Metadata Program," Cato Institute, Cato at Liberty blog, June 16, 2013, http://www.cato.org/blog/reply-epstein-pilon-nsas-metadata-program (condemning the NSA's surveillance under libertarian principles).

20 See Randy E. Barnett, "Libertarians and the War," (opinion column) *Wall Street Journal*, July 17, 2007, http://online.wsj.com/news/articles/SB118463507387568429.

21 Agnieska Jaworska and Julie Tannenbaum, s.v. "The Grounds of Moral Status," *Stanford Encyclopedia Philosophy* (Summer 2013 Edition), introduction, http://plato.stanford.edu/archives/sum2013/entries/grounds-moral-status/.

22 See, for example, Mary Ann Warren, "On the Moral and Legal Status of Abortion" [originally published 1973] and "A Postscript on Infanticide" [1982], in Thomas A. Mappes and David DeGarzia, eds, *Biomedical Ethics*, 5th edn (New York: McGraw-Hill, 2001), 456–62; and Peter Singer, *Practical Ethics*, 3rd edn (Cambridge: Cambridge University Press, 2011), chapter 6.

23 A number of pro-choice philosophers accept that there is no principled way to distinguish the moral status of a newborn and fetus. Rather than conceding that this equivalence implies that (at least a late-term) fetus has FMS, they draw the appalling conclusion that the newborn *also* lacks rights, so that if the parents or other members of the community do not wish to care for the baby, it may be killed or left to die. Warren acknowledges that "It remains true that according to my argument neither abortion nor the killing of neonates is properly considered a form of murder." Warren, "Postscript," 462. She then immediately observes that killing or allowing newborns to die is not wrong if the society into which they are born is so impoverished that it is not possible to care for the newborn "without endangering the survival of existing persons." Ibid. I am unclear if Warren thinks that this observation somehow exonerates her earlier statement or if she just wishes to change the

subject, but it clearly does not. On her logic, killing a newborn with the proverbial silver spoon in its mouth would not constitute murder.

Singer's position is no less chilling. He argues that although the newborn has no rights, as a matter of fact healthy newborns will not be left to die because severely handicapped, and thus unwelcome, fetuses will be aborted, and only those desired by their parents will be carried to term. But as a philosophical position, this is no different than Warren's. The newborn either has FMS or it doesn't, under extremely optimistic empirical assumptions this might not matter, but if a healthy newborn is killed by its parents, they have not committed murder according to Singer. See Singer, *Practical Ethics*, 151–4.

24 See Don Marquis, "Why Abortion is Immoral," *The Journal of Philosophy* 86 (April, 1989), 183–202; and Don Marquis, "Singer on Abortion and Infanticide," chapter 3 in Jeffrey A. Schaler, ed., *Peter Singer Under Fire: The Moral Iconoclast Faces His Critics* (LaSalle, IL: Open Court, 2009).

25 Marquis's account of the harm done by killing is persuasive, less so its analysis of the identity, for normative purposes, of the embryo and the adult. He accepts that "according to the future of value theory, the embryo that was my precursor had the right to life only if that embryo was an earlier stage of the same individual I am." Marquis, *Singer Under Fire*, 150. But I am not convinced that "sameness" is properly determined by biology alone. While a 3-week-old collection of human cells may be the biological precursor of the adult, it is a radically different *being*. Until it is *capable* of consciousness, the embryo is arguably no different from the ethical perspective than a germ or even an inanimate object. Therefore, a very early fetus, regardless of its potential, may not be the *same* individual, in the morally relevant sense, as the person it develops into.

26 Ayn Rand, "Of Living Death," in *The Voice of Reason: Essays in Objectivist Thought* (New York: Plume, 1990), 57–8, http://aynrandlexicon.com/lexicon/abortion.html.

27 Nozick does not expressly address the question of abortion rights, but what he has to say on a somewhat different topic suggests that he rejects Rand's view. He claims that for a being to justly make moral demands on others, it must "be a seeker after value, someone who searches for value and guides her behavior by value considerations." He then adds, "I should emphasize that the characteristic of being a value seeking I is a capacity or

potentiality—infants and unconscious people have it." Robert Nozick, *Philosophical Investigations* (Cambridge: Harvard University Press, 1981), 457.

28 See Mark D. Friedman, *Nozick's Libertarian Project: An Elaboration and Defense* (London: Continuum International, 2011), 11–5.
29 See Ayn Rand, "A Last Survey," in *The Ayn Rand Letter 1971–1976* (New York: Second Renaissance Press 1990), 2–3, http://aynrandlexicon.com/lexicon/abortion.html.
30 Rothbard, *Ethics of Liberty*, 98.
31 Rothbard concedes that while it *might* be morally wrong to abort a healthy late-term fetus, this choice is a matter of personal morality that should be shielded from interference by the authorities. See ibid., 98, Note 2. But this distinction is incoherent in this context. Until an existing (unjust) state can be replaced by something better, those who run it are morally obligated to promulgate and enforce laws against murder and other acts of unprovoked violence against the innocent. Thus, *if* late-term abortion constitutes something close to murder, it should be criminalized.
32 Rothbard is hardly alone in relying on self-ownership as an argument for a pro-choice stance on abortion. In a well-known paper on this subject, the philosopher Judith Jarvis Thomson put forward an argument similar to Rothbard's. See Judith Jarvis Thomson, "A Defense of Abortion," *Philosophy and Public Affairs* 1, no. 1 (Autumn 1971), 47–66. Thomson asks her readers to imagine a case in which you wake up one morning and discover that you have been kidnapped for purposes of saving the life of a famous violinist, whose kidneys have failed. The violinist's circulatory system has been plugged into your own, so for the next 9 months you will rest side-by-side with him until he recovers. At this point he will be cured, and you may then unplug. You should, Thomson declares, find this demand "outrageous" (ibid., 49), because "if a human being has any just, prior claim to anything at all, he has a just, prior claim to his own body" (ibid., 54).

We would find this outrageous, but this situation is not analogous to the abortion choice. First, except for cases of rape, the women carrying the fetus was not "kidnapped." She engaged in sexual intercourse for her own purposes, knowing that if she did not protect herself, she could quite easily end up with a "violinist" attached to her. This fact alone makes the situation facing a woman who became pregnant this way far less outrageous than suggested by Thomson, and strengthens the case for requiring the woman not to abort.

Moreover, if we accept the commonsense view that FMS obtains when the fetus gains consciousness, but not before, then another disanalogy is apparent. Unlike in Thomson's case, a pregnant woman can avoid killing the "violinist" by having the abortion at an earlier point in gestation. In Thomson's analogy, we should imagine that the kidnapped woman is free to unplug immediately, and if she does so, the violinist's friends can save his life by dialysis. On the other hand, if she delays for a few months, this option will be foreclosed. In this scenario, if the woman chooses to wait until dialysis is no longer an option, I think it is clear that she would be doing a serious wrong by unplugging, absent extenuating circumstances. Perhaps these arguments are not decisive, but I believe they are certainly sufficient to show that neither is Thomson's thought experiment.

33 See Matt Zwolinski, "How Not to Argue for Libertarianism," Bleeding Heart Libertarians.com, May 10, 2011, http://bleedingheartlibertarians.com/2011/05/how-not-to-argue-for-libertarianism/.

34 Indeed, academic philosopher Edward Feser argues in-depth that on the most plausible interpretation of "self-ownership," even a fetus in an early stage of development qualifies, and that abortion is therefore morally wrong. See Edward Feser, "Self-Ownership, Abortion, and the Rights of Children: Toward a More Conservative Libertarianism," *Journal of Libertarian Studies* 18, no. 3 (Summer 2004), 95–104.

35 Rothbard, *Ethics of Liberty*, 100.

36 Former Congressman Ron Paul, the most prominent libertarian politician of his generation, is pro-life, and makes the same basic point. See Ron Paul, *The Revolution: A Manifesto* (Grand Central Publishing, 2009), 59.

37 See Rothbard, *Ethics of Liberty*, 85.

38 See, for example, Michael Huemer, "Is There a Right to Immigrate?" *Social Theory and Practice* 36, no. 3 (July 2010), 429–61; Bas Van Der Vossen, "Reasons for Open Borders," BleedingHeartLibertarians.com, August 9, 2013, http://bleedingheartlibertarians.com/2013/08/reasons-for-open-borders/; and Bryan Caplan, "Why Should We Restrict Immigration?" *Cato Journal* 32, no. 1 (Winter 2012), 5–24, http://www.cato.org/cato-journal/winter-2012.

39 See Huemer, "Right to Immigrate."

40 Ibid., 430.

41 Ibid., 433–4.
42 See, for example, John Hospers, "A Libertarian Argument Against Open Borders," *Journal of Libertarian Studies* 13, no. 2 (Summer 1998), 153–65, http://mises.org/journals/jls/13_2/13_2_3.pdf.
43 Caplan, "Should We Restrict Immigration?" 13. Note that by acknowledging that open borders pose the potential for "political externalities," Caplan concedes that citizens have something like a property right in their political culture. In other words, only in the context of property ownership or rights (e.g., to fresh air), does it make sense to speak of externalities. Caplan discusses the possibility that unlimited migration might move our politics in a more statist direction, and concludes that this risk is minimal. He further argues that if we disagree with his assessment, we should simply eliminate or condition the voting rights of the immigrant population. Ibid., 12–7. But Caplan, like Huemer, does not discuss the rights-based argument against open borders made in the text.
44 See Huemer, "Right to Immigrate," 447–50.
45 Ibid., 449.
46 How great an actual (objective) risk must there be to the rule of law before restrictions on immigration are warranted? As in the case of conflicts regarding land usage rights (see Chapter 1), I see no alternative but the resort to the standard established by the affected community's (i.e., our citizenry's) tolerance for risks of this sort. I confess that I do not know an effective way to measure such sentiment with respect to the potential loss of basic rights, other than through the political process.
47 Although he reaches this conclusion on the basis of a Hayekian analysis of the conditions that will promote human flourishing, libertarian-minded economist Julian Simon holds that:

> it seems reasonable and acceptable for a given population of individuals, at the governmental level of the nation-state, to assert that they have a property right in their social and economic organization. That means that under some circumstances, it may be appropriate for them to decide how many and which potential immigrants are allowed to enter. But it is ridiculously easy to concoct a supposed threat from immigrants to the economic stability and predictability of the nation-state.

Julian L. Simon, "Are There Grounds for Limiting Immigration?" *Journal of Libertarian Studies* 13, no. 2 (Summer 1998), 152.

He thinks, therefore, that the ability of the majority to limit entry should be restricted to situations that present a "clear-and-present danger." Ibid. However, apart from his apparent concern that, as a practical matter, the political process will be used to unfairly exclude immigrants, he offers no *philosophical* argument in support of this very stringent standard.

48 The 1.6 billion figure comes from Pew Research Center, "Religion & Public Life Project: The Global Landscape: Muslims," December 18, 2012, http://www.pewforum.org/2012/12/18/global-religious-landscape-muslim/.

49 See Pew Research Center, "The World's Muslims: Religion, Politics and Society," April 30, 2013, http://www.pewforum.org/2013/04/30/the-worlds-muslims-religion-politics-society-overview/. Within this summary are links to more specific data.

50 A majority of respondents in three of the five regions covered believe that women should not have the right of divorce. Majorities in four out of five regions reported (all except Southern-Eastern Europe) believe that a woman must always obey her husband.

51 See Pew Research Center, "Muslim Publics Share Concerns About Extremist Groups," September 10, 2013, http://www.pewglobal.org/2013/09/10/muslim-publics-share-concerns-about-extremist-groups/.

52 See Kristin Powers, "A Global Slaughter of Christians, but America's Churches Stay Silent," TheDailyBeast.com, September 27, 2013, http://www.thedailybeast.com/articles/2013/09/27/a-global-slaughter-of-christians-but-america-s-churches-stay-silent.html; and Christa Case Bryant, "What the Middle East Would be Like Without Christians," *Christian Science Monitor*, December 22, 2013, http://www.csmonitor.com/World/Middle-East/2013/1222/What-the-Middle-East-would-be-like-without-Christians.

53 See Philip Jenkins, "Mystical Power: Why Sufi Muslims, for Centuries the Most Ferocious Soldiers of Islam, Could be our Most Valuable Allies in the Fight Against Extremism," BostonGlobe.com, January 25, 2009, http://www.boston.com/bostonglobe/ideas/articles/2009/01/25/mystical_power/?page=full; and Stephan Schwartz, "How Many Sufis are There in Islam," July 20, 2011, HuffingtonPost.com, http://www.huffingtonpost.com/stephen-schwartz/how-many-sufis-in-world-i_b_902164.html.

54 See Daniel Pipes, *The Rushdie Affair: The Novel, the Ayatollah, and the West*, 2003 edn (Piscataway, NJ: Transaction Publishers), 169–71. See also Wikipedia.com, s.v. "*The Satanic Verses* Controversy," http://en.wikipedia.org/wiki/The_Satanic_Verses_controversy.

55 See Wikipedia, s.v. "*Jyllands-Posten* Muhammad Cartoons Controversy," http://en.wikipedia.org/wiki/Jyllands-Posten_Muhammad_cartoons_controversy.

56 Yale University Press, "Statement by John Donatich, Director of Yale University Press," September 9, 2009, http://yalepress.yale.edu/yupbooks/KlausenStatement.asp.

57 Other reported cases include the threats against the creators of *South Park* for their use of an image of the Prophet Muhammad (which was then censored by the producers), see Soraya Roberts, "South Park Parody of the Prophet Muhammed is Censored Following Radical Islamists' Warning," *NYDailyNews*.com, April 22, 2010, http://www.nydailynews.com/entertainment/tv-movies/south-park-parody-prophet-muhammed-censored-radical-islamists-warning-article-1.169091; the decision by Random House not to publish the novel, *The Jewel of Medina* because of fears of Muslim violence, see Wikipedia.com, s.v. "*The Jewel of Medina*," http://en.wikipedia.org/wiki/The_Jewel_of_Medina; and the admission by MSNBC television host Lawrence O'Donnell that "I would like to criticize Islam much more than I do publicly, but I'm afraid for my life if I do." Hugh Hewitt.com, Transcript, "Theology 101 With Lawrence O'Donnell" [radio interview by Hugh Hewitt], December 11, 2007, HughHewitt.com, http://www.hughhewitt.com/theology-101-with-lawrence-odonnell. No doubt there are many additional instances that never made it into the media.

58 A partial list of murders by legal Muslim immigrants or citizens, inspired by anti-Semitism, would include: the 2009 murder of a military recruiting officer in Little Rock, Arkansas (the perpetrator confessed to an earlier fire-bombing of a rabbi's house in Nashville and firing shots at the home of a Little Rock rabbi), http://en.wikipedia.org/wiki/2009_Little_Rock_recruiting_office_shooting; the 2006 Seattle Jewish Federation murder and other shootings, http://en.wikipedia.org/wiki/Seattle_Jewish_Federation_shooting; the two murders and other shootings committed at the El Al ticket counter in the Los Angeles International Airport in 2002, http://en.wikipedia.org/wiki/2002_Los_Angeles_International_Airport_shooting; the 1997 Empire State Building murder and other shootings, http://en.wikipedia.org/wiki/1997_Empire_State_Building_shooting; and the 1994 Brooklyn Bridge murder and other shootings, http://en.wikipedia.org/wiki/Brooklyn_Bridge_shooting.

59 See Anti-Defamation League, "American Muslim Extremists: A Growing Threat to Jews," updated April 24, 2013, http://archive.adl.org/nr/exeres/d59191ec-39af-498c-ad2c-

8f40ae5a871f,db7611a2-02cd-43af-8147-649e26813571,frameless.html.

60 It is not necessarily true that the global Muslim population is the *only* one that deserves special scrutiny. It is just that the data with respect to this community is more readily available than for other such groups (if any exist).

61 See Nikolaj Nielsen, "UK, Germany Dislike EU 'Welfare Tourism' Plan," EUObserver.com, June 12, 2013, http://euobserver.com/justice/122370.

Chapter 11

1 See David Boaz, *Libertarianism: A Primer* (New York: Free Press, 1997). Chapter 1 is titled "The Coming Libertarian Age;" see especially 1–11. See also Nick Gillespie and Matt Welch, *The Declaration of Independents: How Libertarian Politics Can Fix What's Wrong with America* (New York: Public Affairs, 2012), chapter 1.

2 See Nicholas Elliot, "The Levelers: Libertarian Revolutionaries," *The Freeman*, May 1, 1989, http://www.fee.org/the_freeman/detail/the-levelers-libertarian-revolutionaries#axzz2q1JrTz3p; F. A. Hayek, *The Constitution of Liberty* (Chicago: University of Chicago Press, 1960), 167–8; and Daniel B. Klein, "The Origin of 'Liberalism,'" *Atlantic*.com, February 13, 2014, http://www.theatlantic.com/politics/archive/2014/02/the-origin-of-liberalism/283780/.

3 These include the philosophers and economists who author the Bleeding Heart Libertarians blog, the motto for which is "Free Markets and Social Justice," and those affiliated with the Molinari Institute, http://praxeology.net/anarcres.htm and the Center for a Stateless Society, http://c4ss.org/.

4 Indeed, political scientist Charles Murray has concluded on the basis of exhaustive empirical research that there is scant evidence that the "war on poverty" has had any positive impact, and has perhaps even made things worse. His solution is to terminate all federal antipoverty programs and leave this responsibility entirely to local governments and private organizations. See Charles Murray, *Losing Ground: American Social Policy*, 1950–1980 (New York: Basic Books, 1984), 56–68, 219–20, 227–33.

5 See US Department of Commerce, Bureau of the Census (1960), *Historical Statistics of the United States, Colonial Times to 1957*,

Table Series F 1–5 (Gross National Product, Total and Per Capita, in Current and 1929 Prices: 1869 to 1957), 139.

6 Ibid.

7 See Center for Disease Control, National Vital Statistics Reports 54, no. 14, April 19, 2006 (revised March 28, 2007), "Table 11. Life Expectancy by Age, Race, and Sex: Death-Registration States, 1900–1902 to 1919–21, and United States, 1929–31 to 2003," 30, http://www.cdc.gov/nchs/data/nvsr/nvsr54/nvsr54_14.pdf. I have not found data for years prior to 1900.

8 See the discussion in Chapter 5 regarding the steady decline in workplace accidents and deaths *prior* to the formation of the Occupational Safety and Health Administration in 1971.

9 F. A. Hayek, "Economic Freedom and Representative Government" (Fourth Wincott Memorial Lecture, October 31, 1973), The Institute of Economic Affairs (London), available at http://www.iea.org.uk/sites/default/files/publications/files/upldbook507.pdf.

10 Nozick counters the claim that democratic approval can somehow sanitize immoral demands with his "Tale of the Slave" (see *ASU*, 290–2).

11 See James P. Shenton, "Chapter 78. The Antislavery Impulse in America," in John A. Garraty and Peter Gay, eds, *The Columbia History of the World* (New York: Harper & Row, 1972), 903.

12 Judith Jarvis Thomson, "The Trolley Problem," *Yale L. J.* 94, no. 6 (May 1985), 1395–415.

13 Matt Zwolinski, "Why Not Utilitarianism?" BleedingHeartLibertarians.com, May 2, 2012, http://bleedingheartlibertarians.com/2012/05/why-not-utilitarianism/. This concise piece is an excellent summary of three of the most salient arguments against utilitarianism. For a more extended critique, see Will Kymlicka, *Contemporary Political Philosophy: An Introduction*, 2nd edn (Oxford: Oxford University Press, 2002), chapter 2.

14 This is known to philosophers as the "leveling down" argument. See Richard Arneson, s.v. "Egalitarianism," *Stanford Encyclopedia of Philosophy* (Summer 2013 Edition), section 6, http://plato.stanford.edu/archives/sum2013/entries/egalitarianism/. I have discussed this argument in more detail on my blog. See Mark D. Friedman, "The Leveling Down Argument Levels Its Critics," NaturalRightsLibertarian.com, May 2, 2014, http://naturalrightslibertarian.com/2014/05/the-leveling-down-argument-levels-its-critics/.

15 See James Gwartney et al., *Economic Freedom in the World: 2013 Annual Report*, Fraser Institute, September 8, 2013, chapter 2, http://www.freetheworld.com/datasets_efw.html. Fraser's ranking are based on five criteria: size of government, legal system and property rights, sound money, freedom to trade internationally, and regulation. A more recent comparable analysis conducted jointly by the Heritage Foundation and the *Wall Street Journal* shows the US falling out of the top ten (to twelfth) for the first time in this survey's 21-year history, see Heritage Foundation, "2014 Index of Economic Freedom" (January 2014), http://www.heritage.org/index/.

16 See generally the information available at WorkPermit.com, http://www.workpermit.com/.

17 See, for example, the program described at New Zealand Immigration: New Zealand Now, "Stay to Work After Study," http://www.newzealandnow.govt.nz/new-zealand-visa/already-in-nz/study-to-work-visa.

18 See Neil Parmar, "The Millionaire Residency Visa," *Wall Street Journal*, September 20, 2013, http://online.wsj.com/news/articles/SB10001424127887323665504579032922966616830.

19 See United States Department of State, Bureau of Consular Affairs, "Dual Nationality," http://travel.state.gov/travel/cis_pa_tw/cis/cis_1753.html.

20 See Laura Sanders, "More Taxpayers Are Abandoning the U.S.," *Wall Street Journal*, November 13, 2013, http://online.wsj.com/news/articles/SB10001424052702304243904579195923107439130.

LIST OF USEFUL INTERNET RESOURCES

What follows is a compilation of internet resources that I have found to be both intellectually stimulating and helpful in clarifying my own thinking about libertarian philosophy and the politics that arise from it. I have taken the liberty of placing my own blog first, but beyond this, these sites are in no particular order.

Natural Rights Libertarian.com; http://naturalrightslibertarian.com/. This blog is dedicated to explaining Nozick's rights-based, minimal state libertarianism to the intelligent general reader and addressing philosophical questions and political controversies of interest to libertarians. My mission includes an ongoing discussion of the philosophical and policy issues raised in this study.

Bleeding Heart Libertarians.com; http://bleedingheartlibertarians.com/. Offers carefully argued posts on current topics in philosophy, politics, economics, and culture by a group of prominent libertarian/classical liberal academic philosophers and economists. It boasts of its commitment to "free markets and social justice."

Cato Institute; http://www.cato.org/. The leading libertarian policy think tank, providing economic and (to a lesser extent) philosophical critiques of the welfare/regulatory state, dedicated in its words to: "individual liberty, limited government, free markets and peace." Publisher of the *Cato Journal*, an important interdisciplinary journal of public policy analysis, authored by leading libertarian scholars.

Ludwig von Mises Institute; http://mises.org/. The preeminent venue for anarcho-capitalist thought, providing ongoing commentary on the issues of the day from contemporary followers of Mises and Rothbard. Makes available online a treasure trove of scholarship by these men, as well as archived copies of now inactive libertarian journals, such as the *Review of Austrian Economics*, *Journal of Libertarian Studies*, and others.

Reason.com; http://reason.com/. A libertarian site providing up-to-the-minute, thoughtful coverage of the news from this perspective, and offering access to the content of past print editions of *Reason* magazine.

Library of Economics and Liberty; http://www.econlib.org/. Home of leading libertarian economists Bryan Caplan and David Henderson (and their blogs), as well as *The Concise Encyclopedia of Economics*, which provides hundreds of entries by prominent economists on technical and popular topics, all intended to be accessible to noneconomists.

Libertarianism.org; http://www.libertarianism.org/. A project of the Cato Institute, this site includes blog posts by leading contemporary libertarian thinkers, historians, and policy experts, as well as access to historical publications of interest to libertarians, study guides, and reading lists that provide a comprehensive introduction to libertarian thought.

The Foundation for Economic Education ("FEE"); http://www.fee.org/. One of the first libertarian nonprofit, educational organizations, founded in 1946. It has published the influential periodical, *The Freeman*, since 1950, which is now an online daily that covers events from a libertarian perspective. FEE offers access to its archive of past print editions of this magazine, and provides a cache of valuable educational resources for budding libertarians. Its mission is "to inspire, educate and connect future leaders with the economic, ethical and legal principles of a free society."

The Stanford Encyclopedia of Philosophy; http://plato.stanford.edu/. Invaluable online, peer-reviewed encyclopedia of philosophy, with thousands of entries, including many of interest to libertarians, for example, on libertarianism, rights, Nozick, Locke, and Hayek.

The Independent Institute; http://www.independent.org/. A leading libertarian public policy think tank, whose mission is, "to boldly advance peaceful, prosperous, and free societies grounded in a commitment to human worth and dignity." Publishes the influential periodical *The Independent Review*, as well as books, white papers, and other materials by its affiliated scholars.

Reason Papers; http://reasonpapers.com/home/. This is an online, peer-reviewed "journal of interdisciplinary normative studies" that publishes (usually libertarian themed) essays of the overtly philosophical sort as well as empirical studies with philosophical implications. Also permits access to its archive of print back issues.

Libertarian Papers; http://libertarianpapers.org/. A relatively recently established [2009], online, peer-reviewed journal of libertarian scholarship. Its self-described purpose is "to advance scholarly research in disciplines of particular interest to the libertarian community, broadly conceived." It includes, in addition to traditional philosophical essays, analysis of economic issues from the Austrian perspective.

Learn Liberty.org; http://www.learnliberty.org/about/. This is a project of the venerable Institute for Humane Studies, an organization founded in 1961, and dedicated to the promotion of classical liberal/libertarian ideas through seminars, publications, videos, and so on. Learn Liberty is IHS's educational portal, primarily relying on relatively short videos, for in its words: "learning about the ideas of a free society."

BIBLIOGRAPHY

Abrams, Burton. "Income Tax Turns 100." Opinion column *Washington Times* (October 29, 2013).

Adams, Christopher P. and Van V. Brantner. "Estimating the Cost of New Drug Development: Is It Really $802 Million?" *Health Affairs* 25, no. 2 (2006): 420–8.

Alexander, Larry and Michael Moore. S.v. "Deontological Ethics." In Edward N. Zalta, ed. *The Stanford Encyclopedia of Philosophy* (Winter 2012 Edition).

Alloway, Tracy. "Banks Reap Profits on Mortgages After QE3." *Financial Times* (October 1, 2012).

Alonso-Zaldivar, Ricardo. "Report: U.S. Health Care System Wastes $750B a Year." Associated Press, September 6, 2012.

Anti-Defamation League. "American Muslim Extremists: A Growing Threat to Jews." ADL.com (Updated April 24, 2013).

Arneson, Richard J. "Sophisticated Rule Consequentialism: Some Simple Objections." *Philosophical Issues* 15, no. 1 (2005), 235–51.

—. S.v. "Egalitarianism." In Edward N. Zalta, ed. *The Stanford Encyclopedia of Philosophy* (Summer 2013 Edition).

Balfanz, Robert, John M. Bridgehead, Mary Bruce, and Joanna Hornig Fox. "Building a Grad Nation: Progress and Challenge in Ending the High School Dropout Epidemic, Annual Update." America's Promise Alliance, and the Alliance for Excellent Education (February 2013).

Bandow, Doug. "End the FDA Drug Monopoly: Let Patients Choose Their Medicines." *Forbes* (June 11, 2012).

—. "Where to Cut the Federal Budget? Start by Killing Corporate Welfare." *Forbes*.com (August 20, 2012).

Barendt, Eric. *Freedom of Speech*, 2nd edn. Oxford: Oxford University Press, 2007.

Barnett, Randy E. "Antiwar Libertarians and the Reification of the State." TheVolokhConspiracy.com (July 20, 2007).

—. "Coping With Partiality: Justice, the Rule of Law, and the Role of Lawyers." *Roger Williams University Law Review* 3 (Fall 1997): 1–18.

—. "Does the Constitution Protect Economic Liberty." *Harvard Journal of Law & Public Policy* 35 (2012): 5–12.
—. "Libertarians and the War." Opinion column *Wall Street Journal* (July 17, 2007): A13.
Barone, Michael. "The Tyranny of Good Intentions at U.S. Colleges." Creators.com (2012).
Bastiat, Fredric. "What Is Seen and What Is Not Seen." 1848. In *Selected Essays on Political Economy*. Irvington-on-Hudson, NY: The Foundation for Economic Education, Inc., 1995.
Beito, David T. *From Mutual Aid to the Welfare State: Fraternal Societies and Social Services 1890–1967*. Chapel Hill, NC: University of North Carolina Press, 1999.
Berlant, Jeffrey L. *Profession and Monopoly: A Study of Medicine in the United States and Great Britain*. Berkeley, CA: University of California Press, 1975.
Berlin, Isaiah. "Two Concepts of Liberty." In *Four Essays on Liberty*. Oxford: Oxford University Press, 1969.
Bernanke, Ben. Federal Reserve.gov. "Remarks at the Conference to Honor Milton Friedman" (November 8, 2002).
—. Federal Reserve.gov. "Transcript of Chairman Bernanke's Press Conference, November 3, 2011."
—. Federal Reserve.gov. "Transcript of Chairman Bernanke's Press Conference, September 13, 2012."
Bernstein, David E. "Context Matters: A Better Libertarian Approach to Antidiscrimination Law." Washington, DC: Cato Institute, Cato Unbound (June 16, 2010).
Besharov, Douglas J. "Use of Technology to Improve the Administration of SSI's Financial Eligibility Requirements." Testimony before the Subcommittee on Human Resources, Committee on Ways and Means, House of Representatives, July 25, 2012.
Biggs, Andrew and Jason Richwine. "Overpaid Public Workers: The Evidence Mounts." Opinion column *Wall Street Journal* (April 11, 2012): A13.
Board of Trustees of Social Security and Medicare. *The 2012 Annual Report of the Board of Trustees of the Federal Old-Age and Survivors Insurance and Federal Disability Insurance Funds* (transmitted to Congress on April 23, 2012).
Boaz, David. *Libertarianism, A Primer*. New York: The Free Press, 1997.
Boaz, David and Timothy Lynch. "Chapter 33: The War on Drugs." In *Cato Handbook for Policymakers*, 7th edn. Washington, DC: Cato Institute, 2009: 337–44.
Boldrin, Michele and S. Joshua Swamidass. "A New Bargain for Drug Approvals." Opinion column *Wall Street Journal* (July 27, 2011): A15.

Bragdon, Tarren. "Florida's Medicaid Reform Shows the Way to Improve Health, Increase Satisfaction, and Control Costs." The Heritage Foundation, *Backgrounder* 2620 (November 9, 2011).

Brennan, Jason. "If You Want to Keep Dating Me, You'd Better Let Me Fuck You." Bleeding Heart Libertarians.com (June 7, 2012).

Briones, Ignacio and Hugh Rockoff. "Do Economists Reach a Conclusion About Free-Banking Episodes?" *Economics Journal Watch* 2, no. 2 (August 2005): 279–324.

Brook, Yaron and Don Watkins. "America Before the Entitlement State." *Forbes* (January 16, 2012): 28.

Brown, Russ. "A Deep Secret That Labor Unions Don't Want Workers to Know." *Forbes*.com (August 16, 2012).

Bryant, Christa Case. "What the Middle East Would be Like Without Christians." *Christian Science Monitor*.com (December 22, 2013).

Buettner, Zachary J. "Defense Acquisition Reform: Doing the Same Thing All Over Again." School of Advanced Military Studies, U.S. Army Command and General Staff College (April 19, 2010).

Bunce, Victoria C. "Health Insurance Mandates in the States, 2012." Council for Affordable Health Insurance (April 9, 2013).

Calandrillo, Steven P. "Responsible Regulation: A Sensible Cost-Benefit, Risk Versus Risk, Approach to Federal Health and Safety Regulation." *Boston University Law Review* 81 (December 2001): 957–1032.

Cannon, Michael F. "Chapter 15: Healthcare Regulation." In *Cato Handbook for Policymakers*, 7th edn. Washington, DC: Cato Institute, 2009.

—. "Chapter 16: Health Insurance Regulation." In *Cato Handbook for Policymakers*, 7th edn. Washington, DC: Cato Institute, 2009.

—. "Chapter 14: The Tax Treatment of Healthcare." In *Cato Handbook for Policymakers*, 7th edn. Washington, DC: Cato Institute, 2009.

—. "ObamaCare: The Plot Thickens." *Harvard Health Policy Review* 14, no. 1 (Spring 2013): 36–41.

Caplan, Bryan. "Why Should We Restrict Immigration?" *Cato Journal* 32, no. 1 (Winter 2012): 5–24.

Capretta, James C. "Reforming Medicare Integrated Care: An Alternative to the Obama Administration's Accountable Care Organizations." American Enterprise Institute (August 21, 2013).

Carpenter, Dick M., Lisa Knepper, Angela C. Erikson, and John K. Ross. "License to Work: A National Study of Burdens from Occupational Licensing." Institute for Justice (May 2012).

Carroll, Conn. "Health Care Reform Cost Estimates: What is the Track Record?" Heritage Foundation (August 4, 2009).

Center for Disease Control. *National Vital Statistics Reports* 54, no. 14 (April 19, 2006: revised March 28, 2007).

Centers for Medicare and Medicaid Services. CMS.gov. "National Health Expenditure Projections, 2012–2022" (September 18, 2012).

—. CMS.gov. "National Health Expenditures 2012 Highlights."

Champ, Bruce. "The National Banking System: A Brief History." Federal Reserve Bank of Cleveland. Working Paper No. 07-23R (originally published 2007, revised May 2011).

Child, James W. "Can Libertarianism Sustain a Fraud Standard?" *Ethics* 104 (July 1994): 722–38.

Chingos, Matthew M. and Paul E. Peterson. "A Generation of School-Voucher Success." Opinion column *Wall Street Journal* (August 23, 2012): A13.

Clinton, President William. "Welfare Reform Must Protect Children and Legal Immigrants." In Charles P. Cozic, ed. *Welfare Reform*. San Diego, CA: Greenhaven Press, 1997: 40–4.

Cnossen, Sijbren. "Tobacco Taxation in the European Union." *FinanzArchiv/Public Finance Analysis* 62, no. 2 (June 2006): 305–22.

Cochrane, John H. "What to Do About Pre-existing Conditions." Opinion column *Wall Street Journal*.com (August 14, 2009).

—. "What to Do When ObamaCare Unravels." Opinion column *WallStreetJournal*.com (December 25, 2013).

Cogan, John. "The Millionaire Retirees Next Door." Opinion column *Wall Street Journal* (May 12, 2011): A15.

Conover, Christopher J. "Featured Discussion: Understanding American Health Care: A Conversation With Christopher J. Conover." Interview by J. Paul Howard. American Enterprise Institute (March 29, 2013).

—. "Health Reform Breaks Bad." *Weekly Standard* 19, no. 7 (October 21, 2013).

Coulson, Andrew J. "The Impact of Federal Involvement in America's Classrooms." Testimony before Committee on Education & the Workforce, United States House of Representatives, February 10, 2011.

Cowen, Tyler. "How Far Back Should We Go? Why Restitution Should be Small." In Jon Elster, ed. *Retribution and Restitution in the Transition to Democracy Since 1945*. Cambridge: Cambridge University Press, 2006: 17–32.

Cox, Chris and Bill Archer. "Why $16 Trillion Only Hints at the True U.S. Debt." Opinion column *Wall Street Journal* (November 28, 2012).

Crook, Clive. "The Fed Needs a New, Simpler Mandate." Bloomberg.com (April 12, 2012).

Crouse, Janice Shaw. Beverly LaHaye Institute. "Poverty Rates by Living Arrangements: 2000, 2007 & 2012." In *Data Digest*, XIII, no. 1 (December 2013).

Cunningham, Peter J. and Ann S. O'Malley. "Do Reimbursement Delays Discourage Medicaid Participation By Physicians?" *Health Affairs* 28, no. 1 (January/February 2009): w17–w28.

Dean, Howard. "The Affordable Care Act's Rate-Setting Won't Work." Opinion column *Wall Street Journal* (July 28, 2013).

DeConde, Alexander. *A History of American Foreign Policy*, 2nd edn. New York: Charles Scribner's Sons, 1971.

DeHaven, Tad. "Corporate Welfare in the Federal Budget." Washington, DC: Cato Institute, *Policy Analysis* No. 703 (July 25, 2012).

DeMuth Christopher, Sr. and Cristopher Demuth, Jr. "The FDA Nixes a Pathbreaking Drug for MS." Opinion column *Wall Street Journal* (January 17, 2014).

Dershowitz, Alan M. "Shouting 'Fire!'" *Atlantic Monthly* (January 1989).

DiMasi, Joseph A., Ronald W. Hansen, and Henry G. Grabowski. "The Price of Innovation: New Estimates of Drug Development Costs." *Journal of Health Economics* 22 (2003): 151–85.

Donatich, Don. "Statement by John Donatich, Director of Yale University Press." Yale University Press (September 9, 2009).

Donway, Roger. "The War Over Libertarian Foreign Policy." TheAtlasSociety.org (January 26, 2011).

Driver, Julia. S.v. "The History of Utilitarianism." In Edward N. Zalta, ed. *The Stanford Encyclopedia of Philosophy* (Summer 2009 Edition).

Dworkin, Gerald. S.v. "Paternalism." In Edward N. Zalta, ed. *The Stanford Encyclopedia of Philosophy* (Summer 2010 Edition).

Dwoskin, Elizabeth. "Why Americans Won't Do Dirty Jobs." BloombergBusinessweek.com (November 11, 2011).

Dwyer, Gerald P., Jr. "Wildcat Banking, Bank Panics, and Free Banking in the United States." Federal Reserve Bank of Atlanta. *Economic Review* (December 1996): 1–20.

Eberstadt, Nicholas. "Poor Statistics." *Forbes* (March 2, 2009): 26.

Edwards, Chris. "Food Subsidies." In *Downsizing the Federal Government*. Washington, DC: Cato Institute (July 2009).

—. "Indian Lands, Indian Subsidies, and the Bureau of Indian Affairs." In *Downsizing the Federal Government*. Washington, DC: Cato Institute (February 2012).

—. "Public-Sector Unions." *Tax & Budget Bulletin*, no. 61 (March 2010).

—. "Public Sector Unions and the Rising Cost of Employee Compensation." *Cato Journal* 30, no. 1 (Winter 2010): 87–115.

Edwards, Chris and Tad DeHaven. "Fraud and Abuse in Federal Programs." In *Downsizing the Federal Government*. Washington, DC: Cato Institute (August 2009).

Edwards, James Rolph. "The Costs of Public Income Redistribution and Private Charity." *Journal of Libertarian Studies* 21, no. 2 (Summer 2007): 3–20.

—. "Taxation, Forced Labor, and Theft: Comment." *Independent Review* VI, no. 2 (Fall 2001): 253–7.

Ellickson, Robert C. "Alternatives to Zoning: Covenants, Nuisance Rules and Fines as Land Use Controls." *University of Chicago Law Review* 40, no. 4 (Summer 1973): 681–781.

Elliot, Nicholas. "The Levelers: Libertarian Revolutionaries." Foundation for Economic Education. *The Freeman* (May 1, 1989).

Elwell, Craig K. "Brief History of the Gold Standard in the United States." Congressional Research Service (June 23, 2011).

Epstein, Gene. "What, Me Worry?" *Barron's* (September 30, 2013): 21–3.

Epstein, Richard A. "Physical and Regulatory Takings: One Distinction Too Many." *Stanford Law Review Online* 64, no. 99 (March 1, 2012).

—. *Simple Rules for a Complex World*. Cambridge, MA: Harvard University Press, 1995.

The Federal Reserve Bank of Minneapolis. Minneapolisfed.org. "A History of Central Banking in the United States" (undated).

Feinberg, Joel. "Voluntary Euthanasia and the Inalienable Right to Life." In Sterling McMurrin, ed. *The Tanner Lectures on Human Value*, Vol. 1. Salt Lake City, UT: University of Utah Press, 1980: 221–51.

Feldstein, Martin. "The Fed's Dangerous Direction." Opinion column *Wall Street Journal* (January 13, 2013): A13.

Feser, Edward. "Self-Ownership, Abortion, and the Rights of Children: Toward a More Conservative Libertarianism." *Journal of Libertarian Studies* 18, no. 3 (Summer 2004): 95–104.

Finley, Allysia. "California Prison Academy: Better Than a Harvard Degree." Opinion column *Wall Street Journal* (April 30–May 1, 2011): A3.

Fischel, William A. *The Economics of Zoning Laws: A Property Rights Approach to American Land Use*. Baltimore, MD: Johns Hopkins University Press, 1985.

Fisher, Richard. "We Are Sailing Deeper Into Uncharted Waters." RealClearPolitics.com (September 22, 2012).

Flaherty, Michael. "The Latest Crime Wave: Sending Your Child to a Better School." Opinion column *Wall Street Journal* (October 1–2, 2011): A13.

Forbes, Steve. "Dinosaur U." *Forbes* (February 28, 2011): 13.

Foy, Andrew. "The Medical Marketplace, Free and Unfree." *Mises Daily* (June 17, 2011).

Friedman, Benjamin. "Chapter 19: The Defense Budget." In *Cato Handbook for Policymakers*, 7th edn. Washington, DC: Cato Institute, 2009.

Friedman, Mark D. *Nozick's Libertarian Project: An Elaboration and Defense.* London: Continuum International, 2011.

—. "The Leveling Down Argument Levels Its Critics." NaturalRightsLibertarian.com (May 4, 2014).

Friedman, Milton. *Capitalism and Freedom.* 1962. With the assistance of Rose D. Friedman. Chicago: University of Chicago Press, 1982.

Friedman, Milton and Anna J. Schwartz. "Has Government Have Any Role in Money?" *Journal of Monetary Economics* 17 (1986): 37–62. Collected in Anna J. Schwartz, ed. *Money in Historical Perspective.* Chicago: University of Chicago Press, 1987.

—. *Monetary History of the United States, 1867–1960.* Princeton, NJ: Princeton University Press, 1963.

Friedman, Milton and Rose Friedman. *Free to Choose: A Personal Statement.* New York: Harcourt Brace Jovanovich, 1980.

Furchtgott-Roth, Diana. "If Possible, Fed Forecasts are Worse Than Its Policies." RealClearMarkets.com (December 24, 2013).

—. "Medicare is Unsustainable in Current Form." MarketWatch.com (December 6, 2012).

Gillespie, Nick and Matt Welch. *The Declaration of Independents: How Libertarian Politics Can Fix What's Wrong with America.* New York: PublicAffairs, 2012.

Gokhale, Jagadeesh. "Democrats' Social Security Dilemma." Opinion column *Washington Times* (April 7, 2011).

Gold, Jenny. "FAQ On ACOs: Accountable Care Organizations, Explained." Henry J. Kaiser Foundation, *Kaiser Health News* (August 23, 2013).

Goldberg, Dror. "Legal Tender," Bar-Ilan University. Working Paper 2009-4 (April 2009).

Good, Chris. "Paul Ryan's 2011 Medicare Plan: A Primer." ABC News.com (August 11, 2012).

Goodman, John C. and Laurence Kotikoff. "Medicare by the Scary Numbers." Opinion column *Wall Street Journal* (June 24, 2013): A15.

Gordon, John Steele. *An Empire of Wealth.* New York: Harper Collins, 2004.

Gorman, Linda. "Medicaid Block Grants and Medicaid Performance." Independence Institute (March 2012).

Gottlieb, Scott. "The Doctor Won't See You Now. He's Clocked Out." Opinion column *Wall Street Journal* (March 15, 2013).

—. "Medicaid is Worse Than No Coverage at All." Opinion column *Wall Street Journal* (March 10, 2011): A17.

—. "Meet the ObamaCare Mandate Committee." Opinion column *Wall Street Journal* (February 16, 2012).

Gravelle, Jane. "Do Smokers Have Rights? The Science and Politics of Tobacco." *Cato Policy Report* XVI, no. 6 (November/December 1994).

Green, Kenneth P. "Fostering Quality Science at EPA: Perspectives on Common Sense Reform." Statement before House Committee on Science (November 30, 2011).

Greene, Jay. "Myths of the Teachers Unions." FrontPageMagazine.com (January 9, 2007).

Greenspan, Alan. "Alan Greenspan, Former Chairman of the Federal Reserve Tells *CBS Sunday Morning With Charles Osgood* He Missed Signals That Led to the 2008 Economic Collapse." CBS News.com. Press Release (October 18, 2013).

Grier, Peter. "Millions Losing Health Plans Under Obamacare. Did President Mislead." *Christian Science Monitor* (October 29, 2013).

Gross, Bill. "*Barron's* 2011 Roundtable, Part 1." *Baron's* (January 24, 2011).

Gwartney, James, Robert Lawson, and Joshua Hall. *Economic Freedom in the World: 2013 Annual Report.* Fraser Institute (2013).

Hagopian, Kip. "The Inequality of the Progressive Income Tax." Hoover Institution. *Policy Review*, no. 166 (April 1, 2011).

Hahn, Heather, David Kassabian, and Sheila Zedlewski. "TANF Work Requirements and State Strategies to Fulfill Them." Urban Institute (March 2012).

Hancock, Jay. "FAQ: How Employer-Sponsored Health Insurance is Changing." *Kaiser Health News* (September 17, 2013).

Harris, Samantha. "Speech Code of the Month: Oakland University." Foundation of Individual Rights in Education.org (April 3, 2012).

Hayek, Friedrich A. *The Constitution of Liberty.* Chicago: University of Chicago Press, 1960.

—. *Denationalization of Money.* London: Institute of Economic Affairs, 1976.

—. "Economic Freedom and Representative Government." Institute of Economic Affairs (October 31, 1973).

—. *Law, Legislation and Liberty: Vol. 1, Rules and Order.* London: Routledge, 1973.

—. *The Road to Serfdom*, anniversary edn, with a new introduction by Milton Friedman. Chicago: University of Chicago Press, 1994.

Heath, Allister. "A Wealth Tax Would be Ethically Wrong and Economically Destructive." Opinion column *Telegraph*.co.uk (February 19, 2012).

Helin, Calvin. *Dances With Dependency Trap: Out of Poverty Through Self-Reliance.* Woodland Hills, CA: Cubbie Blue Publishing, 2008.

Henderson, David R. "The Economics and History of Cronyism." *Mercatus Research* (July 27, 2012).

Henry J. Kaiser Family Foundation. "Medicare Spending and Financing Fact Sheet." November 14, 2012.

The Heritage Foundation. "2014 Index of Economic Freedom." Heritage.org (January, 2014).

Herman, Arthur. "What if Apple Designed an iFighter?" Opinion column *Wall Street Journal* (July 24, 2012): A15.

Herper, Matthew. "The Cost of Creating a New Drug Now $5 Billion, Pushing Big Pharma to Change." *Forbes*.com (August 11, 2013).

Higgs, Robert. "Are Questions of War and Peace Merely One Issue Among Many for Libertarians?" *Independent Review* 16, no. 2 (Fall 2011).

—. *Crisis and Leviathan*. Oxford: Oxford University Press, 1987.

Hooker, Brad. S.v. "Rule Consequentialism." In Edward N. Zalta, ed. *The Stanford Encyclopedia of Philosophy* (Spring 2011 Edition).

Horwitz, Steven. Mercatus Center. "An Introduction to U.S. Monetary Policy." (April 2, 2013).

Hospers, John. "Hospers Replies." *The Libertarian Forum* (February 1973): 2–3.

—. "What Libertarianism Is." In Tibor Machan and Douglas B. Rasmussen, eds. *Liberty for the Twenty-First Century*, Latham, MD: Rowman & Littlefield, 1995: 5–17.

—. "A Libertarian Argument Against Open Borders." *Journal of Libertarian Studies* 13, no. 2 (Summer 1998): 153–65.

Huemer, Michael. "Is There a Right to Immigrate?" *Social Theory and Practice* 36, no. 3 (July 2010): 429–61.

Hummel, Jeffrey Rogers. "Ben Bernanke versus Milton Friedman." *Independent Review* 15, no. 4 (Spring 2011).

Hyman, David A. "Rescue Without Law: An Empirical Perspective on the Duty to Rescue." *Texas. Law Review* 84, no. 3 (2006): 653–738.

Independent Institute. FDA Review.org. "Theory, Evidence and Examples of FDA Harm."

Institute for Justice, "Five Years After *Kelo*: The Sweeping Backlash Against One of the Supreme Court's Most-Despised Decision" (2010).

Investor's Business Daily, Editorial, "Yes, Chile's Private Pension Model Works, Big Time." (September 26, 2013).

Jaworska, Agnieska and Julie Tannenbaum. S.v. "The Grounds of Moral Status." In Edward N. Zalta, ed. *The Stanford Encyclopedia of Philosophy* (Summer 2013 Edition).

Jenkins, Holman W., Jr. "Let's Begin Obama's 'Conversation' on Entitlements." Opinion column *Wall Street Journal* (February 26–7, 2011): A15.

—. "The Young Won't Buy ObamaCare." Opinion column *Wall Street Journal* (June 19, 2013): A13.

Jenkins, Philip. "Mystical Power: Why Sufi Muslims, for Centuries the Most Ferocious Soldiers of Islam, Could be our Most Valuable Allies in the Fight Against Extremism." BostonGlobe.com (January 25, 2009).

Johnson, President Lyndon. "Annual Message to the Congress on the State of the Union, January 8, 1964," Transcript, LBJ Presidential Library.org.

—. "To Fulfill These Rights." Commencement Address at Howard University (June 4, 1965).

Johnson, Roger T. "Historical Beginnings . . . The Federal Reserve." Federal Reserve Bank of Boston (2010).

Johnson, Senator Ron. "Obamacare's Coats are Soaring." Opinion column *Wall Street Journal* (March 21, 2012): A11.

Jordan, Jerry L. "Who Will Guard the Monetary Guardians?" Washington, DC: Cato Institute, Cato Unbound (November 12, 2013).

Kaiser Health News. "'Budget Report: More Employers Than Previously Estimated Will Drop Health Coverage." (February 6, 2013).

Kane, Jason. "Health Costs: How the U.S. Compares With Other Countries." PBS Newshour, October 22, 2012.

Kant, Immanuel. *Groundwork of the Metaphysic of Morals*. 1785, Translated and edited by H. J. Paton. New York: Harper & Row, 1964.

Karkkainen, Bradley C. "Zoning: A Reply to the Critics." *Journal of Land Use & Environmental Law* 10, no. 1 (1994): 1–46.

Katz, Lisa. "Scope of Practice of Health Professionals in the State of Michigan." Public Sector Consultants, MSMG.org (2001).

Keating, David and Edward Crane. "Meet the Parents of the Super PACs." Opinion Column *Wall Street Journal* (February 11–2, 2012): A13.

Kekes, John. *The Illusions of Egalitarianism*. Ithaca, CA: Cornell University Press, 2003.

Kessler, Daniel P. "How Health Reform Punishes Work." Opinion column *Wall Street Journal* (April 25, 2011): A15.

—. "ObamaCare's Broken Promises." Opinion column *Wall Street Journal* (February 1, 2013): A13.

Kessler, Glenn. "Does 'Obamacare' Have $1 Trillion in Tax Hikes Aimed at the Middle Class?" *Washington Post*. The Fact Checker blog (March 12, 2013).

King, Teresa T. and H. Wayne Cecil. "The History of Major Changes to the Social Security System." *CPA Journal* (May 2006).

Kirby, David and David Boaz. "The Libertarian Vote in the Age of Obama." *Policy Analysis*, No. 658. Washington, DC: Cato Institute (January 21, 2010).

Klein, Daniel B. "The Origin of 'Liberalism.'" *Atlantic*.com (February 13, 2014).

Kolko, Gabriel. "The New Deal Illusion." *CounterPunch*.org (August 29, 2012).

Konczal, Mike. "Economists Agree: Raising the Minimum Wage Reduces Poverty." Opinion column *WashingtonPost*.com (January 4, 2014).

Kopp, Raymond J., Alan J. Krupnick, and Michael Toman. "Cost-Benefit Analysis and Regulatory Reform: An Assessment of the Science and the Art." Resources for the Future, Discussion Paper 97-19 (January 1997).

Krupa, Carolyne. "Medical Licensure: State Lines Pose Daunting Barriers." American Medical Association. American Medical News (September 17, 2012).

Kukathas, Chandran. "The Mirage of Global Justice." *Social Philosophy and Policy* 28, no. 1 (2006): 1–28.

Kurtz, Annalyn. "This Could be the Largest Fed Stimulus Ever." *Money*. CNN.com (October 28, 2013).

Kymlicka, Will. *Contemporary Political Philosophy: An Introduction*, 2nd edn. Oxford: Oxford University Press, 2002.

Labonte, Marc. "Changing the Federal Reserve's Mandate: An Economic Analysis." Congressional Research Service (August 12, 2013).

Labor Management Relations Act of 1947. Public Law 80-101. Codified at U.S. Code §§ 401–531.

Lambert, Thomas A. "The Case Against Smoking Bans." *Regulation* (Winter 2006–7): 34–40.

Landes, David S. *The Wealth and Poverty of Nations: Why Some Are So Rich and Some So Poor*. New York: W.W. Norton, 1999.

Langlois, Richard N. "Cost-Benefit Analysis, Environmentalism, and Rights." *Cato Journal* 2, no. 1 (Spring 1982).

Ledyard, John O. "Market Failure." In John Eatwell, Murray Milgate, and Peter Newman, eds. *The New Palgrave: The World of Economics*, 1st American edn. New York: W.W. Norton & Company, 1991: 407–12.

Levine, Peter "The Libertarian Critique of Labor Unions." *Philosophy & Public Policy Quarterly* 21, no. 4 (Fall 2001): 17–24.

Levy, Robert A. "Campaign Finance Reform: A Libertarian Primer." Washington, DC: Cato Institute, Commentary (January 29, 2010).

Lewyn, Michael. "How Overregulation Creates Sprawl (Even in a City Without Zoning)." *Wayne Law Review* 50, no. 1171 (Winter 2005).

Libertarian Party 2012 Platform (adopted May 2012). LP.org.
Liebman, George W. "Modernization of Zoning: A Means to Reform." *Regulation* no. 2 (1996): 71–7.
Locke, John. *Two Treatises of Government*. 1702. Student edn. Edited with an introduction by Peter Laslett. Cambridge: Cambridge University Press, 1988.
Lombardi, John V. "Public and Private; What's the Difference?" InsideHigherEducation.com (March 6, 2006).
Machan, Tibor R. *Individuals and Their Rights*. LaSalle, IL: Open Court, 1989.
Machan, Tibor and Douglass Rasmussen, eds. *Liberty for the Twenty-First Century: Contemporary Libertarian Thought*. Latham, MD: Rowman & Littlefield, 1995.
Mack, Eric. "Rights, Just War, and National Defense." In Tibor Machan and Douglas B. Rasmussen, eds. *Liberty for the Twenty-First Century*, Latham, MD: Rowman & Littlefield, 1995: 101–20.
—. "The Natural Rights of Property." *Social Philosophy and Policy* 27, no. 1 (January 2010): 53–78.
—. "Nozickian Arguments for the More-Than-Minimal State." In Ralf M. Bader and John Meadowcroft, eds. *The Cambridge Companion to Nozick's "Anarchy, State, and Utopia."* Cambridge: Cambridge University Press, 2011: 89–115.
Malkiel, Burton G. "Innovation, Competition and the FDA." *Forbes* (August 8, 2011): 16.
Malone, Patrick A. "The Role of FDA Approval in Drug Cases." *Trial* (November 1998).
Mankiw, N. Greg. *Principles of Economics*, 3rd edn. New York: Dryden Press, 1998.
Marquis, Don. "Singer on Abortion and Infanticide." In Jeffrey A. Schaler, ed. *Peter Singer Under Fire: The Moral Iconoclast Faces His Critics*. LaSalle, IL: Open Court, 2009: 133–52.
—. "Why Abortion is Immoral." *The Journal of Philosophy* 86 (April, 1989): 183–202.
Martin, Timothy and Christopher Weaver. "Burden Shifts on Insurance." *Wall Street Journal* (September 18, 2013): A1.
Matthew, Merrill. "Scamming Uncle Sam." *Forbes* (May 10, 2010): 20.
McArdle, Megan. "Is Obamacare in a Death Spiral?" BloombergNews.com (October 21, 2013).
McBride, William. "What is the Evidence on Taxes and Growth?" Tax Foundation, *Special Report* No. 207 (December 12, 2012).
McCluskey, Neal. "Chapter 21: Higher Education Policy." In *Cato Handbook for Policymakers*, 7th edn. Washington, DC: Cato Institute, 2007.

McIntyre, Alison. S.v. "The Doctrine of Double Effect." In Edward N. Zalta, ed. *The Stanford Encyclopedia of Philosophy* (Fall 2011 Edition).

McWhorter, John. "How the War on Drugs Is Destroying Black America." *Cato's Letter* 9, no. 1 (Winter 2011): 1–5.

Mill, John Stuart. *On Liberty*. 1859. London: Longmans, Green & Co., 1913.

Miller, David. "Tiny Little Hope for Tax Reform." HuffPost Business (April 4, 2012).

Miron, Jeffry A. "Anti-Sex School for Johns?" Washington, DC: Cato Institute, Cato at Liberty blog (August 31, 2009).

Miron, Jeffrey A. and Katherine Waldock. "The Budgetary Impact of Ending Drug Prohibition." Washington, DC: Cato Institute, White Paper (September 27, 2010).

Moffatt, Mike. "Why the Fed Should Abandon Its Dual Mandate." Opinion column *Globe and Mail*.com (July 18, 2012).

Moore, Adrian. "Don't Be Fooled, Regulations Cost Jobs." RealClearMarkets.com (August 9, 2012).

Moore, Stephen and Julian L. Simon. *It's Getting Better All the Time: 100 Greatest Trends of the Last 100 Years*. Washington, DC: Cato Institute, 2000.

Morgenson, Gretchen and Joshua Rosner. *Reckless Endangerment: How Outsized Ambition, Greed and Corruption Led to Economic Armageddon*. New York: Times Books, 2011.

Moynihan, Patrick D. "The Negro Family: The Case for National Action." In Lee Rainwater and W. L. Yancy, eds. *The Moynihan Report and the Politics of Controversy*. Cambridge, MA: MIT Press, 1967.

Murphy, Liam and Thomas Nagel. *The Myth of Ownership: Taxes and Justice*. London: Oxford University Press, 2004.

Murphy, Mark. S.v. "The Natural Law Tradition in Ethics." In Edward N. Zalta, ed. *The Stanford Encyclopedia of Philosophy* (Winter 2011 Edition).

Murray, Charles. *Losing Ground: American Social Policy 1950–1980*. New York: Basic Books, 1984.

—. *What it Means to be a Libertarian*. New York: Broadway Books, 1997.

Nagel, Thomas. "Personal Rights and Public Space," *Philosophy and Public Affairs* 24, no. 2 (1995): 83–107.

Narveson, Jan. *The Libertarian Idea*. Philadelphia, PA: Temple University Press, 1988.

National Labor Relations Act of 1935. Public Law 74-198. Codified at 29 U.S. Code §§151-69.

New York Times, Editorial, "The Limits of Property Rights" (June 24, 2005).
Nozick, Robert. *Anarchy, State, and Utopia*. New York: Basic Books, 1974.
—. "On the Randian Argument." In Jeffrey Paul, ed. *Reading Nozick: Essays on "Anarchy, State, and Utopia."* Tolowa, NJ: Rowman & Littlefield, 1981: 206–31.
—. *Philosophical Explanations*. Cambridge, MA: Harvard University Press, 1981.
—. "War, Terrorism, Reprisals—Drawing Some Moral Lines." In Robert Nozick, *Socratic Puzzles*. Cambridge: Harvard University Press, 1997: 300–4.
Obama, President Barack. "Address to a Joint Session of Congress, September 8, 2011." Whitehouse.gov.
O'Donnell, Lawrence. "Theology 101 With Lawrence O'Donnell" [Transcript, radio interview by Hugh Hewitt]. HughHewitt.com (December 11, 2007).
O'Driscoll Gerald P., Jr. "The Fed at 100." Washington, DC: Cato Institute, Cato Unbound blog (November 4, 2013).
Office of Management and Budget. "Fiscal Year 2014 Analytical Perspectives, Budget of the U.S. Government" (2013).
O'Neill, Ben. "How Zoning Rules Would Work in a Free Society." *Mises Daily* (June 17, 2009).
Orend, Brian. S.v. "War." In Edward N. Zalta, ed. *The Stanford Encyclopedia of Philosophy* (Fall 2008 Edition).
Organization for Economic Cooperation and Development. "OECD (2013), Education at a Glance 2013: OECD Indicators." OECD Publishing.
—. "PISA 2012 Results in Focus: What 15-Year-Olds Know and What They Can Do With What They Know." OECD Publishing.
Palumbo, Matt. "How the Free Market Can Cure Health Care." *American Thinker* (December 17, 2011).
Park, Daniel. "Conflicts of Interest: Monitoring the FDA's Relationship with Pharmaceutical Companies." *Yale Journal of Medicine and Law* (November 1, 2005).
Parmar, Neil. "The Millionaire Residency Visa." *Wall Street Journal* (September 20, 2013).
Paul, Jeffrey, ed. *Reading Nozick: Essays on Anarchy, State, and Utopia*. Oxford: Basil Blackwell, 1982.
Paul, Ron. *The Revolution: A Manifesto*. New York: Grand Central Publishing, 2008.
Pennington, Mark. *Robust Political Economy: Classical Liberalism and the Future of Public Policy*. Cheltenham, UK: Edward Elgar, 2011.

Perold, Andre F. "Negative Real Interest Rates: The Conundrum for Investment and Spending Policies." *Enterprising Investor* (July 3, 2012).

Perry, Mark J. "31% of Americans Without Health Insurance Live in Households Making $50k or More, and 38% are Between 18–34 Years Old." American Enterprise Institute blog (October 5, 2012).

Petit, Philip. "Non-Consequentialism and Political Philosophy." In David Schmidtz, ed. *Robert Nozick*. Cambridge: Cambridge University Press, 2002: 83–104.

Pew Research Center. "Muslim Publics Share Concerns about Extremist Groups." PewGlobal.org (September 10, 2013).

—. "Religion & Public Life Project: The Global Landscape: Muslims." PewGlobal.org (December 18, 2012).

—. "The World's Muslims: Religion, Politics and Society." PewGlobal.org (April 30, 2013).

Pham, Nam D. and Daniel J. Ikenson. "A Critical Review of the Benefits and Costs of EPA Regulations on the U.S. Economy." NDP Consulting (November 2012).

Philipson, Thomas and Eric Sun. "Cost of Caution: The Impact on Patients of Delayed Drug Approvals." The Manhattan Institute for Policy Research. Project FDA Report, no. 2 (June 2010).

Phillips, Kerk. "A Flat Tax is Not Incapable of Funding the Government and the Poor." Opinion column *Deseret News* (February 19, 2013).

Pilon, Roger. "Chapter 34: Property Rights and the Constitution." In *Cato Handbook for Policymakers*, 7th edn. Washington, DC: Cato Institute, 2007.

Pilon, Roger and Richard Epstein. "NSA Surveillance in Perspective." Opinion column *Chicago Tribune* (June 12, 2013).

Pipes, Daniel. *The Rushdie Affair: The Novel, the Ayatollah, and the West*. New York: Transaction Publishers, 2003.

Pipes, Richard. *Property and Freedom*. New York: Alfred A. Knopf, 1999.

Plumer, Brad. "These Ten Charts Show the Black-White Economic Gap Hasn't Budged in 50 Years." *WashingtonPost*.com, Wonkblog (August 28, 2013).

Powers, Kristin. "A Global Slaughter of Christians, but America's Churches Stay Silent." TheDailyBeast.com (September 27, 2013).

Public Religion Research Institute. "2013 American Values Survey: In Search of Libertarians in America." PublicReligion.org (October 29, 2013).

Radnofsky, Louise and Damien Paletta. "Health Law to Cut Into Labor Force." *Wall Street Journal* (February 5, 2014): A1.

Rahn, Richard. "Flat Tax? Sales Tax? Value-Added Tax?" Opinion column *Washington Times*.com (July 16, 2013).

Railton, Peter. "Locke, Stock and Peril: Natural Property Rights, Pollution and Risk." In Mary Gibson, ed. *To Breathe Freely*. Tolowa, NJ: Rowman & Littlefield, 1985: 89–123.

Rakowski, Eric. "Can Wealth Taxes Be Justified?" *Tax Law Review* 53 (1999–2000): 262–375.

Rand, Ayn. "The 'Conflicts' of Man's Interests." In *The Virtue of Selfishness*, by Ayn Rand, with additional articles by Nathan Brandon. New York: Signet Books, 1970: 50–6.

—. "A Last Survey." In *The Ayn Rand Letter 1971–1976*. New York: Second Renaissance Press, 1990.

—. "Man's Rights." In Rand, *The Virtue of Selfishness*, 92–100.

—. "The Nature of Government." In Rand, *The Virtue of Selfishness*, 107–15.

—. "The Objectivist Ethics." In Rand, *The Virtue of Selfishness*, 13–35.

—. "Of Living Death," In Ayn Rand, ed. *The Voice of Reason: Essays in Objectivist Thought*. New York: Plume, 1990: 57–8.

Randazzo, Anthony. "How Quantitative Easing Helps the Rich and Soaks the Rest of Us." *Reason*.com (September 13, 2012).

Rector, Robert. "Examining the Means-tested Welfare State: 79 Programs and $927 Billion in Annual Spending." Testimony before Committee on the Budget, U.S. House of Representatives (April 17, 2012).

—. "How the War on Poverty Was Lost." Opinion column *Wall Street Journal* (January 8, 2014): A15.

—. "Obama's End Run on Welfare Reform, Part One: Understanding Workfare." The Heritage Foundation, *Backgrounder*, No. 2730 (September 19, 2012).

—. "Obama's End Run on Welfare Reform, Part Two: Dismantling Workfare." The Heritage Foundation. *Backgrounder*, No. 2731 (September 26, 2012).

Restatement (Second) of Torts, Vol. 4. American Law Institute (1979).

Reuters News Service. "Fed Missed Warning Signs in 2007 as Crisis Gained" (January 18, 2013).

Reznik, Gayle L., Dave Shoffner, and David A. Weaver. "Coping With the Demographic Challenge: Fewer Children and Living Longer." Social Security Administration Office of Policy. *Social Security Bulletin* 66, no. 4 (Winter 2005/2006).

Richman, Sheldon. "The Libertarian Case Against Right-to-Work Laws." *Reason*.com (December 16, 2012).

Richwine, Jason. "The Myth of Racial Disparities in Public School Funding." The Heritage Foundation, *Backgrounder* No. 2548 (April 20, 2011).

Rivkin, David B. and Elizabeth Foley. "An ObamaCare Board Answerable to No One." Opinion column *Wall Street Journal* (June 20, 2013): A21.

Roberts, Soraya. "South Park Parody of the Prophet Muhammed is Censored Following Radical Islamists' Warning." NYDailyNews.com (April 22, 2010).

Rockefeller, Senator John D. and Senator Olympia Snowe. Letter to Rex W. Tillerson (Chairman and CEO, ExxonMobil Corporation), October 27, 2006.

Roosevelt, President Franklin D. "Letter on the Resolution of Federation of Federal Employees Against Strikes in Federal Service," August 16, 1937. Online by Gerhard Peters and John T. Woolley, *The American Presidency Project*.

Rothbard, Murray N. "The Editor Rebuts." *The Libertarian Forum* (February 1973): 4–5.

—. *The Ethics of Liberty*. With a new introduction. New York: New York University Press, 1998. First published in 1982 by Humanities Press.

—. *For a New Liberty: The Libertarian Manifesto*, revised edn. New York: Macmillan, 1978.

—. "Law, Property Rights, and Air Pollution." *Cato Journal* 2, no. 1 (Spring 1982): 55–99.

Rothwell, Jonathan. "Housing Costs, Zoning and Access to High-Scoring Schools." Brookings Institute, Brookings Papers (April 19, 2012).

Roy, Avik. "Four Reasons Why the Oregon Medicaid Results Are Even Worse Than They Look." *Forbes*.com (May 11, 2013).

—. "Yet Another White House Obamacare Delay: Out-of-Pocket Caps Waived Until 2015." *Forbes*.com (August 13, 2013).

Sabia, Joseph J. "Does Raising the Minimum Wage Reduce Poverty?" Opinion column *U-T San Diego* (April 12, 2012).

Samuelson, Robert J. "The Folly of Obamacare." Opinion column *Washington Post* (June 17, 2012).

—. "How We Won—and Lost—the War on Poverty." RealClearPolitics.com (January 12, 2014).

—. "Naive, Hypocritical and Dishonest." Real Clear Politics (June 15, 2009).

Sanchez, Julian. "A Reply to Epstein and Pilon on the NSA's Metadata Program." Washington, DC: Cato Institute, Cato at Liberty blog (June 16, 2013).

Sandel, Michael. "Interview: Michael Sandel on Justice." By Nigel Warburton. *Prospect Magazine* (January 21, 2011).

Sanders, Laura. "More Taxpayers Are Abandoning the U.S." *Wall Street Journal* (November 13, 2013).

Scearce, Carolyn. "A Revolutionary Reading List: The Intellectual Tradition That Influenced the U.S. Founding Fathers." ProQuest Information (April 2010).

Schaeffer, Adam. "They Spend WHAT? The Real Cost of Public Schools." Cato Institute, *Policy Analysis* No. 662 (March 10, 2010).

Schiller, Robert J. "Is Economics a Science?" *Project Syndicate* (November 6, 2013).

Schuler, Kurt. "Note Issue by Banks: A Step Toward Free Banking in the United States?" *Cato Journal* 20, no. 3 (Winter 2001): 453–65.

Schoenbrod, David and Melissa White. "Statutory Arteriosclerosis." In *The Environmental Forum* 28, no. 5 (September/October 2011): 24–9. American Enterprise Institute.

Scholz, John Karl, Robert Moffitt, and Benjamin Cowan. "Trends in Income Support" (September 2, 2008).

Schwartz, Anna J. and Walter F. Todd. "Why a Dual Mandate is Wrong for Monetary Policy." *International Finance* 11, no. 2 (2008): 167–83.

Schwartz, Stephan. "How Many Sufis are There in Islam." HuffingtonPost.com (July 20, 2011).

Selgin, George. "Milton Friedman and the Case Against Currency Competition." *Cato Journal* 28, no. 2 (Spring/Summer 2008): 287–301.

—. *The Theory of Free Banking: Money Supply Under Competitive Note Issue*. Washington, DC: Cato Institute, 1988.

Shapiro, Daniel. *Is the Welfare State Justified?* Cambridge: Cambridge University Press, 2007.

Shapiro, Ilya. "Supreme Court Snubs Citizens Whose Social Security Will Be Confiscated If They Refuse Government Health Care." Cato at Liberty blog (January 25, 2013).

Shelton, Hilary O. "Statement before the House Energy and Commerce Committee, Subcommittee on Commerce, Trade and Consumer Protection," October 19, 2005.

Shenton, James P. "Chapter 78. The Antislavery Impulse in America." In John A. Garraty and Peter Gay, eds. *The Columbia History of the World*. New York: Harper & Row, 1972.

Sherk, James. "Effects of Unemployment Benefits." Heritage Foundation. The Foundry blog (May 13, 2010).

Siegan, Bernard. "Non-Zoning is the Best Zoning." *California Western Law Review* 31 (1994): 127–35.

Simon, Julian L. "Are There Grounds for Limiting Immigration?" *Journal of Libertarian Studies* 13, no. 2 (Summer 1998): 137–52.

Singer, Peter. *Practical Ethics*, 3rd edn. Cambridge: Cambridge University Press, 2011.

Sinnott-Armstrong, Walter. S.v. "Consequentialism." In Edward N. Zalta, ed. *The Stanford Encyclopedia of Philosophy* (Winter 2011 Edition).

Skoble, Aeon J. "War and Liberty." *Reason Papers* 28 (Spring 2006): 43–9.

Slater, Joseph E. "The Assault on Public Sector Collective Bargaining: Real Harms and Imaginary Benefits." American Constitution Society (June 2011).

Slivinski, Stephen. "The Corporate Welfare State: How the Federal Government Subsidizes U.S. Businesses." Washington, DC: Cato Institute. *Policy Analysis*, No. 592 (May 14, 2007).

Smith, Adam. *The Wealth of Nations*, Books I–III. 1776. Edited and with an introduction by Andrew Skinner. London: Penguin Books, 1986.

Smith, Anne E. "Prepared Statement of Anne E. Smith, Ph.D. before the House Committee on Science, Space and Technology." October 4, 2011.

Smith, Bradley A. "The War on Political Free Speech." Opinion column *Wall Street Journal* (January 23, 2012).

Smith, George H. "Thinking About War." *Liberty* (May 2008).

Sowell, Thomas. *The Vision of the Anointed: Self-Congratulation as a Basis for Social Policy*. New York: Basic Books, 1995.

Steiner, Hillel. *An Essay on Rights*. Oxford: Blackwell, 1994.

Steuerle, C. Eugene. "The Widespread Prevalence of Marriage Penalties." Testimony Before the Subcommittee on the District of Columbia Committee on Appropriations, United States Senate, May 3, 2006.

Steuerle, C. Eugene and Stephanie Rennane. "Social Security and Medicare Taxes and Benefits Over a Lifetime." Urban Institute (June 20, 2010).

Stoll, Ira. "Unhappy Labor Day: Obamacare Edition." *Reason*.com (September 2, 2013).

Stovall, Tess and Deirdre Dolan. "Incomplete: How Middle-Class Schools Aren't Making the Grade," Third Way (September 2011).

Stratton-Lake, Philip. "Can Hooker's Rule-Consequentialist Principle Justify Ross's Prima Facie Duties?" *Mind* 106 (October 1997): 751–8.

Stutzman, Marlin and Michael Needham. "The 'Farm' Bill is No Such Thing." Opinion column *Wall Street Journal* (August 2, 2012): A13.

Suderman, Peter. "Obamacare Savings Program Shows Partial Success—But Will It Last?" *Reason*.com (July 19, 2013).

Sumner, Scott. "In Defense of a Flexible Monetary Policy." Washington, DC: Cato Institute, Cato Unbound (November 8, 2013).

Swedish Agency for Growth Policy Analysis. "The Economic Effects of the Regulatory Burden—A Theoretical and Empirical Analysis." (December 2010).

Tahir, Darius. "Narrow-Network Health Plans Expected to Proliferate Under Obamacare." *National Journal*.com (October 9, 2013).

Tanner, Michael D. "The American Welfare State: How We Spend Nearly $1 Trillion a Year Fighting Poverty—and Fail." *Policy Analysis* No. 694. Washington, DC: Cato Institute (April 11, 2013).

—. "The 6.2 Percent Solution: A Plan for Reforming Social Security." *Social Security Choice Paper* No. 32. Washington, DC: Cato Institute (February 17, 2004).

Tanner, Michael D. and Tad DeHaven. "TANF and Federal Welfare." In *Downsizing the Federal Government: Medicare and Medicaid*. Washington, DC: Cato Institute (September 2010).

Tax Policy Center (Urban Institute/Brookings Institution). "Tax Facts: Historical Amount of Revenue by Source."

Taylor, Jerry. "Chapter 44: Environmental Policy." In *Cato Handbook for Policymakers*, 7th edn. Washington, DC: Cato Institute, 2009.

Téson, Fernando R. "Targeted Killing in War and Peace: A Philosophical Analysis." In Claire Finkelstein, Jens David Ohlin, and Andrew Altman, eds. *Targeted Killing: Morality and Law in an Asymmetrical World*. Oxford: Oxford University Press, 2012: 403–33.

Thaler, Richard H. "The Argument Clinic," Washington, DC: Cato Institute, Cato Unbound (April 16, 2010).

Thaler Richard H. and Cass Sunstein. *Nudge: Improving Decisions About Health, Wealth, and Happiness*. New Haven, CT: Yale University Press, 2008.

Thomson, Judith. "A Defense of Abortion." *Philosophy and Public Affairs* 1, no. 1 (Autumn 1971): 47–66.

—. "The Trolley Problem," *Yale L. J.* 94, no. 6 (May 1985): 1395–415.

Tocqueville, Alexis de. *Democracy in America*, Volume II. 1840. Henry Reeve translation. New York: The Colonial Press, 1899.

Trotsky, Leon. *The Revolution Betrayed: What is the Soviet Union and Where is it Going?* Garden City, NY: Doubleday, Doran & Co., 1937.

Tuckness, Alex. S.v. "Locke's Political Philosophy." In Edward N. Zalta, ed. *The Stanford Encyclopedia of Philosophy* (Winter 2012).

US Department of Commerce, Bureau of the Census. *The Historical Statistics of the United States, Colonial Times to 1957* (1960).

US Department of Health and Human Services, Centers for Medicare and Medicaid Services. "Report to Congress: 2012 Actuarial Report on the Financial Outlook for Medicaid." (March 1, 2013).

US Department of State, Bureau of Consular Affairs. Travel.state.gov. "Dual Nationality."

US Department of the Treasury. Treasury.gov. Resource Center, Interest Rate Statistics. "Daily Treasury Real Yield Curve Rates."
US Environmental Protection Agency. EPA.gov. "Summary of the Toxic Substances Control Act" (last updated July 26, 2013).
US Food and Drug Administration. Frequently Asked Questions: Breakthrough Therapies. FDA.gov. "Fast Track, Breakthrough Therapy, Accelerated Approval and Priority Review" (last updated March 3, 2014).
US Social Security Administration. "Research Note #3, Details of Ida May Fuller's Payroll Tax Contributions." SSA.gov. Under "Agency History."
Vedder, Richard. "Right-To-Work Laws: Liberty, Prosperity, and Quality of Life." *Cato Journal* 30, no. 1 (Winter 2010): 171–80.
Vestal, Christine. "Nurse Practitioners Slowly Gaining Autonomy." *Kaiser Health News* (July 19, 2013).
Volokh, Eugene. "Duty to Rescue/Report Statutes." The Voklokh Conspiracy.com (November 3, 2009).
Vossen, Bas Van Der. "Reasons for Open Borders." BleedingHeartLibertarians.com (August 9, 2013).
Walker, Tim. "What Do the 2012 PISA Scores Tell Us About U.S. Schools?" *NEA Today* (December 3, 2013).
Wall Street Journal. Editorial "Forced Into Medicare" (March 24, 2011): A15.
Warren, Mary Ann. "'On the Moral and Legal Status of Abortion.' and 'A Postscript on Infanticide.'" In Thomas A. Mappes and David DeGarzia, eds. *Biomedical Ethics*, 5th edn. New York: McGraw-Hill, 2001: 456–62.
Washington Times. Editorial "The Obamacare Bomb." (September 9, 2013).
Wells, Donald and L. S. Scruggs. "The Free Banking Alternative," Foundation for Economics Education. *The Freeman* (February 1, 1985).
White, Lawrence H. S.v. "Competing Money Supplies" Library of Economics and Liberty. *The Concise Encyclopedia of Economics* (2008).
—. "The Federal Reserve and the Rule of Law." Testimony Before the Subcommittee on Monetary Policy and Trade, House Committee on Financial Services, September 12, 2013.
Wilkerson, Will. "Why Opting Out Is No 'Third Way': The Perplexing Banality of 'Libertarian Paternalism.'" *Reason*.com (October 2008).
Williams, Bob. "Why Government Employee Collective Bargaining Laws Must Be Reformed Now." State Budget Solutions.org (June 5, 2012).

Wilson, Mark. "The Negative Effects of Minimum Wage Laws." Washington, DC: Cato Institute. *Policy Analysis*, No. 701 (June 21, 2012).

Wolf, Milton R., Dr. "After Obamacare." Opinion column *Washington Times* (June 21, 2012).

Young, Andrew and Walter Block. "Enterprising Education: Doing Away with the Public School System." *International Journal of Value-Based Management* 12 (1999): 195–207.

Young, William H. and Nancy K. Young. *The 1930s*. Westport, CT: Greenwood Publishing, 2002.

Znamenski, Andrei. "Native American Reservations: 'Socialist Archipelago.'" *Mises Daily* (April 26, 2013).

Zwolinski, Matt. "How Not to Argue for Libertarianism." Bleeding Heart Libertarians.com (May 10, 2011).

—. "Why Not Utilitarianism?" BleedingHeartLibertarians.com (May 2, 2012).

INDEX

abortion rights 152
   dominant libertarian view on 157
   moral status of fetus,
      importance of 158, 162
   compared to newborn,
      158–61, 238n. 23
   potentiality argument
      regarding 158–9, 239nn. 25, 27
   self-ownership and 160–1, 240n.32, 241n. 34
anarcho-capitalists 5, 28, 37, 154, 188
Aristotle 21–2

Barnett, R. E. 157, 179n. 4, 187n. 3
Bastiat, F. 83
Bennett, W. 134
Berlin, I. 27
Bernanke, Chairman B. 105, 107, 212n. 62
Boaz, D. 91, 169

capitalism,
   definition of 11–12
   nature of 8, 59, 135, 147
   see also property rights
Caplan, B. 163, 242n. 43
Capretta, J. 145
Cato Institute 7, 111, 152
Champ, B. 100

Chase, S. 173
Clinton, President B. 120
Cochrane, J. 148
consequentialism 7–8
   problem of "collapse" 191n. 3
   utilitarianism 7–8, 50, 66, 113, 163, 174, 175, 191n. 3, 202n. 42, 246n. 13
corporate welfare 111
   libertarian condemnation of 112–14
   market failure and 113
   mechanism for ending 114
   total spending on 111–12
   see also crony capitalism
cost benefit analysis (CBA) 25, 73, 74, 76, 79, 90–3, 202n. 42
crony capitalism 12, 113, 142, 214nn. 8, 11

democracy 36, 112, 173, 176
   tyranny of the majority 86–7, 246n. 10
deontological ethics 8
Dershowitz, A. 56
doctrinaire versus nondoctrinaire political
   issues, distinction between 152
doctrine of double effect 153, 236n. 7
Dworkin, G. 63

Eberstadt, N. 117
economic liberty 2, 34, 35, 47, 55, 88, 162, 177
economics,
  economic growth 83, 91, 94, 99, 121, 172, 176, 178
  theory of 7, 8–9, 94, 110, 113, 176
Edwards, J. R. 96, 184n. 26
egalitarianism 4–5, 20, 21, 23–4, 35, 96, 174–5
eminent domain, 95, 97, 169
  history of 36–7
  injustice of 38–40
  public use, meaning of 37
  reform of abusive use of 140
entitlement programs and
national debt 6, 140, 141, 169–70, 176, 228n. 20
entitlement theory (of justice) 17
  justice in acquisition 17–19, 35, 182n. 11
  justice in transfer 19
  rectification 17, 19–20, 35, 57, 58, 182n. 12
  versus patterned principles of justice 19–20
  see also Locke, original appropriation
Epstein, R. 8, 41
externalities, problem of 8, 113
  immigration and 163, 242n. 42
  land use and pollution 25–6, 78, 90–1
  motorcycle helmet laws and 69
  recreational drugs and 74
  smoking, regulation of 71–2

federal income tax 93–4, 204n. 1
  benefit principle of taxation 95
  flat (or proportionate) tax, implication of 97–9
  income vs. wealth alternatives 97–8, 206n. 20
  justice of 96–7
  inequities of current system 94, 98–9, 207n. 23
  progressive tax, libertarian objections to 95–6
Federal Reserve System 93
  alternatives to status quo 108–9
  criticisms of recent policy 106–7
  free banking 109–10, 213n. 71
  gold standard 102–3
  history of 100–4, 211n. 62
  rule of law, and 105–8
federalism 176, 206n. 17
Fisher, R. 104
foreign policy,
  argument against non-interventionism as doctrinaire libertarian view 153–7
  just war theory 152–3
  libertarians preference for non-interventionism 152, 236n. 13
  non-interventionism, meaning of 152
  Westphalian, theory of 153–5
fraud 11, 17, 53, 81, 88, 147, 175
  libertarian theory regarding 26–8, 184n. 22
free association, right of 57
  antidiscrimination laws 57–9, 170
  corporate form, and 59, 193n. 16
  libertarian rejection of 58–60
free speech (and expression), right of 5, 49
  commercial speech 54–5

Islamic extremism and 166
libertarian defense of 49–50, 52
　contrasted with utilitarian
　　defense 50–2
　theoretical issues relating
　　to 55–7
　political campaign
　　contributions 52–4
　private vs. public colleges
　　and 61–2, 191n. 7
　property rights and 188n. 4
Friedman, M. 7, 8, 12, 65, 126
Friedman, M. and R. 84–5, 103

Gokhale, J. 67
Gravelle, J. 71
Greene, J. 129
Greenspan, A. 107
Gross, B. 106

Hagopian, K. 96
Hayek, F. A. 10, 68, 109, 173, 176
　connection between property
　　and
　　autonomy 34, 176
　rule of law, conception of 10,
　　105, 108, 169
　social justice, argument
　　against 23
　Social Security, reform of 66
　spontaneous order, concept
　　of 40–1
health care, US system of 64–5,
　135
　Affordable Care Act
　　(ACA) 141–2
　　mandates, and other
　　　provisions of 142–4
　employer-based insurance 136–7,
　　141, 231n. 35
　free market alternative 147–50
　individual insurance 138, 143,
　　147–8

Medicare,
　efforts to control costs under
　　ACA 145–6, 232n. 44
　fraud in 139
　practical reform of 149
　spending under 140–1,
　　227n. 14, 228n. 20
　violation of rights
　　under 138–40
　out-of-pocket payment for,
　　benefits of 137–8
　expected to fall under ACA 146
　international comparison
　　of 137
　overall spending on 141, 146
　perceived flaws in 142
　poor performance of 141
　regulations, harms of 135–7
　third party payment
　　model 137–8, 141, 144
　uninsured population 148,
　　233n. 49
　veterans, care of 64, 150,
　　236n. 53
　violation of rights under 135–6,
　　147
Higgs, R. 156
Horwitz, S. 103, 108
Huemer, M. 162–4
Hummel, J. 105

immigration, right of 162
　dominant libertarian view 162
　Muslim fundamentalism,
　　and 164–6, 244n. 57
　open borders, libertarian
　　argument
　　against 163–6, 242n. 46
　open borders, libertarian
　　argument
　　for 162–4
　policy recommendation
　　regarding 167

inheritance, institution of 99, 208n. 25

Jaworski, A. (and B. Tannenbaum) 158
Jenkins, H. 137
Johnson, President L. B. 115–16
Johnson, R. 101

Kant, I. 16, 21, 26, 27
Karkkainen, B. 46
Kekes, J. 30

Labonte, M. 104, 108
labor unions 86
  campaign finance reform and 52, 54
  private sector 87–8, 201n. 35
  public sector 88–9, 127, 129, 202n. 40
Ledyard, J. 113
Libertarian Party 1, 152, 157, 162, 236n. 4
libertarianism (rights-based) 1, 5–11 *passim*, 24, 30, 34, 69, 159, 170, 179n. 1
  common arguments against, rebuttals to 169–75 *passim*
  international options for 177–8
  issues wrongly thought to have doctrinaire libertarian positions 157–66 *passim*
  see also natural rights; property rights; rights, negative rights
Locke, J. 2, 13, 171
  natural law views 2–3
  original appropriation 3, 9, 17–18, 29, 171, 182n. 11
  property, understanding of 2
  social safety net and 30
  state of nature concept 2, 29, 155, 173

Machan, T. 33
McIntyre, A. 153
Marquis, D. 158–9, 239n. 25
Medicaid 115, 116, 117, 119, 139, 149
  expansion under the ACA 142, 234n. 50
  Florida's reform of 123
  reasons for poor performance of 217n. 27
Medicare 64, 68, 72, 226n. 11, 229n. 22
  coercion under 138–9
  unfunded liabilities under 140–1
  see also health care, US system of
Mill, J. S. 50, 126
minimal state 57, 97
  coercive funding of 28–9, 184n. 26
  definition of 5
  social safety net, provision of 29–31, 171
  see also public goods
Miron, J. 74
moral (or value) pluralism 30, 171
Mulligan, C. 146
Murphy, M. 13
Murray, C. 78, 116, 217n. 24, 245n. 4

Nagel, T. 49
natural law 2, 3, 13–14
natural rights 2–6, 10, 13–14, 152, 157, 163, 170–5 *passim*
  definition of 2
  libertarian conception of 153
  Nozick's argument for 6, 15–17, 35
  state's violations of 6, 41, 42, 50, 53, 64, 66, 93

New Deal, the 2, 6, 172–3, 176
nondoctrinare political positions, meaning of 152
Nozick, R. 6, 9, 13, 138, 152, 236n. 7, 246n. 11
  criticism of Locke 14
  entitlement theory of justice 17
    justice in acquisition 17–19, 182n. 11
    justice in transfer 17, 19
    recitifcation 17, 19–20
  Lockean proviso 9, 18–19, 22, 29–30, 171
  luck egalitarians, argument against 23–4
  minimal state, justification of 28
  rational agency 15–16, 24, 27, 49, 58, 64, 95, 98, 178, 182n. 7
  side constraints on coercion 16, 22, 24, 26, 30–1, 66, 175
    moral catastrophe exception 22, 30, 171
  Wilt Chamberlain argument against distributive justice 20–1 see also Locke, orignal appropriation

paternalism 63
  antismoking laws 70–3
  definition of 63–4
  libertarian objection to 64–5
  motocycle helmet (and seatbelt) laws 68–70
  recreational drugs, and prostituion 73–4
  Social Security system, and 65–8
  soft variety of 75–6
Paul, R. 152, 241n. 36
Petit, P. 6

Pipes, R. 36
politics 52–4, 68, 70, 82, 93, 94–5, 123, 139
  comparison of US with other nations' 177
  contemporary US trends 1, 169–70
    prosepcts for changing 176
  moral theory, and 180n. 6
pollution control 25–6, 78
  see also regulations, environmental
private charities 118, 121–2, 216n. 23
Progressive Era 93
property rights,
  benefits of 9–10, 18, 35, 73, 120–1, 176
  definition of 33–4, 179n. 4
  immigration and 162–3
  pollution and risk, issues regarding 25–6
  relationship to economic liberty 34, 187n. 3
  relationship to freedom generally 36
  smoking, right to permit 73
  stringency of 22, 26, 30, 34–5, 38, 151, 163, 187n. 1
  violations of 39, 41, 69, 90
  see also economic liberty; natural rights
public education, US system of 125
  higher education 132
    harms caused by 133–4
    libertarian objection to status quo 133
    libertarian proposal for 134
    spending on 133
  K-12 system,
    charter schools 130–1, 223n. 13

coercive taxation for 126, 131, 222n. 4
liberal values justification for 127
libertarian alternative to 131–2
monopoly nature of 127–8
moral principles relating to 125–6
poor performance of 129–30
public good argument for 126–7
school vouchers 126, 224n. 17
spending on 130, 223n. 12
public goods 8, 29, 95–7, 113
definition of 185n. 27
education 126
free riders, problem of 184n. 26, 187n. 27
law enforcement 28–9, 205n. 11
national defense 28–9

Rand, A. 1, 151
abortion rights, views on 159–60
nonaggression principle 14–15, 24, 27, 154
Objectivism 15
Rector, R. 114, 120
regulations (administrative) 77–8, 120–1, 176
environmental 78
libertarian analysis of 90–3
tort system, as alternative to 90–1, 203n. 44
health and safety 78
costs of compliance with 83
FDA, case study of 79–83
free market alternatives to 78–9
labor laws 86–9
licensure laws 85–6, 127, 135–6
minimum wage laws 84–5, 170
regulatory capture 82, 136
regulatory takings 40–1

rights 10, 36–7, 151, 173
immigration 162
negative rights 4, 13
positive rights 4, 31, 151
of foreigners 186n. 33
required rescue laws and 186n. 32
see also natural rights; property rights
Rothbard, M.,
abortion rights, views on 160–1, 240n. 31
foreign policy, views on 152–3
property rights, view of 188n. 4
self-ownership thesis 151
rule of law, conventional understanding of 11, 105

Schaeffer, A. 132
self-ownership principle 3, 151, 153, 160–1, 184n. 22
Shapiro, D. 115
Siegan, B. 44
Sinnott-Armstrong, W. 145
Skoble, A. 154
Smith, A. 10
Smith, G. 153
social justice,
arguments against concept of 22–4
definition of 21
Social Security system,
financing of 65–7, 194n. 10
redistributions under 67, 194nn. 7, 8
Suderman, P. 145

Tanner, M. 114, 118
taxation,
coercive 5, 15, 28–9, 33, 65, 92, 121, 171, 185n. 27
redistributive 6, 69, 141, 160, 187n. 1
violating rights by 65, 69, 72, 95–7, 111, 113, 115, 121, 126, 131, 136–46 *passim*, 141

Thaler, H. and Sunstein, C. 75
Thomson, J. J. 174
Tocqueville, A. 64
Trotsky, L. 36

Van Roekel, D. 129

welfare (public assistance)
   programs 111
  libertarian alternative to 120–3
  libertarian objections to 116, 117–20
  total spending on 111, 114
  war on poverty 115–16
    components of 116–17
    dependency, creation of 118–20, 219n. 39, 220n. 41
    failure of 116–20, 171–2
    fraud in programs comprising 117–18, 218n. 33
    rectification and 182–3n. 12
    reduction in poverty prior to 116, 217n. 24
Wells, D. and Scruggs, L. S. 109
White, L. 109
Wilkerson, W. 78

zoning,
   definition of 42
   infringement of natural rights 42–4
   nuisance, tort of 46–7
   operation of 42–3
   practical improvement to 47
   rights-based alternatives 45–6
   utilitarian costs of 44–5
Zwolinski, M. 174

www.ingramcontent.com/pod-product-compliance
Ingram Content Group UK Ltd.
Pitfield, Milton Keynes, MK11 3LW, UK
UKHW021900220326
469204UK00008B/80